UNDERSTANDING
THE PURPOSE AND POWER OF
AUTHORITY

DR. MYLES MUNROE

UNDERSTANDING
THE PURPOSE AND POWER OF

AUTHORITY

A CULTURE-CHANGING LOOK AT POSITIVE LEADERSHIP AND CALLING

WHITAKER
HOUSE

UNDERSTANDING THE PURPOSE AND POWER OF AUTHORITY:
A Culture-Changing Look at Positive Leadership and Calling
(Previously published as *The Purpose and Power of Authority: Discovering the Power of Your Personal Domain*)

Munroe Global
P.O. Box N9583
Nassau, Bahamas
www.munroeglobal.com
office@munroeglobal.com

ISBN: 979-8-88769-152-7• eBook ISBN: 979-8-88769-153-4
Printed in the United States of America
© 2011, 2024 by Munroe Group of Companies Ltd.

Whitaker House
1030 Hunt Valley Circle • New Kensington, PA 15068
www.whitakerhouse.com

The Library of Congress has cataloged the original trade paperback edition as follows:
Munroe, Myles.
The purpose and power of authority / Myles Munroe.
     p. cm.
   Summary: "The author dispels widely accepted but counterfeit and destructive concepts of authority, explains the nature of genuine authority and submission, reveals how one can discover and exercise one's personal authority, and provides principles for establishing legitimate authority in the world"—Provided by publisher.
   ISBN 978-1-60374-262-7 (trade pbk. : alk. paper) 1. Authority—Religious aspects—Christianity. 2. Power (Christian theology) I. Title.
   BT88.M83 2011
   262'.8—dc22
                          2010045311

1 2 3 4 5 6 7 8 9 10 11 ⨆⨆ 31 30 29 28 27 26 25 24

DEDICATION

To the emerging leaders and stewards of the next generation.

To my beloved wife, Ruth, and to my outstanding children, Charisa Makaria and Myles "Chairo" Jr., who allowed me to exercise my authority as a father in guiding them into the challenging land of adulthood. You continue to make me proud.

To my sister Sheila, who, while holding the lofty position of being the eldest of eleven siblings, recognized the unique destiny on my life and chose to submit to the authority of my gift.

To my most outstanding, distinguished leadership team, who submitted to my inherent authority and who, by so doing, allowed us together to build a global organization that affects millions of lives: Richard and Sheena Pinder, Henry and Sheila Francis, Jay and Euturpia Mullings, Dave and Angie Burrows, Allan and Nyoka Munroe, Wesley Smith, Angie and the late Eme Achara, Burton and Barbara Smith, Barbara Lockhart, Gloria Seymour, and Charles and Cassandra Nottage.

I could not have achieved the measure of success that I have to date without your understanding and submission to the authority of my gift.

ACKNOWLEDGMENTS

Creating this book has been a personal journey of discovery, in the course of which I have met many old and new guides to help me along the way. I am always conscious that whatever we accomplish or achieve in life is the sum total of all the people, situations, and circumstances we have encountered in our lives. This book is evidence of that reality.

I would not even have started the journey without the inspiration of the leadership team, staff, and members of Bahamas Faith Ministries International (BFMI) and the International Third World Leaders Association (ITWLA). If they are the leaders of the future, then the future is in good hands.

I would not have had the courage and drive to start and complete this book without the motivational support of my publisher Bob Whitaker and his team.

Most important, words fail to express how grateful I am once again to my very dedicated, skillful, and talented editor, Lois Puglisi, for her assistance in getting this material out of my heart and onto these pages. I will forever be indebted to you for any success our collaboration achieves.

In the course of researching the material for this book, I have drawn on the time and support of many outstanding leaders and friends in the public, private, and voluntary sectors. Thank you all for your practical insights, inspiration, and education. May this book give back to you more than you invested in me.

CONTENTS

PART THREE: RESTORING TRUE AUTHORITY IN THE WORLD

MAXIMIZING YOUR PERSONAL AUTHORITY

THE (UN)REALITY SHOW

Nothing in life is more disturbing than to interact with a counterfeit character. We have all felt the frustration, deep disappointment, and even trauma of the violation of trust we have placed in a person who was later exposed to be a fraud. It seems that in our fast-paced, plastic-driven, Web-based societies, it is increasingly difficult to find authentic people. Many people are taught—directly or through observing the general values of their societies—that it is acceptable to scheme, play games, and promote private agendas in order to achieve personal success, at the expense of honesty, integrity, ethics, moral convictions, and principled character. It's as if everybody is performing a role in the game of life and not genuinely *living* life. Consequently, many don't know whom they can truly depend on. Religious leaders, elected officials, corporate investors, various public institutions, and even spouses whom we trusted have deeply hurt us through betrayal, abuse, or abandonment.

Meanwhile, the level of disappointment resulting from our largely superficial societies is at an epidemic level. Even our so-called reality shows on television are not "real"; they are staged and edited. This lack of authenticity is not an isolated crisis but a worldwide one. People change like the weather and live lives based on expediency alone. Strangely, our cultures often openly display their defects with seeming pride and glory in their failures and immorality through television, radio, and Internet programming.

What the world needs right now are authentic people. Authenticity is not a quality one can learn through a general educational process or through experimentation. This is because true authority is *natural*—it is the natural manifestation of the inherent authority in a human being. In other words, authenticity can be discovered only because it already exists in one's personal authority. A human being becomes authentic when he discovers his true self and makes a specific and ongoing decision to reveal that self to the world.

Authenticity cannot be counterfeited. It is the true "reality show." Being authentic means living, working, and serving humanity in your personal domain in life. An authentic person never *tries* to be something; he just *is*. Being authentic, therefore, is being yourself—not as society has dictated you should be, but what you are in your essence.

I invite you to embark on the discovery of your true self. As you do, you will find your personal authority and live it out in all areas of your life. This is the only path to authenticity.

INTRODUCTION:
AUTHORITY TURNED UPSIDE DOWN

Industrial nations fear it, emerging nations hate it, but few understand it. The very word *authority* conjures up images of oppression and abuse, and yet life in the universe and on planet earth cannot function without it.

There are many benefits and opportunities connected to authority that most people have never dreamed of. I am therefore coming to believe that the greatest problem in our world today is a basic disrespect for authority with an accompanying disregard and dismissal of it. The fundamental reason for this problem is that most people harbor basic false ideas about the nature of authority. I have discovered over the years that there is much confusion and misunderstanding about this concept. Confusion comes first—people have been taught or have experienced conflicting notions of what it is. And misunderstanding is the result—they aren't aware of its personal benefits or its value to their social institutions and nations as a whole.

Because we misunderstand what authority really is—and because this misunderstanding perpetuates the abuse of authority and its consequences—we are always somewhat suspicious of it.

We may have a passing (superficial) knowledge of authority, but we have totally missed the richness of its true nature. Consequently, we deal with it as a necessary evil. For example, when people go to their jobs, many do what the boss tells them to do—not because they want to or feel that it will benefit them in any way, but rather so they can keep their positions and their paychecks or maintain working relationships with their supervisors. In another example, some people grudgingly submit to the laws of the land while driving their cars, but if they run a red light or exceed the speed limit and get stopped by the police, they try to negotiate or argue with the officers. They recognize them as representatives of the law, but they want to challenge the law to see what they can get away with. A similar attitude toward authority can be found in other realms of life.

Entire cultures have developed that are suspicious of authority. For instance, throughout the entire Western world and in developing countries, authority is looked on distrustfully, though for different reasons.

I believe that in the Western, developed world, people have what you might call "an affair" with authority—they use it when it's convenient, but they don't want to give it permanent status in their lives. In the developing world, authority has become a hated enemy, one that represents the chains and whips of slavery and oppression.

The Western world keeps authority at arm's length and even fears it because Westerners highly value the concept of freedom, which has become synonymous with individualism. The ideals of the democratic psyche have evolved down through the years to the point where freedom means liberty or license without control or restriction. Anything that seems like control or restriction must be contained. That is why, if you were to suggest to Westerners that they create boundaries for their behavior, many of them would rebel against that recommendation. In short, the masses are suspicious of authority in all its forms, largely as a result of the evolution of ideas derived from, or influenced by, the Reformation, the Enlightenment, the American and French Revolutions, governmental involvement in scandals and unpopular wars, relaxed moral and ethical standards, and the emergence of democracy as the dominant political force in the world.

Meanwhile, in the minds of many people who live in Third World nations, due to those countries' histories of colonization and slavery, authority has come to represent not just restriction or control but outright domination. Those in the Third World revile the idea that anyone could have authority over them. Many former colonies are now emerging democracies with nationals in positions of leadership, or they desire to move in that direction, and the last thing they want is to have to submit to some outside authority that could reverse the progress they have made.

In this way, the concept of authority has slowly come to be seen in a negative light—sometimes, a fiercely negative one—throughout the earth. Again, one part of the world fears authority, while another hates it, and the result is that few people trust it. Much of the problem is that authority has been misinterpreted, misused, and abused by a great number of individuals, leaders, groups, and nations over the centuries. And large numbers of people have experienced demeaning and even deadly treatment from this misuse and abuse so that few would imagine embracing authority as a valuable and necessary component of a peaceful, productive life.

Yet, even though most of us want to exist without authority being exercised over us, I believe we suffer from an inner contradiction because, somewhere deep within us, we recognize that we need authority in our lives. We don't want authority to control us, but we want our lives to be stable, orderly, and fruitful—the result of established and consistent authority. We've all seen a microcosm of this dilemma in children who seem to enjoy a chaotic atmosphere where there is little adult supervision but who then become fretful until someone comes along who gives them structure and parameters to live by. Suddenly, they are more relaxed and content and are able to interact with others in a constructive way.

As adults, we hope to have learned to govern our personal behavior to a large extent. Yet, we may be living in a larger version of the above scenario as we interact with others in our homes, our workplaces, our churches, and our nations, where structures and parameters are spiraling out of control, preventing us from enjoying the rich and fulfilling lives we were meant to live. We may be in the middle of the chaos, in which case we cannot fully realize the effects that this type of stressful environment is causing. Or, we may be well aware that things are not right with us and with our societies.

The purpose of this book is to unveil the beauty of true authority and to restore authority to its place of dignity in our personal lives, our cultures, and our nations. Authority needs to be reintroduced to both the individual and to society at large as a true friend—no longer the object of a transitory, arm's-length relationship or a deadly enemy.

Authority has been turned upside down so that it has come to represent the opposite of what genuine authority is. Instead of control, authority promotes real freedom and opens the door to possibilities. Instead of domination and death, authority ignites the personal potential within each person, while bringing protection and life.

The cultures and nations of our world are experiencing unnecessary conflict and wasted potential because so many people misunderstand authority. It is impossible for us to maximize our lives apart from a clear understanding of the character of true authority—that it is not only good but also beneficial and necessary for maximum fulfillment and achievement in our individual purposes, in our family relationships, and in the broader social structures of our nations and the world.

PART ONE

WHAT IS AUTHORITY?

ONE

AUTHORITY IS WITHIN YOU

YOU HAVE PERSONAL AUTHORITY AND POWER TO FULFILL YOUR PURPOSE IN LIFE

Neither the judges nor the audience expected anything from the plain-looking, middle-aged, unemployed woman from Scotland who was a contestant on the reality television show *Britain's Got Talent* in the spring of 2009. When asked what her dream was, Susan Boyle answered, "I'm trying to be a professional singer." As she talked with the judges before her performance, they were openly skeptical, and many of the audience members rolled their eyes and shook their heads incredulously, perhaps thinking the producers of the show included this contestant for a comic element. When the introductory notes of her song started to play—"I Dreamed a Dream," from the musical *Les Miserables*—some audience members even looked as if they were anxiously holding their breath, afraid that this unassuming, naive woman would humiliate herself before millions of people.

Then, she began to sing.

With lyrical tones, compelling emotion, and a professional delivery, she sang the song as if she had written it herself to describe her unfulfilled life up to that point and her hopes for the future. Most of the audience members were clapping, cheering, and standing when she had sung just a few lines, and she received a resounding standing ovation at the conclusion of her performance. In minutes, she went from being perceived as a joke to being considered an inspiration and a role model for all who are seeking a second chance in life, or for all who want a first chance to manifest to the world who they are on the inside.

Susan Boyle became an international phenomenon overnight through her television appearance, the popularity of the video of her performance on YouTube, and the overwhelming attention of the media. People were captivated by her voice and moved by her story of decades of struggling and longing to make something of her life.

Though her instantaneous rise to fame has caused inevitable stress for her along the way, she seems to have come to terms with the crush of attention. After finishing the contest in second place, she went on to build the professional singing career she had always dreamed of. Her debut album, *I Dreamed a Dream*, has sold over eight million units worldwide as of this writing. The apex of her dream came to pass when, during the historic visit of Pope Benedict XVI to England and Scotland in September 2010, she was chosen to sing for the Pontiff at the conclusion of his open-air Mass in Glasgow, which was attended by sixty-five thousand people.

What does *authority* have to do with a television performance or even a singer? Doesn't authority have to do with exercising some jurisdiction or control over other people? Doesn't it involve, for example, leaders and followers, bosses and employees, parents and children, teachers and students, law enforcement officers and lawbreakers—in other words, those in charge and those under them who are instructed, directed, ordered, or made to do something?

EVERY PERSON ON EARTH HAS AUTHORITY

There is an underlying aspect of authority that has not often been acknowledged or addressed by leaders, corporations, governments, and individuals but that is crucial for effective and fulfilling human endeavor. It provides the key not only for individual accomplishment but also for corporate success.

Susan Boyle's story illustrates the essence of authority, as well as the heart of this book: true authority is *personal*, and true authority *comes from within.*

> PERSONAL AUTHORITY IS INHERENT WITHIN EVERY HUMAN BEING, WHETHER THAT PERSON IS CONSIDERED THE ONE "IN CHARGE" OR THE ONE FOLLOWING ORDERS.

Authority does not mean having power or control over others.

Authority is not something you automatically receive with a title, either, such as "manager," "boss," "CEO," or "president."

Personal authority is inherent within every human being, whether that person is considered the one "in charge" or the one following orders. Authority is also inherent within every living thing created on earth. It is natural. It does not have to be "worked up," and it cannot be given to someone—only released and developed.

Personal authority can be defined as the intrinsic gifts a person or thing possesses in order to fulfill the purpose for which that person or thing was placed on this earth. Because authority is intrinsic, every person or living thing already has the ability to fulfill his/her/its authority in the area, or the domain, of his/her/its gifting.

You have personal authority that enables you to fulfill your purpose on earth. Have you identified your own personal authority? If you believe you have, are you functioning in it to the fullest extent that you would like to and that you are able to?

FOUR FOUNDATIONAL PRINCIPLES FOR UNDERSTANDING AUTHORITY

In this book, you will discover how to apply four foundational principles for understanding authority and entering into the power of your personal domain:

1. *The Principle of the Author*: The release of your personal authority is linked to the origin of your gifts and power, by which you can fully carry out your life's purpose through your personal domain. Once you discover the true source of the authority that is inherent within you, opportunities for experiencing fulfillment and for contributing your unique gifts to the world will open wide.

2. *The Principle of Authorization*: You not only have personal authority within you, but you also have the *permission* and the *right* to carry it out in the world. No matter what your past experiences have been, or no matter what restrictions you have previously felt, you have the authorization you need to start fulfilling your life's purpose. You'll discover the key to that authorization in coming chapters.

3. *The Principle of Authenticity*: No person is truly authentic until he is manifesting his inherent authority. Once you understand and become your true self—who you were born to be—your life takes on authenticity. In other words, you are real, or authentic, while you are being who you were meant to be and doing what you were meant to do. In the following pages, you will learn how to identify and develop your authentic self.

4. *The Principle of Authority*: The above three principles lead to this fourth and foremost principle of authority, which is twofold. First, *everyone and everything is designed to fulfill its purpose*. Because your authority is inherent, you are automatically equipped to be what you have been authorized to be and to do what you have been authorized to do. You have been designed to fulfill your life's purpose. Your personal authority guides the focus of your life and enables you to accomplish what you were born to accomplish. Second, *everything depends on and must yield to something else in order to function, grow, prosper, and succeed*. As you read this book, you will increasingly see how you can tap into your unique design and begin to apply it to the various aspects of your life. Your personal authority will emerge, and you will be able to live an effective life as you work in collaboration with others to fulfill each other's purposes.

AUTHORITY IS PERSONAL BUT NOT EXCLUSIVE

Because authority is in essence personal, some people make the mistake of thinking that it is therefore exclusive to them and has nothing to do with others. They may think, "I'm following my personal authority, so don't get in my way." Or, they may tend to pursue their unique gifts and abilities only for what they can get out of them. Yet that perspective does not reflect the nature of personal authority, which is designed to operate in concert with other people and for the benefit of others, as well.

Since authority is within every person, and since humans are social beings who interact in social institutions, what happens when my authority meets your authority in the family, in the government, in the church, in the business world, and in other relationships and realms of human interaction? Authority works in such a way that people's personal authorities are interrelated and function interdependently in corporate life. This isn't just an observation but a vital principle: we need each other's authority to fulfill our own.

Personal authority is carried out in the context of many realms of life and in association with a variety of human interactions and organizations. It operates in conjunction with collective human endeavors, such as we experience in families, communities, governments, churches, nonprofit organizations, schools, small businesses, and large corporations.

Yet none of these relationships and endeavors can truly thrive and be successful unless each individual associated with them understands his personal authority and is operating under it. Personal authority empowers each person to contribute his greatest gifts and skills for his own fulfillment and for the benefit of the whole community—no matter how large or small that community may be.

WHAT IS YOUR DREAM?

What is your dream for yourself, your family, your business, your organization, or your nation? Many people don't know how to live out their dreams or find their true place in the world because they don't understand how to put into practice the above principles of authority. You may have some idea of your personal authority but are not fulfilling the vast potential still inside you; you recognize that you are living well below your abilities.

What is true on a personal level is also true on a corporate level. Most of our corporate, community, and national problems come from the fact that people do not truly understand or live in their personal authorities or function in the interdependent nature of authority, which occurs when people blend their gifts to work together for the good of the whole.

THREE KEYS TO ACTIVATING PERSONAL AUTHORITY

In Susan Boyle's case, her potential to inspire and entertain people through her inherent gift of music had been limited by a series of setbacks, not the least of which was early rejection by her peers and the low self-esteem that resulted. Apparently, as she grew older, even though she sang locally, she increasingly had a sense that life was passing her by.

What led to the change in her circumstances?

First, she was aware of her inherent, inner authority—her tremendous singing ability—and had not let that talent fall by the wayside but had tried to develop it as best she could. *Personal authority is dependent upon your truly knowing yourself, knowing the authority inside you.* It is impossible to exercise your authority if you do not know yourself.

> ## PERSONAL AUTHORITY IS DEPENDENT UPON YOUR TRULY KNOWING YOURSELF, KNOWING THE AUTHORITY INSIDE YOU.

Second, although circumstances in her life had prevented her from having a professional singing career in the past (she had even sent demo CDs to music companies, without success), Susan tried one more time. *She made a conscious decision to act on her inherent authority.* In fact, she had promised her mother, who had passed away, that she would "be someone." Her success at "being someone" was not initiated by the fame and acclaim she received but because she exercised her inherent authority—who she was gifted to be—and the world took notice. When she employed her authority, she discovered the very real power of her personal domain.

Third, even though it was outside of her comfort zone, *she submitted to placing herself in a situation where others could recognize her personal authority and enable her to pursue and develop it to the highest extent.* Once she was willing to let that happen, her obvious talent commanded attention. The discovery of Susan Boyle's outstanding musical gift serves as an excellent example of the nature of one's personal authority and its interdependence with the personal authority of others. Please note carefully that I did not say her gift was created but rather "discovered." The *Britain's Got Talent* television show did not give authority to her singing gift but simply provided the stage for the release of her authority. In essence, she had always possessed the authority of her gift in the domain of singing, but she needed an audience and an opportunity to serve it to the world. Yet she almost didn't try to be a contestant on the television program because she thought she was too old to pursue her dream. You are never too old or too young or too poor or too rich or too anything to pursue your inherent authority. What is natural within you will manifest itself if you allow it to.

YOUR PERSONAL DOMAIN

King Solomon, one of the wisest people who ever lived, wrote, *"A gift opens the way for the giver and ushers him into the presence of the great"* (Proverbs 18:16), and *"Do you see a man skilled in his work? He will serve before kings"* (Proverbs 22:29). Susan Boyle's gift made a way for her—it brought her before influential people who opened doors that enabled her to fulfill the inner dreams and longings she had held all her life. Although she had already exercised her gift in various ways in her local community, there was an even greater realm in which she was meant to share it.

Your authority also has a domain in which you are to exercise it. The size or scope of that domain, and whether you become "well-known," is not the issue. The issue is whether you will recognize what is inherent within you and exercise your gift for yourself and others. Your authority is your unique leadership ability in the world.

Many people allow their true authority to remain untapped. They have neither discovered nor pursued their special ability to contribute to their generation. Whether one is genuinely operating in one's gifts is not necessarily measured by outward success. Both a multimillionaire businessman and a single mother struggling to make ends meet can still have hidden, untapped authority that, once released and manifested, will bring something of tremendous value to their lives and the lives of others.

The only way you can exercise true authority is to recognize and start functioning in the power of your personal domain.

COUNTERFEIT AND AUTHENTIC PURSUITS

When people violate the principles of authority, it is usually because they don't have a foundational understanding of what genuine authority really is. Many individuals who have great gifts, talents, dreams, and promise have destroyed their futures by failing to implement these principles.

For example, many people pursue prosperity or fame for their own sakes, but these pursuits are not authentic. Instead, people should be pursuing their inner authority. They will discover that when they do so, prosperity will come toward them. Our prosperity is found where our authority is.

True authority is *the right and the power* to be who you were created to be. You can be a more effective parent, carpenter, hairdresser, entrepreneur, CEO, teacher, student, pastor, government official, or any other role or calling—you can be a more effective *person*—if you discover your true authority and understand and live out its principles.

If you have already discovered your personal authority and are pursuing it, you can be even more effective in it by applying the principles of authority delineated in this book. You can discover how these principles operate and what they can do in your life and vocation as you interact with others in various realms of life and learn how to blend your personal authority with theirs for greater results. You'll also learn the origins of your personal authority, why authority works, how authority works, and how to implement it.

If the concept of personal authority is new to you, or if you have been frustrated because you know you have something to contribute to your generation but don't feel you have been exercising your personal authority and want to be effective in it, you will find the tools you need in this book. Everyone can exercise authority because authority is within each of us.

WHY MANY PEOPLE ARE AFRAID OF AUTHORITY

Although everyone has personal authority, and although all the major realms of human interaction involve the use of authority, personal authority is still one of the most misunderstood principles in human relations.

Because of this, most people I meet are afraid of authority to some degree. You may be one of them. You may have picked up this book with some measure of apprehension. That is understandable, considering the way authority has been modeled for many of us. Most people misunderstand authority because they have never *seen* it in its true form. Authority has been misconceived, misdefined, misrepresented, and misused. We're afraid of it because we don't understand its nature and purposes. As a result, it is seen as a negative element rather than a positive one.

You may have had a bad experience with a parent, a teacher, an employer, or another "authority figure." You may be a woman or a member of a race or community who has been told you are inferior and who has been prevented from developing your abilities to the fullest. Perhaps you have been a victim of oppression in which religious authority was used to control your life or, even worse, a religious authority figure took advantage of your trust and mentally or physically abused you. If that is the case, your distrust, fear, and hatred of authority are understandable. Or, you may be among those who believe that only people who have a certain title or a type A personality or who reach a certain "level" in life can have authority.

Authority as an aspect of life has been misunderstood and misused to the point that it has often become the *opposite* of what it was meant to be. Yet you will discover in this book that the nature of genuine authority is the antithesis of suppression and oppression and is actually the source of true freedom and fulfillment.

> YOU HAVE THE OPPORTUNITY, RESPONSIBILITY, AND ABILITY TO DEVELOP YOUR OWN PERSONAL AUTHORITY AND CARRY OUT YOUR UNIQUE PURPOSE IN LIFE IN CONJUNCTION WITH OTHERS.

In the next chapter, we'll explore some of the distorted and restricted views of authority that people have accepted, and the misconceptions they breed, which have brought us to what I believe is an actual crisis in authority. In every country of the world, people misunderstand, misuse, or abuse authority. As a result, we have too much of the *wrong* kind of authority and too little of the *right* kind of authority. Our failure to understand authority has led to a decreasing quality in people's lives and a lack of true order, peace, and progress in societies and cultures of the world.

WHAT ARE YOU AUTHORIZED TO DO?

Authority is therefore the key to fulfillment and effective living, the means to proper function in life, and the guarantor of success. Authority is the law of maximum performance. It is also the means of powerful, positive influence in other people's lives. If authority is all of these things, then is it imperative that we all understand this critical concept? Obviously, yes.

Unless you know what you're authorized to do in life, you will always experience some degree of dissatisfaction, uncertainty, frustration, and perhaps even anger in regard to your circumstances. Yet, you have the opportunity, responsibility, and ability to develop your own personal authority and carry out your unique purpose in life in conjunction with others.

You are uniquely designed for what you were born to do through your gifts, abilities, and personality. No matter what other people may have told you in the past about your potential, you can release the principles, power, and protection of authority into your life.

Each of the following chapters is designed so that, as you proceed through this book, you will gain a more complete picture of true authority and the many applications of authority to your life that will free you to be all you were meant to be. You'll learn about the basic realms of authority and how to live fruitfully in each.

Through *Understanding the Purpose and Power of Authority*, you will come to...

+ recognize what true authority is—and what it is not

+ understand your own personal, inherent authority

+ discover how to identify the "territory" or area of life you are authorized to oversee

+ learn the origins of true authority

+ gain order, simplicity, and peace in your life

+ respond constructively to others in their own realms of authority

+ exercise your intrinsic power and gifting

+ lead others into their own personal authority

+ live confidently and purposefully

+ be true to your life calling

+ maximize your gifts, talents, and skills

+ find true prosperity

+ work with joy

Susan Boyle determined to do something with her life after years of disappointment and therefore exercised the authority within her. "I made a promise to be someone," she said. I want you to make that same promise to be someone. That "someone" is your true self manifested to the world. Susan Boyle not only has used her authority, but she *is* an authority. True authority is self-manifestation.

In the next few chapters, we will look at some foundational principles of authority that are an essential background for understanding and implementing your personal authority.

TWO

SHARKS AND OTHER "ROLE MODELS" OF POWER

WHY AUTHORITY HAS BECOME THE ENEMY

Were you surprised at my description of authority in chapter one as being personal and coming from within? Many people think of authority as something only outside of them—even imposed on them.

What do you normally think of when you hear the word *authority?* Do you have a positive or negative image of it?

HOW OUR IDEAS AFFECT THE WAY WE LIVE

Our perspectives in life are largely developed by our firsthand experiences. Sometimes, our experiences have a positive effect on us and lead to life-affirming thoughts and actions. Other times, they have a negative effect on us and can cause us to adopt mindsets that limit us. We therefore have to be careful about basing our lives solely on our experiences. Otherwise, our deductions may prevent us from having full, rewarding lives if they lead us to live in discouragement, fear, distrust of others, and so forth.

Whenever I drive in a particular area in my neighborhood, I am reminded of an accident I had there one time, and those memories and feelings associated with the accident still come back to me. Sometimes, returning to a certain location or environment in our lives can reawaken a discomfort or fear we thought we had overcome. We have to decide not to let those feelings control us and affect the way we live.

All of us collect certain fears throughout our lives from experiences that have caused us discomfort, dissatisfaction, or pain. To use a simple example, suppose a child got stuck in an elevator for two hours and developed a fear of enclosed spaces. Then, when he was a young man, he was involved in several car accidents and became fearful whenever he was driving. As he grew older, he fell and suffered a bad break in his arm, and so he developed a fear of falling. Everyone experiences issues such as these.

While we have to use normal precautions and common sense as we go about our lives, fears of enclosed spaces and accidents are not inherent but learned fears. When someone experiences any type of fear, it is very real to that person, whether or not others feel that the fear is justified. We are dealing with emotions that have begun to affect our behavior and that need to be addressed.

In a similar way, we have developed our attitudes and reactions toward authority—whether negative or positive—from our past experiences with "authority figures" rather than from really stopping to think about the concept. I don't think that most people naturally fear or reject true authority. If someone is uncomfortable with, fears, or despises the idea of authority, he's likely had a negative experience at some point that precipitated it.

Our attitudes and perspectives toward authority have a direct effect on our outlooks on life and on ourselves, and on what purposes and goals we pursue. Therefore, our discomfort with and fear of authority likewise need to be acknowledged and addressed if we are going to pursue our personal authority.

Unfortunately, most of us have had opportunities for negative experiences with authority. Many of our parents, extended family members, teachers, employers, and civic and religious leaders have unknowingly contributed to our misunderstanding of authority because of their own lack of understanding of what genuine authority is. Our spouses may have contributed to our confusion over authority because of their own background and personal experiences, which they bring to the relationship. Our cultures have contributed to our misconceptions about authority through established traditions based on misinterpretations of authority. In the religious realm, many people perceive God as a monster because of what they were taught as children; they were told that He is a tyrant looking for someone to catch so He can punish him in hell. Finally, we ourselves have perpetuated our misunderstandings of authority by reinforcing the erroneous ideas we have absorbed. Again, much of what we've experienced has built up a picture of authority in our minds and hearts that is intrusive or frightening. If a whole race or generation fears authority, it's because somewhere in their collective past, they experienced pain, discomfort, or dissatisfaction as a result of an apparent authority.

OPINIONS ABOUT AUTHORITY

People's widely different experiences with authority in our contemporary world, as well as in previous eras, have led to quite diverse opinions about it. That is why, if you browse quotations about authority on the Internet and in books, you will find as opposite views as Oscar Wilde's seeming rejection of it—"Authority is quite degrading"—to Albert Einstein's ironic observation—"To punish me for my contempt for authority, fate made me an authority myself"—to Daniel Webster's passionate warning: "[I]f we and our posterity reject religious instruction and authority, violate the rules of eternal justice, trifle with the injunctions of morality, and recklessly destroy the political constitution which holds us together, no man can tell how sudden a catastrophe may overwhelm us, that shall bury all our glory in profound obscurity."

It seems as if people divide into certain camps when it comes to authority. To some, it represents order and structure. To others, it represents a lack of freedom of thought and action. Authority is considered by many to be a negative force that stifles people's freedom—or at best a necessary evil to keep life functioning.

> GENUINE AUTHORITY CREATES AN ENVIRONMENT FOR PEOPLE TO THINK, TO DREAM, TO DISCOVER AND REFINE THEIR GIFTS AND TALENTS, TO BUILD OTHERS UP, AND TO DEVELOP THEMSELVES FULLY.

Yet authority in its true form is not stifling or restrictive. Genuine authority creates an environment for people to think, to dream, to discover and refine their gifts and talents, to build others up, and to develop themselves fully. Authority has therefore been hijacked, and the result is that it has been misconceived, misdefined, and misrepresented across the globe.

SWIMMING WITH THE SHARKS

I was born in the tropical, sun-drenched islands of The Bahamas in the Caribbean, which is considered by millions to be surrounded by the most beautiful waters in the world. Obviously, water activities are very popular. I sometimes like to go spearfishing in the ocean, and I've seen sharks a number of times. Whenever I'm underwater and see a shark, however, I still get chills all over, especially if the shark is larger than I am! There have been a few times when all indications have pointed to the fact that the shark was very interested in me, and I felt totally helpless.

One time, I had speared a fish, the fish was still moving on my spear, and a shark came by and apparently decided, "You've stolen my meal." Let me tell you, I was very accommodating. I dropped the spear as I thought, "Mr. Shark, you can have the fish and the spear." At the same time I was thinking this, I was swimming away. I knew that if the shark wanted to overtake me and get a piece of me, he could do so without any problem. Why? I was not born to swim, so it was not as easy for me to move through the water as it was for him. It took much more effort on my part than it took the shark because swimming is one of his natural abilities, and the ocean is his natural domain. It is his realm of authority. Sharp teeth are also a part of his authority. It's an authority I am aware of and respect, and so I protect myself accordingly.

There are many stories and proven cases of shark attacks in which people have been maimed and others have lost their lives. Do we or can we blame the sharks for these incidences, or do we accept them as a natural result of the authority within nature at work? It seems that the shark considers his behavior natural and well within his authority. In essence, we are trespassing on *his* domain of authority, and that violation results in a natural display of his authority.

It is interesting to note that we do not condemn all sharks for the actions of one. We do not cancel the value of sharks or dismiss the vital role they play in the broad scheme of things. We see them as simply exercising their authority in nature. Maybe we should rethink our fear of sharks and exchange it for respect for their authority. Every time I am in the ocean and see the magnificent beauty and power of the shark, I am reminded that it is I who am trespassing on his domain of authority, and so I honor that fact by keeping my distance and being ready to leave his domain at a moment's notice. Through understanding, my fear of authority has become a respect for authority.

HUMAN "SHARKS"

I've run into certain people who have pretty sharp teeth, as well. We can experience a whole set of problems when we deal with human "sharks" in the guise of authority figures who do serious damage to our lives. The difference between these people and the sharks in the ocean is that they are operating *outside* the parameters of true authority and beyond their natural environments of authority. They misuse and abuse authority as they rule over others in various capacities and realms of life. They grab what doesn't belong to them, and, because they have become adept at doing so and are able to wield their sharp teeth, those around them have to drop their own natural authority and swim for their lives.

Considering the bad experiences with authority many of us have had, we need to be careful not to "throw the baby out with the bathwater." In this book, we will explore many reasons why genuine authority is very good and, in fact, essential to a life of productivity and fulfillment. Yet because it has been abused by those who were the custodians or usurpers of authority throughout history, people have been burned so badly that they reject what they believe has caused that pain—"authority"—rather than the misuses of it.

Some people have used knives as weapons to kill people, but the knives themselves were not the issue. The problem was with those who wielded the knives. Likewise, if you are burned while you are ironing clothes, the iron is not the problem but whatever absentmindedness, accident, or mechanical malfunction caused you to be burned by it. So, the problem is not authority but rather how people have treated it. Most people do not recognize exactly what they're reacting to when they resist so-called authority. Yet focusing on their bad experiences can prevent them from having good experiences with authority in the future.

COMMON MISCONCEPTIONS OF AUTHORITY

Because these false but commonly accepted concepts of authority have so permeated the nations and cultures of the world, we first need to explore what true authority is *not* so that we can become free of our misconceptions and clearly understand what true authority is.

See if you recognize any human "sharks" represented in the following concepts of authority. Some of these terms may overlap, but each also has a distinct aspect to it that is worth noting.

A PERSON WHO WIELDS POWER

One of the false conceptions of authority that has led to its misuse and abuse is that *power* is synonymous with authority. Many people have come to see authority as a greater strength that is able to subdue others.

Power is the capacity to move something by force or energy, whether it is an object, an idea, or a person. It is the ability to cause, activate, initiate, transform, or impact. Power can be exercised through position, knowledge, strength, force, integrity, influence, personality, or threats. But power is not the same thing as authority. The difference is that true authority is always sanctioned, or authorized, whereas power can be illegitimate, or unauthorized. Power that is used to harm people in some way is clearly unauthorized; it has then become a weapon. Bullies of all ages use power in this way.

Many people who have come into contact with power that is oppressive and even abusive develop a fear of authority because, in their minds, they have transferred that experience to authority itself. For example, if a child is physically abused by a parent, he may try to protect himself from further abuse by rejecting any adult whom he sees as an authority figure. If a wife is repeatedly emotionally abused by her husband, she can become suspicious of others who make suggestions or offer direction, equating their motives with the same kind of control.

On a societal or national level, history is unfortunately strewn with examples of unauthorized power. One of the most obvious examples is Adolf Hitler, who seized control of Germany through intimidation and overpowering force and then turned his weapons of abuse on much of Europe. Those who wield power without authority are forced to subject people to their wills. When we see a person oppressing other people, whether by a carrot-and-stick approach or by controlling their destinies because he has something the people need, that's an abuse of authority. Slave owners use power to the point of "owning" other human beings and overwhelming them by physical force.

POWER IS MERELY ENERGY AND ABILITY, BUT AUTHORITY IS PERMISSION AND RIGHT TO USE THE POWER.

Power was never meant to exist for or by itself but as a tool for good. Power has to be protected and regulated, and genuine authority does this. For example, electricity without conductivity or grounding can be destructive; yet, with these things, it can give us light and energy to run appliances, equipment, electronic devices, and so forth. The same power that could destroy us becomes a service to us if it is regulated, or submitted to the right purpose.

Power is merely energy and ability, but authority is permission and right to use the power. Power without authority is energy without authorization; it is illegal force. The key to success is not power alone but knowing and using authorized power. Someone acting with true authority empowers and protects people. True authority converts power into service.

That is why the greatest protection against misdirected power is genuine authority. When people operate in an authorized way, they will use power to serve constructive ends.

We must also recognize, however, that authority without power is ineffective; it is essentially permission to do something without the ability to carry it out. Authority is responsibility but power is ability. Have you ever appealed to a government official or worked for a supervisor at your job who had no ability to take action or make needed changes or corrections? You cannot give authority without also empowering the recipient to act, or that authority is useless. A person should delegate authority only if he has the capability to back it up.

Authority and power are therefore inseparable. If they are separated, the purpose of each becomes weakened, distorted, or nullified. Each has its place.

A PERSON WHO HAS THE "BOSS SPIRIT"

The concept of the "boss spirit" is related to power, but its main attribute is the abuse of position through manipulation. The word *manipulate* is defined as "to control or play upon by artful, unfair, or insidious means."

The boss spirit is the idea that having authority means you can take advantage of people, order them around at will, and get them to do what you want through coercion.

Such a perspective is unnatural and antithetical to true authority. When someone in a leadership position embraces this false idea of authority, he engages in actions that intimidate, discriminate, exploit, oppress, suppress, and abuse people. Many people have either treated others according to the boss spirit or have been on the receiving end of it, to some extent.

The opposite of the boss spirit is to use authority for the good of all concerned and to seek others' cooperation and contributions rather than trying to maneuver them.

A PERSON WHO RULES OR IS "IN CHARGE"

Many people think that because someone rules over them or is "in charge," that person automatically has authority. Since authority needs legitimacy and authorization, however, those who usurp the role of leader actually have no genuine authority, even though they are in positions where they can rule.

Any attempt to be in charge without authorization cancels authority. Many governments in nations around the world have had unauthorized rulers. Some of those rulers may have done extraordinary things, but they were still illegitimate.

People who overthrow legitimate rule for the sake of taking power always have to keep looking over their shoulders for those who might do the same to them. They have established a precedent of disregard for established authority. They often have to kill people to get and keep their power because everyone is aware that it is not valid.

A person can legitimately be "in charge," but he has to earn his position and be authorized for it—through legal election, proper succession, a group's consensus, and so forth. There is an account in the ancient Scriptures of a young shepherd named David who received authorization from God to succeed King Saul as the next king of Israel. A prophet was sent to tell him of his appointment and to anoint him for his rule. However, even with this divine sanction behind him, David did not take the throne until it was time for him to do so. He did not kill the current ruler, King Saul. As long as Saul was still alive, he did not usurp the throne, even though Saul sought to take his life. David stated, *"I will not lift my hand against my master, because he is the LORD's anointed"* (1 Samuel 24:10). After Saul died, David then became the legitimate ruler of Israel.

A PERSON WHO DOMINATES

While the "boss spirit" mainly refers to manipulation, and "in charge" refers to usurpation, the domination concept has to do with control. Many people confuse authority with domination.

There are those who operate entirely through control. Some of these people are so insecure that the only way they feel they can hide their vulnerability and have others' respect is (ironically) to be heavy-handed.

Those who operate according to this approach threaten others or use some of the negative techniques discussed above in order to maintain a state of control: they may exhibit a boss spirit, use force, and refuse to delegate because they don't trust anyone else. They centralize all activity with themselves and become the hub of all power and decisions, micromanaging the activities of their organization, family, church, or nation. People who equate such domination with authority may grow to mistrust any parameters others try to put on them or their actions.

> GENUINE AUTHORITY DOESN'T CONTROL BUT RELEASES PEOPLE TO EXERCISE THEIR OWN AUTHORITY.

Genuine authority doesn't control but releases people to exercise their own authority. A true leader feels no need to dominate others but immediately shares his authority with them. He wants to delegate authority and encourage others to develop their own abilities.

A PERSON WHO FUNCTIONS AS A DICTATOR OR TYRANT

Some people think that a person who wields absolute power is in a place of authority. The very nature of a dictator cancels authority, however, because true authority does not demand unconditional rule over others.

A dictatorship incorporates the domination approach, to a great extent. It does not allow freedom of expression or permit people to explore ideas and fully partake of opportunities for personal and professional growth—in essence, they are denied the ability to be fully human. People may confuse dictatorship with authority if they have lived under an oppressive system for a period of time so that it has become familiar, even though repressive.

A dictator and a tyrant are similar in that instead of exhibiting true authority, they are *authoritarian*. One of the meanings of *authoritarian* is "of, relating to, or favoring blind submission to authority." Someone with an authoritarian approach demands unquestioned obedience from others. The tyrant spirit is one of ultimate corrupt power that wants others to submit without thought or question. A tyrant is not only a usurper of power, but he also especially wields power for his own personal gain and security.

Again, the very nature of dictatorship and tyranny cancels genuine authority. Any perceived submission that is a result of force or threat is not real submission but surrender. Wherever there's true authority, there will be true submission—which, as we will see in a later chapter, is a voluntary act and part of the inherently interdependent nature of authority. Surrender is in stark contrast to this and is always a result of manipulation and fear.

When people are so fearful of another person that they are afraid to do what they actually desire to do because that person has "authority," they are functioning under a dictatorship. That is not authority; it is intimidation. True authority allows people to express themselves and to develop to the full extent of their potential. It doesn't restrict but provides instruction, advice, or counsel to build others up. The opposite of a tyrant is someone who seeks the good of others, not his own gain, and even makes personal sacrifices on their behalf.

A PERSON WHO HAS A TITLE

Some people think that authority automatically accompanies a person's title. We tend to respect and honor people who have titles that seem to elevate them. In this way we confuse labels with legitimacy. It does not necessarily follow that a person with a title is exercising authority. For example, a person may connive, manipulate a system, or even kill to obtain a certain title or role. This person's rule is unauthorized. Only genuine authority makes rule or power legal.

A true leader may have a title, but he does not operate from the title. He operates from his inner authority, and people respond to his natural authority rather than to his label.

A PERSON WHO IS LOUD OR "LARGER THAN LIFE"

At times, people automatically attribute authority to someone who speaks the loudest or appears "larger than life." This aspect of false authority has to do with a person's personality—he or she may come across as strong, opinionated, overbearing, charismatic, articulate and persuasive, threatening, or obnoxious. Yet, just because a person or even a group speaks the loudest or the most forcefully doesn't necessarily mean they have legitimate authority over others. Many people are intimidated by such individuals and therefore succumb to them. They allow them to make decisions and to cause everyone connected with them to move in a certain direction, which may or may not be healthy.

> YOU KNOW YOU HAVE EFFECTIVE AUTHORITY WHEN YOU SAY NOTHING OR ARE VERY QUIET, AND PEOPLE RESPOND POSITIVELY TO YOU AND YOUR INFLUENCE.

In contrast, I have noticed that true authority is often quiet or even silent. It takes greater natural authority to lower your volume and still be effective. Often, the greater the true authority that is present, the quieter the atmosphere. You know you have effective authority when you say nothing or are very quiet, and people respond positively to you and your influence.

I taught junior high school for five years, and I learned early on that if I had to shout at my students to maintain order, I had no real authority. So, I quickly established boundaries and communicated the values by which my classroom would be run, making it clear on the board and on signs posted around the room what the laws of the learning environment would be. I had been authorized by the school to teach the students, so my authority in that situation was legitimate, but then I had to create the context for that authority. Once the students understood my standards and values, they knew they would have to submit to them if they wanted a good relationship with me. The students responded well and respected my authority, and so there was a good environment for learning.

A similar principle can be seen in many effective leaders of countries, companies, and even families. The measure of their authority is what happens in the midst of their silence—or even their absence. For instance, if a mother goes on an errand, leaving an older child to oversee the household, the measure of her true authority will be reflected in how that older child responds during her absence. Does he run wild through the house, or does he make sure his younger siblings are taken care of? If the household is at peace when the mother returns, the children have respected her authority even when she was out of sight. Or, suppose you are in a meeting at your workplace at which fifteen people are present, but the president of the company is not. Perhaps there is confusion about what should be done regarding a certain matter or who should do it. Then, the president walks in and sits in the back, and the whole discussion and environment change as people calm down and begin to make constructive suggestions. That is an example of silent authority that is put into motion just by one's presence.

Jesus of Nazareth had this inherent authority. Once, when the religious leaders of His day wanted to trap Him, they brought to Him a woman who had been caught in adultery to see if He would agree that she should be stoned to death, which was the punishment according to the law. He responded with silence, while they kept demanding an answer. Then, He quietly asked them one question, which decisively defeated them, and they went away. That's authority.

They were using this question as a trap, in order to have a basis for accusing him. But Jesus bent down and started to write on the ground with his finger. When they kept on questioning him, he straightened up and said to them, "If any one of you is without sin, let him be the first to throw a stone at her." Again he stooped down and wrote on the ground. At this, those who heard began to go away one at a time, the older ones first, until only Jesus was left, with the woman still standing there. Jesus straightened up and asked her, "Woman, where are they? Has no one condemned you?" "No one, sir," she said. "Then neither do I condemn you," Jesus declared. "Go now and leave your life of sin."

(John 8:6–11)

Jesus was later dragged before the Roman governor, Pontius Pilate, and falsely accused. He didn't say a word in response. His silence unnerved Pilate. It's interesting that Pilate's response was to threaten Jesus with authority, telling Him that he had the authority to release Him or to kill Him. Jesus told him, *"You would have no authority over Me, unless it had been given you from above"* (John 19:11 NASB). Jesus was operating under an authority that was higher than the Roman government's, and even Pilate had to submit to that authority, whether he was aware of it or not.

A PERSON WITH TRUE AUTHORITY DOESN'T HAVE TO FLAUNT IT; IT SELLS ITSELF.

Confidence or composure, such as Jesus demonstrated, comes from a sense of true authority. Authority creates its own confidence. A person with true authority doesn't have to flaunt it; it sells itself. Likewise, when a person has legitimate authority, he doesn't have to use force or volume to demand that he be heard. People will listen to true authority, whether they agree with it or not. The religious leaders of Jesus's day kept questioning His authority because they wanted to undermine Him. Yet many of the people responded to Him. *"The crowds were amazed at his teaching, because he taught as one who had authority, and not as their teachers of the law"* (Matthew 7:28–29).

WHAT AUTHORITY IS NOT

The accepted concepts of authority listed above have nothing to do with real authority, yet the problem is that the majority of the world's population *believes* that one or more of these ideas represents authority, and that is why we are experiencing an authority crisis. These false ideas are what many people think of when they hear this word because *authority* has been defined or modeled for them in distorted ways, and their experience of it has been oppressive, negative, stifling, and even deadly.

We must understand that authority is not…

+ dominating others

+ overpowering others

+ dictating to others

+ oppressing others

+ mastering others

+ forcing people to do what you want them to do

+ manipulating people to do what you want them to do

+ controlling others

+ restricting others

+ tyrannizing others

+ subjecting other people to your will

To summarize, we often perceive authority as any person, party, or position that dominates, controls, or manipulates other people or situations, usually to that perceived authority's advantage. And all of us hate to be dominated, manipulated, and controlled!

Those who exhibit false authority not only hurt everyone around them but also stifle the true authority that is within themselves and that they could be offering to others. They are not operating in their proper authority and domain but in a false domain of abuse. While we naturally side with the victims of false authority, we must realize that both perpetrators and victims of erroneous perceptions of authority need to find and live in the freedom that comes only through true authority.

RESULTS OF THE MISUSE AND ABUSE OF AUTHORITY

People react in different ways to the neglect, misuse, or abuse of authority, but our negative conceptions of and experiences with authority produce life-draining emotions and attitudes. Think about specific negative experiences in your life in which you have dealt with people in alleged authority or found yourself in circumstances that seemed to control you. Now, consider how you have reacted to them as you read through the following list of reactions people may have to false authority:

- *Fear*: They are afraid of being ruled and controlled.

- *Intimidation/Timidity*: They are unsettled by those who claim to have authority over them and may go along with their orders or suggestions only because they feel they have no choice.

- *Distrust/Caution*: They keep themselves at arm's length from others because they don't want to be taken advantage of or have their lives run by someone else.

- *Suspicion*: They are distrustful of those who *want* to be in charge, and so they steer clear of them.

- *Friction*: Their relationships with those who are "in charge" are tense; they have difficulty finding common ground on which to connect with supervisors, teachers, parents, and colleagues.

- *Antagonism/Contentiousness/Defiance*: They are disagreeable and belligerent in their interactions with others.

- *Defensiveness*: They are easily offended and try to protect themselves from criticism.

- *Resentment*: They develop a bitter spirit toward those whom they perceive as "management" or "executives."

- *Protest*: They object to suggestions, thinking, "Nobody's going to tell me what to do," so they immediately dispute any attempt to influence their lives.

- *Avoidance*: Because of their negative experiences with authority, they avoid exercising initiative or taking supervisory roles themselves.

- *Threat*: They feel in danger from and vulnerable to those who have power.

- *Stress/Anxiety/Worry/Dread*: They experience distress when interacting with authority figures.

What a terrible way to live!

As a result of the misuse and abuse of authority, our world—especially the present generation—has an underlying current of distrust, disrespect, and fear of authority. Some people have come to even reject any semblance of authority. Others have come to believe that suppression and oppression are natural components of authority, or at least ones that are to be accepted, tolerated, or endured. These long-established concepts of authority and the behavior that results from them are the fundamental cause of many of the problems we face in the world today. They are essentially destroying people, preventing them from becoming all that they were born to be.

Even though we can understand and sympathize with the above reactions and emotions, they are not healthy, and they will do nothing toward helping us to exercise our own inherent personal authority.

THE BEAUTIFUL PRINCIPLE

The negative experiences we've had with authority inevitably have an effect on our fulfillment and effectiveness in life. Therefore, let's leave behind our prior misconceptions of authority and move past our reactions to the misuse and abuse of authority and instead discover the nature and principles of true authority.

I like to call authority the "beautiful principle" because it's not about "lording it over" others. It's about making smooth paths for people. It's a means of providing the resources, protection, refreshment, enlightenment, growth, happiness, fulfillment, satisfaction, and contentment we all need.

In the next chapter, we will explore the nature of true authority and what this nature is based on.

THREE

THE SOURCE OF AUTHORITY

THE ESSENTIAL RELATIONSHIP BETWEEN AUTHOR AND AUTHORIZED

In the last chapter, we looked at some poor and destructive substitutes for authority. To recognize and understand true authority, we need to explore the source, or origin, of human authority and the inherent purposes of that authority.

THE AUTHOR

THE "COPYRIGHT OWNER" OF THE EARTH

The English word *authority* comes from a Latin word, *auctor*. *Auctor* means "promoter, originator, or author." What is an author? A simple dictionary definition is "one that originates or creates: source." An author is the originator or creator of something. In many countries, the copyright of authors of literary or musical works and the patents of inventors are highly valued and protected by law.

Let me say here that every human being has the right to believe what he wishes to believe, and I respect and would defend his right to do so. In our modern age of so-called enlightenment, many have opted to believe that they are by-products of an evolutionary process and are children of apes. However, it is my firm conviction and belief that human beings have an Author—the Creator of the world—who is the source of our very lives, in addition to our authority. Our Creator, or God, is the originator of the world and everything in it. We call God "God" because He is the natural author of all creation. The word *God* refers to "the supreme or ultimate reality: as the Being perfect in power, wisdom, and goodness who is worshipped as creator and ruler of the universe." Though many people have tried to infringe on or deny His "copyright" on them, it still remains His and always will. This principle of the Creator's authority is fundamental and essential to understanding the nature and power of your personal authority.

THE RIGHT OF THE SOURCE

God, the self-sufficient One, is the Author, the Originating Cause, the Creator of all things seen and unseen. He is the absolute rightful Sovereign over all He has created. It is God "*for whom and through whom everything exists*" (Hebrews 2:10).

The Creator gave everything existence, and He has the power of life itself—the ability to give life and to take it away. From our perspective as human beings, there's no greater authority than that! Many people are literally looking for a fountain of youth, and, figuratively, they are looking for eternal life. Yet only God can give eternal life. Jesus of Nazareth said, "*The Father has life in himself*" (John 5:26).

In the first book written by Moses, the great leader and lawgiver, it says, "*In the beginning God created* [authored] *the heavens and the earth*" (Genesis 1:1). David, the musician-king of Israel, wrote, "*The earth is the* Lord's, *and everything in it, the world, and all who live in it*" (Psalm 24:1). Everything that exists on the earth—plants, animals, birds, reptiles, oceans, land, human beings—as well as everything in the vast universe is owned by God. Nobody has a right to counterfeit what He has "written" in the foundations of the world or to usurp what He has made.

OUR AUTHORITY COMES FROM OUR SOURCE'S AUTHORITY

An author or creator is always the authoritative source of his work, whether it is a book, an appliance, a car, a house, or an aircraft. For example, I am the author of a number of books, and I could teach all of my books without looking at the published volumes or my original notes for them because I'm the source of them. People may use my books to teach others, but as the author, I can speak conclusively about what is in them and my purpose for writing them. Everything an author or inventor produces is created because there is something he desires to communicate or to make that initiates its production. It is created for a reason.

The source of a product therefore has the legitimate right to state the framework of the authority he puts into his product and the way the product functions best. This framework is what we call the principles or laws governing it and through which it operates. For a product produced by a company, the framework for that product's authority would be its user's manual. In this way, not only is the company or creator itself the authority, but its documentation of the principles and laws governing the product become the authority, as well. The product manual is not produced by a wholesaler, retailer, or consumer but by the one from whom the product originated. Their opinions and preferences for the working of a product may be interesting, but they are not the authority; they are not authorized by the maker and can't be guaranteed.

The Ultimate Authority and Source of all human authority is therefore the Creator, as well as the principles and laws He has established concerning humanity, which are recorded in the Scriptures. Anything that doesn't correspond to them or reflect their essence and spirit is not true authority. Opinions that don't correspond to the Creator's original design cannot be guaranteed. What people theorize about humanity and creation is not the question. The question is, What did the Manufacturer say about it?

If we want to live in the reality that comes from following the principles governing true authority, we must get in touch with the Source and find out His parameters for our lives. This is how we protect and preserve ourselves as human beings.

A *principle* is an established law or fundamental rule under which something functions due to its nature and design. The principles we need to apply to our lives are inherent in creation, timeless, and permanent. They were established by the Creator to secure and protect the functions and fulfillment of His creation. Scripture uses various terms to refer to principles, such as *commandments, precepts, statutes,* and phrases like *the ways of God.*

Authority is a principle in itself, but it also functions according to specific precepts that we must understand in order to appreciate and benefit from it.

SHARED AUTHORITY

Under the copyright laws of the United States, even though an author is the owner of his work and has full authority in relation to it, he also has the power to share the rights of that work with someone else or to transfer those rights entirely, so that the other person becomes a "copyright claimant" in relation to the work. This occurs through a written document by which the author grants permission for the transfer of full or joint ownership of the rights. Rights can also be legally transferred by will or inheritance; if the author dies, the rights are bestowed on a designated relative or friend.

Similarly, the Creator, as the Author of our world, and having ownership of it, delegated some of His authority by entrusting it to human beings. He shared authority in relation to His "copyright" of the earth so that we could exercise that authority both in and over the earth. It was He who designed us with the ability to carry out our individual and collective authorities in the world.

AUTHORITY IS BUILT INTO OUR VERY EXISTENCE

In what manner did the Creator grant us this shared ownership of the world? He did not give us authority as a form of transaction between business associates. He shared it with us in the way a father would share what is his with his children. We were made to share in the Creator's inherent authority by being made in His own image, by being made as His "offspring." In this way, authority has been built into our very existence as human beings:

> WE WERE MADE TO SHARE IN THE CREATOR'S INHERENT AUTHORITY BY BEING MADE IN HIS OWN IMAGE, BY BEING MADE AS HIS "OFFSPRING."

Then God said, "Let us make man in our image, in our likeness, and let them rule over the fish of the sea and the birds of the air, over the livestock, over all the earth, and over all the creatures that move along the ground." So God created man in his own image, in the image of God he created him; male and female he created them.

(Genesis 1:26–27)

To show human beings the authority He had placed within them and to instruct them in it, "*God blessed them and said to them, 'Be fruitful and increase in number; fill the earth and subdue it. Rule over the fish of the sea and the birds of the air and over every living creature that moves on the ground'"* (Genesis 1:28).

We were made—literally—for authority. Human beings have been given both a general authority over the earth and a personal authority that is specific to each one of us.

The Creator operates in the universe in conjunction with His authority. We were made to receive authority from Him and, in turn, to operate according to this authority and the principles He has established for the earth.

Our authority is manifested in a number of ways and in various realms of human interaction and endeavor as we are fruitful with our lives, as we fill the earth, and as we rule over it. Our understanding of the Creator's authority and purpose, and our response to them, are demonstrated by the extent to which we fulfill our authority.

AUTHORITY IS BUILT INTO ALL OF CREATION

It is not only human beings who function through authority but also all of creation. In nature, we can clearly see some of the ways in which the Creator has established authority to be a principle on earth. For example, when He designed the world, He created it to function under two distinct periods, day and night. Interestingly, Moses described their purposes in terms of authority:

> *And God said, "Let there be lights in the expanse of the sky to separate the day from the night, and let them serve as signs to mark seasons and days and years, and let them be lights in the expanse of the sky to give light on the earth." And it was so. God made two great lights—the greater light to govern the day and the lesser light to govern the night. He also made the stars. God set them in the expanse of the sky to give light on the earth, to govern the day and the night, and to separate light from darkness. And God saw that it was good.* (Genesis 1:14–18)

Our life on earth is governed by days that are approximately twenty-four hours in length, and by seasons, both which were established at humanity's origin. We obviously don't have the ability to change the reality of days and seasons. We have to respect the "authority" of the sun and the moon—the two lights that "oversee" our world. Generally, things slow down at night, not only because people are tired and have a biological need for sleep, but also because night is a less conducive time to work. The world also takes on a different atmosphere after dark. It is quieter and a time for reflection and rest rather than production. Of course, we can work with artificial lights, but no one can keep up round-the-clock activity indefinitely. In addition, fewer people are available to interact with at night because they, also, are governed by the parameters of this daily cycle. So, we are governed by the nature of days.

Seasons also have "authority" over our lives, affecting when and how we do things. Even in locations like the Bahamas where it is warm year-round, seasons govern the times during which we engage in certain activities. For example, although many tourists visit during the fall and winter seasons and swim in the ocean, most Bahamians think they're a little crazy to do so. They won't go swimming until it's good and hot—at least 90 degrees! In regions where the seasons go from one temperature extreme to the other, people alter their behavior to fit the changing weather conditions. We all have certain habits and behaviors and patterns of life according to the seasons, and, in that sense, seasons exercise authority over our lives.

In another example of authority in nature, God created animals and plants in various genuses and species—He made them *according to their kinds*" (Genesis 1:11–12; 21, 24–25). Each species is unique and was created to fulfill God's purpose under its own authority of existence.

WE MUST CONSULT THE AUTHOR

If we really want to know the purposes for which God created the heavens and the earth, therefore, we have no choice but to consult Him as the Author. The sciences can provide us with some answers regarding how things function and what they consist of, but scientists can research only what has already been made. When a scientist discovers an aspect of life that has been functioning since creation, we sometimes seem to give him almost as much credit as if he had created it! We may award him a Nobel Prize or other award. While we can value scientists and their findings, we need to think of them with proper perspective. Again, science can simply discover what the Author had already put into creation.

> **I BELIEVE THAT MOST PEOPLE HAVEN'T REALLY BEEN "DISCOVERED" YET IN TERMS OF KNOWING WHY AND HOW THEY WERE CREATED.**

Moreover, discovering something is one thing. Understanding why it was created is something else. I believe that most people haven't really been "discovered" yet in terms of knowing why and how they were created. Few people understand who they really are because they are not in touch with the Creator. Only an author truly knows his work and why he wrote it. Only an inventor really knows his invention and why he created it.

It is one thing to know that God created you in His image and likeness, but there is something beyond the act of creation itself, and that is *why* He created you and *what authority* He has given you to accomplish your purpose on earth.

As the Ultimate Authority, the Creator is the Source of the authority within you, within me, and within everyone else in the world. We need to recognize and exercise the authority He has placed inside us and carry out what He has authorized us to be and do.

PURPOSE DETERMINES DESIGN

IN THE PHYSICAL WORLD

To begin to recognize and exercise the authority within us, let's explore one of the foundational principles of authority that we noted in chapter one: *everyone and everything is designed to fulfill its purpose*. We can also word it in this way: the purpose for which a product is designed determines the design of the product itself. Everything (at least, everything that is well made) is designed so that it will fulfill the purpose for which it was created.

This foundational principle is built into all of creation. Everything was made because there is something that the Creator wanted on earth that required its existence.

For example, in the physical world that He created, God needed something that would prevent people and objects on earth from drifting off into space, and so He established gravity, with its associated laws.

God knew He would need something to produce light rays that would cause photosynthesis in plants, and so He built this capacity into the sun.

God's purpose was to perpetuate life on earth, and so He provided for the sustenance and perpetuation of life in a number of ways.

Although many flowers are beautiful to look at, and although appreciating beauty is valuable in itself, there is more to flowers than their beauty. Certain insects are genetically designed to respond to certain colors of flowers, and those colors are connected to what the insects need to feed on for survival. When the insects feed from the blossoms, they pick up pollen from the plants and then transfer that pollen to other plants. This causes the plants to create blossoms and fruit, which produce new plants so that life can be carried on through subsequent generations. God was therefore not only thinking about the beauty of the plants but also of the new plants that would come later as a result of them. He has created everything for a purpose, and He has given everything its own authority to carry out that purpose.

God created the human body with various purposes in mind, and so He designed it to function according to certain processes. For example, He knew the body would need a method of taking in oxygen while breathing out carbon dioxide, so He first designed plants with the capacity to take in carbon dioxide while emitting oxygen. Then, He created the human body to produce carbon dioxide, which the plants need, so the plants could produce oxygen, which the body needs. He also designed human lungs to act as an exchange mechanism for this process. He made everything because there was something that would require its existence.

Every aspect of the human body was designed with a specific assignment so that it could function in a healthy way. The entire world was created to function in such a manner that everything had what it needed to sustain life. And the Creator has been keeping the world going ever since.

For by [God] all things were created: things in heaven and on earth,
visible and invisible, whether thrones or powers or rulers or authorities;

all things were created by him and for him. He is before all things, and
in him all things hold together. (Colossians 1:16–17)

IN THE "WORLD" OF HUMAN RELATIONSHIPS AND VOCATION

God planned not only the interactions and interrelationships of the physical world according to His purposes, but also human relationships and human vocation according to His purposes. By *vocation*, I do not mean just people's jobs. I am referring to the concept of vocation as "the special function of an individual or group" or "a summons or strong inclination to a particular state or course of action." There is something that God desires to accomplish that made your existence necessary and valuable. If you're ever tempted to feel that you're not important, remember that your purpose is what caused you to be born. God has an assignment in mind that made you essential.

> ## YOUR BIRTH IS EVIDENCE THAT GOD WANTED TO ACCOMPLISH SOMETHING THAT HE HAD TO CREATE **YOU** TO DO.

I believe that every single person on the planet—approaching seven billion of us, young and old, at the time of this writing—was created because there was something God wanted done that required that person's existence. Your birth is evidence that God wanted to accomplish something that He had to create *you* to do.

Everyone was created to have dominion over an area or a specific "territory" of life that only he can "govern." When you find the area or territory that you're supposed to oversee, you will find the secret to your fulfillment in life and to your particular contribution to the human race. This territorial assignment is your authority.

A Greek word for *authority* in the Scriptures is *exousia*, and one meaning of this word is "delegated influence."

Therefore, your authority determines your influence in the world.

This means that whatever you were created to do is your territory, or area of authority. Your unique gifts and qualities are the special tools that allow you to function in your authority.

THE SOURCE SUPPORTS AND IS RESPONSIBLE FOR ITS PRODUCT

AUTHORITY IS FROM THE AUTHOR AND FOR THE AUTHOR

Authority is therefore an inherent purpose of human beings. Moreover, along with authority, we have been given the ability to fulfill the intent of our Author, or Source. Thus, authority is both *from* the Author and *for* the Author. Authority is fulfilled successfully when the Author is pleased. When you manifest your authority, that is your measure of success.

The Creator supports His delegated authority. He is responsible for making sure that the authority He gave you is successful. One who has true authority will never abandon those to whom he delegates authority. He will enable them to fulfill it. *"The* LORD *will fulfill his purpose for me"* (Psalm 138:8).

A MATTER OF REPUTATION

One of the reasons the Creator supports the authority He has given us is that His reputation is on the line. For example, in the commercial world, the products you buy are supported by the manufacturers because their names are on them, and they want to protect their reputations in the minds of consumers. A company wants its products to succeed and to sell well. Its name and its image are synonymous in the customers' minds, and therefore, if a product is faulty, the company's name can be tarnished— sometimes to the point of causing the business to fail.

When the Toyota company had technical problems with its popular energy-conserving car, the Prius, as well as other models, their previously excellent name in the automobile business was weakened. In addressing the situation and trying to regain consumers' trust, one of the things they did was to run television advertisements saying that they were working hard to correct the problems. To further protect the brand name of Toyota, the company sent the president of the company, who is the grandson of the founder, to meet with the Congress of the United States to discuss the issues directly and to explain the steps the company was taking to resolve the problems and to manage quality control. All of this was done to protect the name of the company and to regain its authority in the marketplace.

When the international banking industry took a tailspin through, among other things, poor lending practices, causing banks to fail and prompting governments to offer grants and loans to help banks weather the crisis, some banks displayed signs on their buildings stating that they were "Bail-out Free." They wanted their customers to know that they had not engaged in risky banking policies, were in sound financial shape, and had not needed to accept governmental funds. The signs were one attempt to protect their names in the minds of their customers.

Similarly, whenever there are issues with the quality of certain foods or with an outbreak of food poisoning, some grocery stores and restaurants post signs that indicate that their products were not affected by whatever was causing the problem. They want people to know they still have quality goods for sale, so that their own reputations won't be affected by the problems of other companies.

These examples reflect the fact that a responsible source or manufacturer of a product desires to guarantee the quality of the product so that it is safe and functions according to design.

The Creator backs up the authority He has given us as we operate according to the principles He has established for humanity. He tells us, "I am watching to see that my word is fulfilled" (Jeremiah 1:12), and "The LORD will not forsake his people for his great name's sake" (1 Samuel 12:22 KJV).

THE AUTHORITY DILEMMA

As it was established by the Creator, authority is inherently good. It allows us to fulfill our collective and individual purposes as human beings. Yet, historically, we have seen how authority has been abused by those who were supposed to be its custodians, as well as by those who usurped authority for their own purposes and selfish goals. Again, false authority has hurt some people so badly that they reject the very concept of authority.

In our contemporary world, because of our negative experiences with "authority figures," we face the issue of needing to be friendly with authority to get along in life but never quite trusting it. We don't want to accept any vestiges of absolute authority. Nevertheless, we find ourselves in a dilemma: as human beings, we were created to operate under legitimate authority and its principles, and our lives can't function properly without them; yet, at the same time, we're afraid of authority.

RECAPTURING THE ORIGINAL PURPOSE FOR AUTHORITY

In the face of this dilemma, how do we recover genuine authority in our lives? The Creator says, *"My people are destroyed from lack of knowledge"* (Hosea 4:6). Therefore, let us move forward to discover how to recapture the true nature of authority for ourselves and our world.

FOUR

THE BETRAYAL AND RESTORATION OF AUTHORITY

AN IMITATION LIFE IS COSTLIER THAN THE DESIGNER'S LIFE

Our authority is found in what the Creator planned and designed for us to do, but most of us are not living according to our personal authority. To recapture our true authority, we need to discover how humanity's confusion about authority began and why it persists. We have to start again at the beginning.

> God said, "Let us make man in our image, in our likeness, and let them rule over the fish of the sea and the birds of the air, over the livestock, over all the earth, and over all the creatures that move along the ground." So God created man in his own image, in the image of God he created him; male and female he created them.
>
> (Genesis 1:26–27)

When human beings were made in the image and likeness of the Creator, they were designed to be like Him, act like Him, and function like Him. Just as He rules, humans were to rule the earth—under His ultimate authority, His established principles for the earth. This authority did not *belong* to human beings; it was *entrusted* to them by the Creator. A shared authority was delegated to them.

You can never "take" true authority. It is always delegated and therefore can only be received with gratitude and acted upon. You can seize power, but authority has to be given to you. Moreover, if you transfer some of the authority that you have received to someone else, then he, too, can only receive it. He can't take your authority from you.

THE BETRAYAL OF AUTHORITY

We noted in the last chapter that true authority corresponds to the principles and laws the Creator has established concerning humanity. If we fail to follow these principles and laws, we will find ourselves outside of the protection of His authority, and therefore we will be at risk. Whatever is not authorized by the Creator can't be guaranteed to function as designed.

Unfortunately, the first human beings went outside the parameters of the authority that the Creator God had given to them and did exactly what He had told them not to do. Why? Because they desired power more than authority.

God has an enemy, Satan (meaning "accuser" or "adversary"), also called the devil, who tempted the first human beings to do this. Satan is a created angelic being who rebelled against God's authority himself. His goal is to cause human beings to lose their true selves by forfeiting the precious life and authority that God has given to them. He tempted the first human beings by asking them, in effect, "Wouldn't you like to be like God?" Yet Adam and Eve were *already* like God; they were created in His image and reflected His nature. They had His delegated authority. But Satan wanted them to doubt who they inherently were and to become something else, something unnatural. And this is exactly how he has been tempting human beings ever since.

This is how the initial temptation transpired:

The LORD God took the man and put him in the Garden of Eden to work it and take care of it. And the LORD God commanded the man, "You are free to eat from any tree in the garden; but you must not eat from the tree of the knowledge of good and evil, for when you eat of it you will surely die."… Now the serpent was more crafty than any of the wild animals the LORD God had made. He said to the woman, "Did God really say, 'You must not eat from any tree in the garden'?" The woman said to the serpent, "We may eat fruit from the trees in the garden, but God did say, 'You must not eat fruit from the tree that is in the middle of the garden, and you must not touch it, or you will die.'" "You will not surely die," the serpent said to the woman. "For God knows that when you eat of it your eyes will be opened, and you will be

*like God, knowing good and evil." When the woman saw that the fruit
of the tree was good for food and pleasing to the eye, and also desirable
for gaining wisdom, she took some and ate it. She also gave some to her
husband, who was with her, and he ate it.* (Genesis 2:15–17; 3:1–6)

Again, true authority is always a trust that we are given. It isn't ours;
we don't own it. Any attempt to misuse or discard it is a betrayal of that
trust. Whenever a person is given authority, he must always be aware that
it is not his personal property. It is not for sale; it is never to be gambled,
sold, or used for personal gain. This is the behavior we examined in chapter
2 among those who wield false authority—the one who "rules" through
overpowering force, the one with the "boss spirit," the dictator, and so
forth. Instead, entrusted authority must always be used for the purpose for
which it was given. And because it is never owned by the one who receives
it, it can always be recalled if necessary.

Instead of regarding the trust they had been given, Adam and Eve
handed over their authority—and the authority of the whole human race—
to an illegitimate ruler. Their action was the equivalent of treason because
they betrayed their trust and broke their allegiance to their Creator and
Sovereign.

The fundamental source of all of mankind's deficiencies and problems,
therefore, was the original violation of the Creator's ultimate authority—it
was a betrayal of devotion and trust toward the Creator by His creation.
This violation is what the Scriptures call "sin." Everything that is wrong in
the world today is a consequence of the abandonment of authority.

THREE FUNDAMENTAL RESULTS OF THE BETRAYAL

Have you ever bought an imitation brand of a product that you
thought you'd like? Sometimes, we think we are saving money when we do
this. Yet, often, we get what we pay for. The knockoff product wears out,
breaks down, or fades much more quickly or doesn't function as effectively
because it is made of cheaper materials. Then, we have to buy another one
to replace it. Going for the imitation can end up being costlier than buying
the brand-name or designer version in the first place.

EVERYTHING THAT IS WRONG IN THE WORLD TODAY IS A CONSEQUENCE OF THE ABANDONMENT OF AUTHORITY.

Adam and Eve were taken in by imitation authority—a cheap version of authority—when they played into the hands of the imitation-authority salesman, Satan. The results were disastrous and far costlier than being true to the life the Master Designer had given them:

1. *The Forfeit of Authority.* When human beings abandoned God's authority, they forfeited their shared authority of the earth; they gave it over to God's enemy, and that is why Satan is called *"the god of this age ["world" KJV]"* (2 Corinthians 4:4). Through Adam and Eve's disobedience, Satan seized power on the earth and could now wreak havoc on it. From that point on, humanity has had to live under a false and usurped authority that is bent on its complete ruin.

2. *The Shock of the Unauthentic.* Under false authority, life is hard, complicated, disappointing, and burdensome. *"Cursed is the ground because of you; through painful toil you will eat of it all the days of your life. It will produce thorns and thistles for you"* (Genesis 3:17–18). There is a high cost to living in a shadow of the original authority humanity once had. Yet, human beings brought all these things on themselves as the natural result of choosing to live outside of their true authority. An unnatural action led to an unnatural existence.

3. *Ultimate Self-Destruction.* Anyone who forfeits true authority will ultimately self-destruct because he is no longer under the protection and safeguard of that authority. This is why Adam and Eve—and all subsequent human beings—had to die. It was the very thing that God had warned them of: *"And the LORD God commanded the man, 'You are free to eat from any tree in the garden; but you must not eat from the tree of the knowledge of good and evil, for when you eat of it you will surely die'"* (Genesis 2:16–17). It is what the false authority said would *not* happen: *"'You will not surely die,' the serpent said"* (Genesis 3:4). And it is exactly what *did* happen: *"By the sweat of your brow you will eat your food until you return to the*

ground, since from it you were taken; for dust you are and to dust you will return" (Genesis 3:19).

CONSEQUENCES OF LOST AUTHORITY

The above three fundamental results of the betrayal led to these additional consequences:

HUMANITY LOST ITS TRUE HOME

An additional outcome of the relinquishment of authority was that humanity lost its true home. The author of the book of Jude gave us insight into this sobering consequence. He wrote about how God gave authority to certain angels, who subsequently discarded it. Let us look at Jude 1:6 using several translations so that we get the full impact of his insight:

> *And the angels who did not keep their **positions of authority** but abandoned their own **home**—these he has kept in darkness, bound with everlasting chains for judgment on the great Day.* (NIV)

> *And angels who did not keep their own **domain**, but abandoned their proper **abode**, He has kept in eternal bonds under darkness for the judgment of the great day.* (NASB)

> *And the angels which kept not their first **estate**, but left their own **habitation**, he hath reserved in everlasting chains under darkness unto the judgment of the great day.* (KJV)

God had given positions of authority to these angels—authority for various assignments—but the angels left these assignments when they rebelled against His ultimate authority as Creator. From this verse in Jude, we can conclude that the angels' authority was not just something they *had*; it was integral to who they *were*—to their very nature and existence. It gave them their place in God's reign. When they forfeited their authority, therefore, their existence was fundamentally changed.

Note in the above Scriptures that the words *position*, *domain*, and *estate* are linked with the words *home*, *abode*, and *habitation*. When the angels abandoned their authority, it was the equivalent of a person abandoning his home and family. Once again, it was a betrayal of trust—and the loss was incalculable.

Jude went on to talk about *"godless men"* who act in the same way as these angels did and who *"reject authority"* (Jude 1:4, 8). When Adam and Eve disobeyed God's word, humanity fell from its place of authority, and life on earth was fundamentally altered. Consequently, human beings lost their place in life.

> ## OUR TRUE "HOME" AS HUMAN BEINGS IS THE PLACE WHERE WE WERE CREATED TO LIVE OUT OUR PERSONAL AUTHORITY.

Our true "home" as human beings is the place where we were created to live out our personal authority. Your domain of authority is not a literal building but a place of being, a position. It is where you belong and where you will find all you need to experience fulfillment, refreshment, and renewal. When you discover your inherent authority, you find your true place. You feel at home, you feel comfortable functioning from that position. Why? Again, because true authority is natural. The angels who rebelled and left their true home chose darkness over the light of God. Likewise, when you don't know who you are, where you're supposed to be, and what your authority is, then you are ignorant or "in the dark." You stumble along in life rather than walk purposefully in it.

These angels voluntarily left their positions of authority. Demons are therefore angels who are out of position. They are still angels, but they are out of order and separated from their former authority. A human who is out of order is still human, of course, but is out of his domain or realm of authority; his life isn't what it was meant to be.

Similar to the angels who abandoned their authority, people who are not exercising their authority and using their inherent gifts are often emotionally and mentally "tormented." They can tend to be irritable, start fights with others, and suffer from anxiety because they're not doing what they're supposed to be doing, and it's unsettling, disheartening, and frustrating to them. They're not demons, of course, but the word *demonic* seems to define their experience. And because they are out of order, they also have the tendency to torment those around them.

The difference between the angels who abandoned their authority and human beings, as we will see, is that human beings don't have to remain in darkness. They can be restored to their former authority.

THE PERPETUATION OF FALSE AUTHORITY ON THE EARTH

Without genuine, absolute authority, there is only false, transitory authority—an "authority" based on circumstances, mere speculation, opinion, tradition, whim, and so forth, even in religious matters. This has been a characteristic of the world since the betrayal.

As part of His restoration plan, the Creator gave to humanity the Scriptures to guide them back to Him and to their original authority. Again, the Scriptures are the "user's manual" for humanity. They are reliable, in contrast to the fickleness of human beings. This is why Jesus taught the people to listen to the teachers of the law when they quoted the "manual," or the law, but not to act in the ways they did, because the teachers' lives didn't reflect what they taught. He said,

> The teachers of the law and the Pharisees sit in Moses' seat. So you must obey them and do everything they tell you. But do not do what they do, for they do not practice what they preach. They tie up heavy loads and put them on men's shoulders, but they themselves are not willing to lift a finger to move them. (Matthew 23:2–4)

These religious leaders were not living according to the principles and standards established by the Creator, even though they knew what these principles and standards were. At another time, Jesus said directly to the religious leaders, "You have let go of the commands of God and are holding on to the traditions of men" (Mark 7:8). Again, we see human beings giving more credence to opinion and tradition than to the truth from their Creator.

Jesus also warned His disciples about another aspect of false authority— a method of ruling over people that was practiced by those who were outside of Israel, who were generally referred to as "the Gentiles," a word that means "the nations."

> Jesus called [His disciples] together and said, "You know that those who are regarded as rulers of the Gentiles lord it over them, and their

high officials exercise authority over them. Not so with you. Instead, whoever wants to become great among you must be your servant, and whoever wants to be first must be slave of all. For even the Son of Man did not come to be served, but to serve, and to give his life as a ransom for many." (Mark 10:42–45)

The term *"lord it over"* in this passage has the connotation of "control" or "subjugate," and the phrase *"exercise authority"* denotes "wielding full privilege over." As Jesus moved His disciples toward restored relationships with God and renewed authority, He showed them that the nature of true authority is not about having total control by "lording" it over others but about using the gifts you have been given to *serve* others.

> TRUE AUTHORITY IS NOT ABOUT HAVING TOTAL CONTROL BY "LORDING" IT OVER OTHERS BUT ABOUT USING THE GIFTS YOU HAVE BEEN GIVEN TO SERVE OTHERS.

As we can see, the whole human race was thrown off course because our first human parents, Adam and Eve, abandoned their authority. Because of their rebellion against the Creator, the nature of humanity was altered so that all human beings who were born from them were also corrupt and prone to seeking their own false authority—collectively and individually.

The conflict and abuse we see in our world today on a wide scale is what happens when authority is misconceived and misused. And, again, this is what has led many people to misunderstand and fear authority in general.

The good news is that the Creator had no plans to leave humanity in this state. He provided a way of reconciliation and restoration.

HUMANITY IS UNAUTHORIZED TO CHANGE ITSELF

Let's consider how the Creator went about this reconciliation and restoration through the analogy of an authorized dealer versus an unauthorized dealer, which is similar to the designer versus imitation concept.

Few people are more dangerous than an unauthorized dealer. Many of us have had the experience of taking a piece of equipment, an appliance, or a car to someone who didn't know what he was doing. He claimed he could fix it, but we found out afterward that he was "experimenting" with our valuable possession. Why? He was unauthorized to deal with that specific device. He didn't have either the authority as one connected with the company that made it or the innate ability to fix it.

THE UNAUTHORIZED MERELY EXPERIMENT

The unauthorized must experiment because they don't have access to the original plans. They can have only a trial-and-error approach to repair. This is why, when they take apart your equipment, they can't always put it back together again—or back the same way. Therefore, whenever you take a malfunctioning piece of equipment to someone who is not authorized, you walk away just hoping that everything will be fine. And if you've had a bad experience with a similar situation, your confidence level in the unauthorized can be even lower. Where there is no sense of authority, there is no confidence. In fact, an absence of authority produces confusion and even chaos.

The effects of the unauthorized can be seen in a variety of realms of life. For example, have you ever been in a restaurant that is so well run that you never have to ask for refills on your water or coffee, your food comes in a timely manner, and the atmosphere is peaceful? The opposite experience is being in a restaurant where the serving staff seem agitated and confused, your order isn't taken correctly, other patrons are fidgeting around the hostess stand because they have been waiting for a long time to be seated, and the atmosphere is generally uneasy. That is the difference between an environment governed by authority—an authorized environment—and an environment where authority is absent—an unauthorized one.

The value something holds for you often determines whether you will pay the cost to have an authorized dealer fix it. The dealer always seems to be more expensive, but it can also often be more secure. Why? The dealer is not experimenting. The company has authorized him to work on the product, and he has access to the company's knowledge and experience in relation to it.

The authorized can provide maximum performance, or function, while the unauthorized may only misuse and abuse valuable things. After sending something to be repaired and getting it back, have you ever said,

"It was better before I sent it to be fixed"? It was bad, but it wasn't as bad as it is now. What you had sent was at least working somewhat until an unauthorized person began to deal with it.

THE AUTHORIZED DEALER

To repair human authority, we need to return to the Authorized Dealer, not to any substitute. Think about your life as being a product of The Creator, Incorporated. He is our Manufacturer.

If you've purchased products that have come with warranties, you may have noticed that manufacturers are very particular about authorization and the need to follow the instructions carefully. Someone gave me an audio device as a gift, and it came with a user's manual. On the back of the manual was a card that read "Limited Warranty/Guarantee." Most warranty and guarantee certificates are worded in a similar way. For example, a "Limited Warranty" often covers ninety days for labor and two years for parts. Within the first three months of your owning the product, if anything goes wrong, the manufacturer will fix it free of charge—at no cost for labor. For two years, if anything goes wrong, the manufacturer will replace any faulty or broken parts, but you have to pay for the labor. It doesn't sound like a bad deal, but you have to look at the fine print, which includes the word *conditions*. Every manufacturer has conditions: if you do this, we will guarantee or do that. If you keep this, we will perform that.

THE MANUFACTURER'S CONDITION

What is the condition of The Creator, Incorporated? The Manufacturer will replace defective parts at no charge to the original owner. He guarantees free replacement; it is what the Scriptures call grace. There is a grace period for the restoration of our relationship with the Creator and of our original authority, and we are now still within that grace period. If we reconnect with the Creator during this grace period, then the warranty is eternal and unlimited. A manufacturer's conditions usually say that parts used for replacement are warranted for the remainder of the original, limited warranty period. Therefore, as long as this product exists, parts will exist for it. With The Creator, Incorporated, no matter how old you are, no matter how many mistakes you have made, He still has a warehouse full of "parts" waiting to replace your defective ones anytime you come to Him.

A manufacturer will provide labor for the repair or replacement of defective parts without charge. Similarly, only our Authorized Dealer can do the work of restoration. We have to place our faith in Him alone to do the work that needs to be done.

Let's look at the even finer print that is usually included in a manufacturer's manual. The free labor and parts are subject to the following conditions: the owner must provide verification of the date of purchase when requesting limited warranty service. There has to be a point, sometime, when you bought the item or received it as a gift, so that you own it. The company doesn't want to fix a product that you stole.

Likewise, we can't just ask the Creator to reestablish authority in us when we have no intention of being restored to Him and following His Manual (the Scriptures) for our lives. The Creator will say, "There has to be a relationship between us." There has to be a point in your life when you make a specific decision to accept the grace offered to you so that you belong to the Creator once more.

> THERE HAS TO BE A POINT IN YOUR LIFE WHEN YOU MAKE A SPECIFIC DECISION TO ACCEPT THE GRACE OFFERED TO YOU SO THAT YOU BELONG TO THE CREATOR ONCE MORE.

Salvation is a personal thing, just as inherent authority is personal. That means that what we are (which has been given as a trust) belongs to Him, and what we will be is also His.

Another condition of a manufacturer, which I alluded to earlier, is that all repairs must be performed by an authorized dealer or facility connected to the company. The user's manual provides information on the locations of authorized service agents and how to reach them. The Creator, Incorporated, functions in a similar way. If you want restoration and repair for your life, you must go to His Authorized Dealer. No experimentation with the product is allowed.

The Manufacturer's Manual is very clear about who the Authorized Dealer is because there is only one: Jesus the Christ, the Son of the Owner of the company. He is the only way, the only truth, the only life. No one can be restored except by Him. (See John 14:6.) If anyone tries to be restored by any other means, he is the equivalent of a robber who climbs through windows or breaks into houses to gain access to what is inside. (See John 10:10.) You can attempt to come to the Manufacturer by another way, but you will have no verification, no certificate of authorization. Jesus said, *"My Father will give you whatever you ask in my name"* (John 16:23). Many people are not receiving what the Creator desires for them because they are coming in unauthorized ways.

If you live according to the conditions of the warranty, you can expect to receive the benefits of the guarantees, or the promises. People continually try to change the Creator's warranty. Some people assert that "all roads lead to the same place" when it comes to connecting with God. Yet that is never the case with any other destination. For example, if you wanted to go to the airport, would you drive down every road within one hundred miles of it in order to get there? There has to be a route that will lead where you want to go. That route is the Authorized Dealer, Jesus Christ.

Usually, a manufacturer's conditions further state, "No person, agent, distributor, dealer, facility, or company is authorized to change, modify, or amend the terms of this warranty." Similarly, when God has spoken, the warranty is closed. We are not to add to, subtract from, or alter what He has established because that would be unauthorized and unauthentic. Unauthorized ways of thinking and living will prevent us from fulfilling our original authority.

The Scriptures are very clear that we need a new nature in order to be restored to the Creator and to our true authority. Jesus said,

> I tell you the truth, no one can enter the kingdom of God unless he is born of water and the Spirit. Flesh gives birth to flesh, but the Spirit gives birth to spirit. You should not be surprised at my saying, "You must be born again." (John 3:5–7)

> For God so loved the world that he gave his one and only Son, that whoever believes in him shall not perish but have eternal life. For God did not send his Son into the world to condemn the world, but to save the world through him. (verses 16–17)

"Born again" is a term that has been thrown around casually so that its meaning has been lost. But it originated with Jesus Christ, and it means that you have received a new nature, through Him as the Authorized Dealer, that allows you access to the Creator and His full plan for your life.

There is usually a final statement in a manufacturer's warranty that says, "If you violate any of these specific conditions, this warranty is cancelled." Again, can it be any clearer than that? We need to operate under the principles and laws of the Creator to reap all the benefits He offers to us.

You may have been trying to receive God's help for your life without realizing that you're not under warranty. You know you're not living right, but you're asking Him to fix you up. The warranty is activated when we tell God we want to live according to His principles instead of the way we have been living. The Creator, Incorporated, is always available, and you can come under His warranty at any time by receiving the gift offered through the Authorized Dealer.

THE GIFT OF THE AUTHORIZED DEALER

Jesus is the Authorized Dealer, and He says He will repair our defective authority by giving us a new life according to the nature of the Creator Himself. In this way, He restores what Adam and Eve lost through their abandonment of authority and disobedience of the Creator's principles. Jesus said, *"I am the light of the world. Whoever follows me will never walk in darkness, but will have the light of life"* (John 8:12).

The way this restoration occurred was in accordance with the principles of authority: the Ultimate Authority is responsible for His product, and only He can save it.

Why does He want to save you? *"To all who received him* [Jesus Christ], *to those who believed in his name, he gave the right to become children of God"* (John 1:12). The Greek word translated *"right"* in this verse is the same word that is sometimes translated as "authority" or "power." In other words, the authority of the Creator provides you with the authority to be His child, to have a relationship with Him in which you can call Him not only "Creator" but also "Father."

THE AUTHORITY OF THE CREATOR PROVIDES YOU WITH THE AUTHORITY TO BE HIS CHILD, TO HAVE A RELATIONSHIP WITH HIM IN WHICH YOU CAN CALL HIM NOT ONLY "CREATOR" BUT ALSO "FATHER."

Why is Jesus the Authorized Dealer who can make this happen? Why is it that those who receive Him obtain this right or authority or power to become children of God?

He is the Authorized Dealer because He is also the Manufacturer. In John 10:30, Jesus said, *"I and the Father are one."* Jesus's disciple John also recorded:

> *In the beginning was the Word, and the Word was with God, and the Word was God. He was with God in the beginning. Through him all things were made; without him nothing was made that has been made. In him was life, and that life was the light of men.… The Word became flesh and made his dwelling among us. We have seen his glory, the glory of the One and Only, who came from the Father, full of grace and truth.* (John 1:1–4, 14)

Jesus is the Manufacturer who came to earth to rescue His broken products. The only way they could be forgiven and restored from their abandonment and rebellion was by someone paying the price on their behalf. Just as the grandson of the founder of Toyota represented both the company and the product before Congress, Jesus Christ, as the Son of God—the Word made flesh—was the only One who could represent both the Creator and His created beings in order to fix the breach between the two and bring about full reconciliation and restoration. The redemptive work of the Creator required the sending of His own Son to earth to secure the reputation of His image in humanity.

RESTORED TO YOUR TRUE PLACE

When Jesus Christ died on the cross, He paid the price for our fallen human nature, which we inherited from our first human parents. He also paid the price for all the times when we ourselves have acted contrary to the nature and principles of our Creator. Treason is punishable by death, and Jesus Christ took that punishment for us, enabling our restoration.

But His action provides only the warranty. You have to accept the gift of being a brand-new "product" in order to come under the warranty. You have to respond to it by making a personal decision to come under the Manufacturer's offered warranty in order to receive the necessary forgiveness and restoration.

The book of Hebrews states:

Although he [Jesus Christ] was a son, he learned obedience from what he suffered and, once made perfect, he became the source of eternal salvation for all who obey him. (Hebrews 5:8–9)

"*Perfect*" in this sense indicates complete maturity, complete submission. The word for "*source*" refers to an original cause. We obey God because He is the source or cause of our eternal salvation, and it is He who enables us to live according to our original authority, as well.

Let us fix our eyes on Jesus, the author and perfecter of our faith, who for the joy set before him endured the cross, scorning its shame, and sat down at the right hand of the throne of God. (Hebrews 12:2)

The word translated "*author*" here also has the meaning of "founder" or "leader." Jesus Christ was the only One who fulfilled complete obedience to the Creator's principles and laws. He therefore leads us into and is the model for our complete obedience to them, as well, so that we can live according to our authority.[1]

Someone might ask, "Why would God send His Son to be a sacrifice for us? Why would God experience punishment for us? Why would God raise Jesus from the dead and establish Him as King of Kings?" He did all of this to redeem us, because the authority we are carrying inside us is so awesome that He considered it worth His death. Do you really understand that the earth needs you? It needs your purpose and your gift. It needs your authority.

DRAWN TO HIS GOODNESS

There are people who want to be restored to the Creator God but are frightened of Him. They believe that to "fear" the Lord means to be afraid of Him. But to fear in regard to God means to respect Him, to have an awareness of all the power He has on your behalf. He can do great things for you through His power.

If you have developed a fear of authority in relation to God over the years, this fear may have hindered you from receiving the restoration He offers you. In my own life, it took me a long time to understand and accept the truth that God isn't mad at sinners. Paul of Tarsus, the great first-century theologian, wrote, *"But God demonstrates his own love for us in this: While we were still sinners, Christ died for us"* (Romans 5:8). God is not angry at you for what you did that was wrong. He is hurt by it. Why? Because He knows that it hinders you from doing what is right. He knows that if He doesn't help you, you will hurt yourself.

God's goodness should therefore bring us to Him. He is not a tyrant or a dictator—He is a Savior! He is not a monster and a destroyer—He is a redeemer and a restorer. Remember that *"God did not send his Son into the world to condemn the world, but to save the world through him"* (John 3:17). Understanding the truth about God's love and provision to restore us will eliminate our fear of Him and His authority.

> GOD'S GOODNESS SHOULD BRING US TO HIM.
> HE IS NOT A TYRANT OR A DICTATOR—HE IS A SAVIOR!

JESUS'S PERSONAL AUTHORITY

Jesus functioned by His personal authority, and He is our model of true authority as we are restored to our Creator and begin to live in our delegated authority. Let us look at some of the ways in which He demonstrated these things.

1. Jesus understood His authority. He said, *"For as the Father has life in himself, so he has granted the Son to have life in himself. And he has given him authority to judge because he is the Son of Man"* (John 5:26–27). Most of the confrontations Jesus experienced with the religious leaders of His day were about authority. These leaders were agitated at Him, asking, in effect, "Who authorized You to do and say these things?" Authority seemed to be their major concern about Him, but He knew His own authorization. Jesus was

only in His early thirties during His ministry on earth, and most of the Pharisees were older than He, but they didn't have true authority. Jesus was singled out because He spoke with authority, and the scribes and the Pharisees spoke as those without authority. (See, for example, Matthew 7:28–29.) They only talked about the Scriptures (as well as other teachings), but Jesus *was* the Word. He spoke *as* the Source, not in references to the Source.

> **WHEN YOU TRULY UNDERSTAND YOUR AUTHORITY, IT WILL GIVE YOU THE CONFIDENCE TO FOLLOW IT.**

2. Jesus's confidence was a result of His authority.

    [Jesus said,] *"The reason my Father loves me is that I lay down my life—only to take it up again. No one takes it from me, but I lay it down of my own accord. I have authority to lay it down and authority to take it up again. This command I received from my Father."* At these words the Jews were again divided. Many of them said, *"He is demon-possessed and raving mad. Why listen to him?"* But others said, *"These are not the sayings of a man possessed by a demon. Can a demon open the eyes of the blind?"*
    (John 10:17–21)

    When you truly understand your authority, it will give you the confidence to follow it.

3. Jesus equated understanding and operating under authority with having faith, as we see from this account of the centurion who asked Jesus to heal his servant:

    [The centurion said,] *"Say the word, and my servant will be healed. For I myself am a man under authority, with soldiers under me. I tell this one, 'Go,' and he goes; and that one, 'Come,' and he comes. I say to my servant, 'Do this,' and he does it."* When Jesus heard this, he was amazed at him, and turning to the crowd following him, he said, *"I tell you, I have not found such great faith even in Israel." Then the men who had been sent returned to the house and found the servant well.* (Luke 7:7–10)

4. Jesus was authorized to give life.

[Jesus prayed to the Father,] *For you granted [Your Son] authority over all people that he might give eternal life to all those you have given him. Now this is eternal life: that they may know you, the only true God, and Jesus Christ, whom you have sent. I have brought you glory on earth by completing the work you gave me to do.* (John 17:2–4)

[Jesus said to the people,] *Do not work for food that spoils, but for food that endures to eternal life, which the Son of Man will give you. On him God the Father has placed his seal of approval.... All that the Father gives me will come to me, and whoever comes to me I will never drive away. For I have come down from heaven not to do my will but to do the will of him who sent me. And this is the will of him who sent me, that I shall lose none of all that he has given me, but raise them up at the last day. For my Father's will is that everyone who looks to the Son and believes in him shall have eternal life, and I will raise him up at the last day.* (John 6:27, 37–40)

5. Jesus was authorized to forgive sins.

But that you may know that the Son of Man has authority on earth to forgive sins.... (Mark 2:10)

Then Jesus said to her, "Your sins are forgiven." The other guests began to say among themselves, "Who is this who even forgives sins?" Jesus said to the woman, "Your faith has saved you; go in peace." (Luke 7:48–50)

6. Jesus is authorized to make us children of God.

But as many as received Him, to them He gave the right to become children of God, to those who believe in His name. (John 1:12)

How great is the love the Father has lavished on us, that we should be called children of God! And that is what we are! (1 John 3:1)

7. Jesus is authorized to restore authority.

For just as the Father raises the dead and gives them life, even so the Son gives life to whom he is pleased to give it. Moreover, the Father judges no one, but has entrusted all judgment to the Son, that all may honor the Son just as they honor the Father.

(John 5:21–23)

All that belongs to the Father is mine. That is why I said the Spirit will take from what is mine and make it known to you.

(John 16:15)

The scroll of the prophet Isaiah was handed to [Jesus]. Unrolling it, he found the place where it is written: "The Spirit of the Lord is on me, because he has anointed me to preach good news to the poor. He has sent me to proclaim freedom for the prisoners and recovery of sight for the blind, to release the oppressed, to proclaim the year of the Lord's favor." Then he rolled up the scroll, gave it back to the attendant and sat down. The eyes of everyone in the synagogue were fastened on him, and he began by saying to them, "Today this scripture is fulfilled in your hearing." All spoke well of him and were amazed at the gracious words that came from his lips.

(Luke 4:17–22)

8. Jesus gives us authority. One of the last words Jesus used on earth in speaking to His disciples was *"authority"*:

All authority in heaven and on earth has been given to me. Therefore go and make disciples of all nations, baptizing them in the name of the Father and of the Son and of the Holy Spirit, and teaching them to obey everything I have commanded you. And surely I am with you always, to the very end of the age.

(Matthew 28:18–20)

It is not for you to know the times or dates the Father has set by his own authority. But you will receive power when the Holy Spirit comes on you; and you will be my witnesses in Jerusalem, and in all Judea and Samaria, and to the ends of the earth.

(Acts 1:7–8)

Often, the greatest obstacle to people living according to their authority is a lack of understanding that they have real *authorization* to carry it out. This prevents them from believing and undertaking what they were created to do, and so they settle for something much less than what they could be and do. They allow outside forces and influences rather than their internal authority to determine how they live their lives. This is why they don't contribute their gifts to their generation. As a result, they and their generation lose out.

In chapter three, I described how an author has the copyright to his work and how he has the right to share the copyright claim with someone or to provide for an inheritance of it. When Jesus died on our behalf, giving us the authority and power to become children of God, we received the full inheritance of rights that He obtained. *"Christ is the mediator of a new covenant, that those who are called may receive the promised eternal inheritance—now that he has died as a ransom to set them free from the sins committed under the first covenant"* (Hebrews 9:15). Authority is the principle of rights.

Authority is the Author's permission for you to be what He designed you to be. You not only have permission but also the commission and the power to fulfill your purpose. With this knowledge and understanding of authority, you can experience God's plan for your life and not just dream about it.

THE PRIVILEGE OF AUTHORITY

The angels from the book of Jude we discussed earlier were not restored to the place they abandoned, but God has made provision for human beings to be restored to theirs. What will you do with the authority that has been provided for you? You have a choice to accept it or to discard it.

I know many individuals, and you probably do, too, who have tremendous gifts, talents, and dreams, and who had great promise for their lives, but who destroyed their futures by violating genuine authority in some way.

The prisons are filled with potentially great leaders who are confined for life because they violated the authority of society, which has established laws for order and peace. The drug houses are filled with talented people who will never fulfill their potential because they are violating the authority of their bodies by abusing them with harmful, illegal substances.

Many people currently have great ideas, dreams, and plans for their lives, but they are on a collision course with destruction because they are—or are contemplating—violating the privilege of authority the Creator has given them by seeking their own authority for selfish purposes.

> **WE HAVE NOT ONLY THE PRIVILEGE OF RECEIVING AUTHORITY FROM GOD BUT ALSO THE RESPONSIBILITY OF REMAINING IN IT AFTER WE RECEIVE IT.**

Why do people end up ruining their lives in this way? They have left (or have never known) the place of authority where they truly belong—just like their original human parents did.

The commentary from Jude tells us that living in our God-given authority is like being home or coming home, like settling into our own habitation. We have not only the privilege of receiving authority from God but also the responsibility of remaining in it after we receive it. This honors our Creator and preserves order and peace in our own lives and in the lives of people around us.

I encourage you to pray this prayer to the Creator: "Lord, show me my authority. I come to You on the basis of the sacrifice of the Authorized Dealer, Jesus Christ. I receive His gift of restoration and come under His offered warranty in order to receive forgiveness, restoration, and eternal life. I don't want to waste another day out of position. I want to be in order. I want to know the authority You have for me so that I can be in the right place in life. So that I can maximize myself and be a support to those around me. So that I can fulfill Your pleasure and be what You created me to be. Help me, Lord, not to leave my position. In the name of the Authorized Dealer, amen."

FIVE

A VITAL PRINCIPLE OF AUTHORITY

EVERYTHING SUBMITS TO SOMETHING ELSE IN ORDER TO FUNCTION, GROW, AND PROSPER

In this chapter, we will explore a major principle of authority that will make a significant difference in your life. It's a principle that we touched on in chapter one: *everything depends on and must submit to something else in order to function, grow, prosper, and succeed.*

This principle was established in the very essence of the created world. Nothing that the Creator made can exist without submission to some authority because authority, by nature, involves dependence and interdependence. The first manifestation of authority is that everything depends on the Creator to exist because everything came from Him. Colossians 1:16–17 states,

> By him all things were created: things in heaven and on earth, visible and invisible, whether thrones or powers or rulers or authorities; all things were created by him and for him. He is before all things, and in him all things hold together.

All things exist and are still held together by the Creator's power. Not only was the universe—seen and unseen—produced by Him, but it also depends on Him for its continued existence. Everything in creation must refer to the Creator for its life and success. Everything in creation was designed to function by the principle of authority.

A seed must "submit" to being planted in the soil if it is to grow; in this sense, the soil is the authority of the seed. Fish must "submit" to living in water in order to survive, so the fishes' authority is the water; if they didn't submit to it, they would die. The planets of our solar system submit to the gravitational pull of the sun as their authority; if they didn't, the solar system would no longer be intact, and the planets would spiral out of control in space.

> WE NEVER GROW OUT OF THE NEED FOR AUTHORITY ITSELF. THIS IS TRUE FOR ALL OF CREATION AND IN ALL HUMAN EXPERIENCES.

Everyone and everything must submit to someone or something in order to function and be successful. It is impossible to outgrow authority. We may transfer our accountability to different kinds of authority, such as when a child grows up and moves out from under his parents' authority, starts his own family, and interacts with others in the world, but we never grow out of the need for authority itself. This is true for all of creation and in all human experiences.

Anyone who refuses to be governed by genuine authority is illegitimate and malfunctioning in the world. For example, a criminal is one who refuses to submit to society and violates the authority of others' lives or property. He crosses others' boundaries or realms of authority. If he is caught and punished, jail becomes forced authority over him. He is made to submit to society through a severe restriction of his activities. If a child refuses to acknowledge the authority of his parents in teaching him positive and constructive ways to live his life, then he will suffer the consequences of some kind of self-destruction to mind, body, or soul.

You are living with dangerous illegitimacy if you are not submitted to any authority so that other people cannot trust you or safely submit to you when needed. We should submit only to those who are submitted themselves.

THE GREATEST EXAMPLE OF THE VITAL PRINCIPLE OF AUTHORITY

I believe that the greatest example of someone who understood and lived out the principle, the power, and the purpose of authority is Jesus Christ, and that there is much to gain in one's understanding of authority from looking at how He lived His life.

The key to the success, effectiveness, efficiency, power, and perfection of His life on earth was His complete understanding of, and adherence to, authority. We see Jesus's submission to authority throughout His life on earth. Let us look at several key examples.

JESUS SUBMITTED TO HIS OWN ESTABLISHED LAWS

First, His willingness to come to earth as a man, even though He was God (see John 1:1–4, 14), was an extraordinary act of submission! In theologian Paul of Tarsus's writings, we read, *"But when the time had fully come, God sent his Son, born of a woman, born under law, to redeem those under law, that we might receive the full rights of sons"* (Galatians 4:4–5).

God's first step in correcting humanity's problem of authority was His own submission to authority. What did He submit to? The very laws pertaining to the authority He had established for the physical creation and for the spiritual life of His people:

- He voluntarily came into this world physically, as a baby, through the womb of a woman, as all other people do.

- He was born *"under law,"* so that, even though He Himself had instituted the law for the Israelites, He was subject to its regulations and requirements. Since God had established all authority, He knew the indispensability of submitting to authority, including the protection it provides for a person's spirit, soul, and body.

JESUS SUBMITTED TO BAPTISM "TO FULFILL ALL RIGHTEOUSNESS"

Second, I want to focus particularly on the accounts of His baptism in relation to His submission to authority because this submission was the inauguration of His ministry. If we desire to be all we were born to be, we need to understand what Jesus knew about authority and how He responded to it, as well as the remarkable results that came from it.

Then Jesus came from Galilee to the Jordan to be baptized by John. But John tried to deter him, saying, "I need to be baptized by you, and do you come to me?" Jesus replied, "Let it be so now; it is proper for us to do this to fulfill all righteousness." Then John consented. As soon as Jesus was baptized, he went up out of the water. At that moment heaven was opened, and he saw the Spirit of God descending like a dove and lighting on him. And a voice from heaven said, "This is my

Son, whom I love; with him I am well pleased." Then Jesus was led by
the Spirit into the desert to be tempted by the devil.

(Matthew 3:13–4:1)

This incident is loaded with meaning.

Do you know how far the site of Jesus's baptism in the Jordan River
is from the region of Galilee? It is approximately seventy or eighty miles.
That would be more than a week's walk over a terrain of rocks and hills.
Jesus didn't come for a casual visit. He *came looking* for John.

We have seen that many people's experiences with authority have been
negative, and that they are therefore wary of it. Yet submitting to *true*
authority is something desirable and essential for our lives, and one of the
ways we know this is that Jesus went looking for what we tend to avoid. He
sought out what we run from. He requested what we are suspicious of. He
confidently sought John the Baptist in order to submit to his authority.

"*But John tried to deter him, saying, 'I need to be baptized by you, and do
you come to me?' Jesus replied, 'Let it be so **now**; it is proper* ["*fitting*" NKJV] *for
us to do this to fulfill all righteousness*'" (Matthew 3:14–15). "*All righteousness*"
means "all right standing, or positioning." Jesus was saying that this was
necessary for Him to be in proper relationship to the Ultimate Authority,
God the Father.

AUTHORITY NEEDS AUTHORITY TO RELEASE ITS POWER

John had previously distinguished his authority from the authority of
Jesus. Before Jesus came to be baptized by him, John had told the people,
"*After me will come **one who is more powerful than I, whose sandals I am
not fit to carry**"* (Matthew 3:11). John knew well the powerful authority of
Jesus. He had also said, "*I baptize you with water for repentance.... He will
baptize you with the Holy Spirit and with fire*" (verse 11).

What kind of baptism did Jesus come for? Water baptism. And it
was John who was authorized to baptize with water. Jesus couldn't baptize Himself because He was not the water-baptizer. As great as He was,
He had to submit to the authority that had been established by God the
Father for this time in His life on earth.

The following Old Testament prophecy in Malachi reveals what authority Jesus was submitting to when He was baptized by John:

"See, I will send my messenger, who will prepare the way before me. Then suddenly the Lord you are seeking will come to his temple; the messenger of the covenant, whom you desire, will come," says the LORD Almighty. But who can endure the day of his coming? Who can stand when he appears? For he will be like a refiner's fire. (Malachi 3:1–2)

Two "messengers" are mentioned in this passage. The first messenger would prepare the way for the Lord, and this refers to John the Baptist. The second messenger is the messenger of the covenant, and this refers to Jesus.

John's authority was in his assignment—to prepare the way for the Lord. He declared, *"The reason I came baptizing with water was that he* [the greater Messenger] *might be revealed to Israel"* (John 1:31).

THE SECRET TO LIFE IS TO CONSTANTLY SUBMIT TO GOD AND HIS AUTHORITY, EVEN THOUGH YOU DON'T ALWAYS UNDERSTAND WHAT HE IS DOING.

The account in the book of Matthew says that when Jesus answered John in terms of authority—*"Let it be so now; it is proper for us to do this to fulfill all righteousness"*—*"then John consented"* (Matthew 3:15).

The secret to life is to constantly submit to God and His authority, even though you don't always understand what He is doing. John told Jesus, in effect, "I cannot baptize You. You should baptize me." He didn't fully understand his authority at first, which is the case with many people today. Your authority is found in what God has prepared for you to do. If anyone needs what God has gifted you to provide for them, then there are no substitutes; they have to come to you. Some people might not like that fact, but God has sent them to you. We may sometimes feel uncomfortable with our own authority, as John was, but we need to obey God in it to fulfill the purposes only He fully knows.

Since John was operating under the authority of God, he understood when Jesus appealed to authority, and he then agreed to baptize Him.

The result of Jesus's submission to the established authority is striking:

As soon as Jesus was baptized, he went up out of the water. At that moment heaven was opened, and he saw the Spirit of God descending like a dove and lighting on him. And a voice from heaven said, "This is my Son, whom I love; with him I am well pleased."

(Matthew 3:16–17)

A voice from heaven spoke. When? *"As soon as"* Jesus submitted to authority. *"As soon as"* means immediately.

We should consider whether our ability to hear from God regarding His purposes for our lives is directly related to our response to His authority. If you are not receiving guidance from God, perhaps it is because you keep violating some authority He has established in your life.

What pleased God the Father so much that He spoke audibly? He witnessed Jesus, God the Son, submitting to a human in obedience! He confirmed that this obedience was pleasing. Of course, Jesus didn't submit to a human being alone but to the authority from God that had been given to that human being. We see Jesus's submission to other earthly authorities in various instances in His life as well, as He was led by God the Father, for the sake of order, peace, and purpose. A few examples are:

+ Submission to His parents' authority. (See Luke 2:40–52.)

+ Submission to the requirement of the temple tax and to taxation by the Roman emperor Caesar. (See Matthew 17:24–27.)

+ Submission to the Roman governor, Pontius Pilate. (See John 19:10–11.)

SUBMISSION TO AUTHORITY LEADS TO TRUE GREATNESS

The vital thing to understand is that Jesus could not begin or accomplish His work until John "released" Him. The fact that many of us haven't understood or had good experiences with authority, prompting our avoidance of it, may be causing us to miss out on the full release of our own authority. We may not have had the opportunity to exercise our authority to its full potential because it is authority that *releases* our authority. We submit first to the authority of our Creator and then to the authority He has given other human beings in various realms and aspects of life. In a later chapter, I describe how you can respond to "authority" that is not in line with God's purposes and still receive His blessing and benefit from it.

There is ample evidence that no one understood authority more than the Authority of Life Himself, who established authority on earth. Jesus had the power to change the world, but that power depended first on His submission to John. John held the authority in his hand to release Jesus. If Jesus Himself needed to submit to God the Father and to John as an earthly authority, why do we often think we don't need to submit to anyone?

No one had a greater impact on the world than Jesus, yet He didn't seek a "ministry" or followers for Himself independently. He knew and lived in the authority He had been given and which had been confirmed in various ways at His birth. (See, for example, Luke 2:25–32.) At age twelve, He was discussing deep questions about God and the Scriptures with the teachers in the temple. (See Luke 2:42–47.) When He felt God prompting Him to be baptized by John, He left the region where He had grown up and went to the Jordan River. He didn't come to check out John. He didn't come to see if John was the kind of preacher He liked. He didn't come to see if John had the kind of ministry He would want to connect with. Jesus, God the Son, the Creator of the world, came looking for an authority He knew He was to submit to.

Likewise, no matter how "great" you were born to be, someone has to release you.

> GREATNESS DOES NOT COME FROM GIFTS AND TALENTS ALONE. IT COMES FROM BEING WHERE YOU'RE SUPPOSED TO BE IN TERMS OF PERSONAL AUTHORITY AND OPERATING IN YOUR UNIQUE DOMAIN.

Moreover, greatness does not come from gifts and talents alone. It comes from being where you're supposed to be in terms of personal authority and operating in your unique domain. John had said, *"After me will come one who is more powerful than I"* (Matthew 3:11). Jesus came along, the One whom John had said was more powerful, and Jesus said to him, in effect, "I need to submit to you now as the authority in this situation. In this circumstance, you are 'greater' in that you are to administer the authority that God has given you to administer."

Acting on your authority from God brings you greatness. Yet the authority that brings greatness is often not what we think it is. It means serving others. At a later time, Jesus told His disciples,

> *Whoever wants to become great among you must be your servant, and whoever wants to be first must be your slave—just as the Son of Man did not come to be served, but to serve, and to give his life as a ransom for many.* (Matthew 20:26–28)

Becoming what you are meant to be and doing what you are meant to do makes you great. It doesn't matter what other people may say about you, there's something they have to come to you for because you have been given that authority. Remember that authority is independent of titles. Some people have titles, but they don't have any real authority. Authority goes beyond titles; it is what God has placed inside you. When Jesus told John, "*Let it be so now; it is proper for us to do this to fulfill all righteousness*" (Matthew 3:15), He was saying, in effect, "John, let's not get into titles. Let's just follow proper authority."

SUBMISSION TO AUTHORITY BRINGS SPIRITUAL POWER AND PROTECTION

What would have happened if Jesus had not been willing to submit to John's authority in baptism, if John had refused to baptize Jesus because Jesus was greater than he, or if Jesus had baptized John in water instead? The heavens would not have opened, the Holy Spirit would not have come down in the form of a dove, God's voice would not have confirmed who Jesus was before the people, and Jesus wouldn't have been able to begin His ministry.

The Scripture says that, right after God spoke from heaven, "*Jesus was led by the Spirit into the desert to be tempted by the devil*" (Matthew 4:1). After Jesus's authority was confirmed by God, He was immediately tempted by the devil to forsake that authority and to take up a false authority. Don't be surprised if you, too, are tempted to give up legitimate authority to take what seems the easy way out in living your life.

Note how the devil's temptations were directly related to authority:

+ The temptation to turn stones into bread can be seen as an attack on God as the Source and Sustainer of life. Jesus's response was, *"It is written: 'Man does not live on bread alone, but on every word that comes from the mouth of God'"* (Matthew 4:4).

+ The temptation to recklessly throw Himself from the pinnacle of the temple and have God save Him can be seen as an enticement to go beyond the parameters of authority that God had given Him. Jesus's response was, *"It is also written: 'Do not put the Lord your God to the test'"* (verse 7).

+ The temptation to bow down and worship the devil in exchange for *"all the kingdoms of the world and their splendor"* (verse 8) can be seen as a ploy to cause Jesus to reject the established and righteous authority of the kingdom of heaven, or the kingdom of God, in favor of the counterfeit, transitory, and decayed authority of earth. This was an especially powerful temptation because the message Jesus came to bring was that the *kingdom of heaven* had come to earth—*through Him.* (See, for example, verse 17.) Jesus's response was, *"Away from me, Satan! For it is written: 'Worship the Lord your God, and serve him only'"* (verse 10).

In response to each of these temptations, Jesus cited the Word of God, the "Manual" for how human beings are to live. That Manual is the authoritative Word of the Creator.

If Jesus had refused to be baptized by John before going into the desert to be tempted, then He wouldn't have been able to overcome these temptations as He did. Satan would have won. Why? Jesus would have been operating in a manner that was out of order in relation to authority. He would have been acting in disobedience, or in violation of God's ways and purposes. He would have broken His relationship with God the Father, forsaken His Word, and damaged the credibility of God. Spiritual strength and the ability to withstand the devil come from obedience to God's ways and from remaining in His established authority.

How many people go out to "fight against the devil" but haven't done what they were supposed to do before they left? Without proper authority from heaven, they will fail. One time, seven sons of a man named Sceva, a

Jewish chief priest, were trying to drive out demons in the name of Jesus, but because they lacked the authority of being in right standing and relationship with God, they utterly failed:

> *One day the evil spirit answered them, "Jesus I know, and I know about Paul, but who are you?" Then the man who had the evil spirit jumped on them and overpowered them all. He gave them such a beating that they ran out of the house naked and bleeding.*
>
> (Acts 19:15–16)

Having the right words isn't enough. You need the authority behind them.

Finally, if Jesus hadn't been baptized by John, it would have interfered with history, and we would today be *"without hope and without God in the world"* (Ephesians 2:12). It would have prevented the restoration of humanity to a relationship with God and to a recovery of its authority.

JESUS'S VERY NATURE DISPLAYS HIS AUTHORITY AND SUBMISSION

There is a passage in Philippians 2 that is startling in its revelation of both Jesus's own authority and His humbleness in submitting to authority:

> *Your attitude should be the same as that of Christ Jesus: who, being in very nature God, did not consider equality with God something to be grasped* [held on to, maintained], *but made himself nothing* ["of no reputation" KJV], *taking the very nature of a servant, being made in human likeness. And being found in appearance as a man, he humbled himself and became obedient to death—even death on a cross!*
>
> (Philippians 2:5–8)

"He humbled himself" is a key phrase. Having all authority as God, Jesus humbled Himself!

> ## TRUE AUTHORITY DOES NOT HUMBLE PEOPLE BUT WAITS FOR PEOPLE TO HUMBLE THEMSELVES.

Authority doesn't work if someone has to humble you. True authority does not humble people but waits for people to humble themselves. Jesus did exactly what we are expected to do. He humbled Himself. *"Humble yourselves before the Lord, and he will lift you up"* (James 4:10).

The passage from Philippians continues,

> *Therefore God exalted him to the highest place and gave him the name that is above every name, that at the name of Jesus every knee should bow, in heaven and on earth and under the earth, and every tongue confess that Jesus Christ is Lord, to the glory of God the Father.*
>
> (Philippians 2:9–11)

*"**Therefore** God exalted him to the highest place."* Jesus humbled Himself; therefore, God did something. He didn't just exalt Him, but He *"exalted Him to the **highest** place."* The Scriptures say that promotion in life does not come from men. *"For promotion cometh neither from the east, nor from the west, nor from the south. But God is the judge: he putteth down one, and setteth up another"* (Psalm 75:6–7 KJV). This means that advancement, progress, and development in your life do not come from man's doing but from God's.

Jesus knew authority in a way that we need to understand and live by so that we not only can experience God's "therefore" but also know that we have authority from God ourselves. What do we learn from Jesus's humble nature?

We learn that even though we know who we are and what our authority is, we choose not to hold on to our rights so that we can accomplish the greater purpose of fulfilling God's will in our lives and lifting others up. Jesus could have said, "I'm God. I'm not going to become a human being." Yet His own confidence and contentment in the knowledge of who He was enabled Him to "[make] *himself nothing,* [take] *the very nature of a servant,* [and be] *made in human likeness"* (Philippians 2:7). As a human being and the Savior of the world, He endured verbal abuse, the emotional pain of betrayal, all human temptations, and excruciating physical suffering, especially through His death on a cross. His choice to humble Himself was not an easy one, but He had no doubts about it.

I have discovered that people who don't know who they are cannot submit to authority. When you know who you are, then you understand that no one can degrade or devalue you. Submission is possible and becomes easier when you are in touch with your own worth. When you know you are of great value to God, other people's opinions and treatment of you do not influence you, even though they may hurt deeply.

PEOPLE WHO DON'T KNOW WHO THEY ARE CANNOT SUBMIT TO AUTHORITY.

Jesus knew that…

+ He was called.
+ He had anointing.
+ He had power.
+ He could work miracles.
+ He had revelation knowledge.

However, He also knew that His authority came from God the Father, and He lived to serve God and to fulfill His purpose on earth. *"'My food,' said Jesus, 'is to do the will of him who sent me and to finish his work'"* (John 4:34).

POINTS FOR PROMOTION

"He humbled himself…. Therefore God exalted him to the highest place" (Philippians 2:8–9). If you want to live in the authority of your personal domain, if you want God to promote you, if you want to be successful in life and fulfill the Father's will, you must understand these points, which are derived from the principle of authority:

1. *When you know who you are in your God-given authority, the first thing you look for is the authority that God has placed in your life to benefit and protect you and to release your authority.* This is the last thing that most people do. Instead, they look for reputation, fame, and power over others; they seek to build organizations, gain followers, and so forth.

    The Creator gives all people inherent authority in various realms and for specific reasons, and we are to respond to other people in recognition of their authority, respecting God's order. John the Baptist was God's established authority to prepare people for the coming of the kingdom of God on earth. Jesus recognized and accepted John as the authority sent from God, through His understanding of the prophetic Scriptures and John's testimony.

2. *Without authority, there can be no (other) authority.* Jesus went to John before He began His ministry and submitted to his authority. Jesus told John, in effect, "John, the order is you, then Me. It doesn't matter who I am; it's the way we work together that counts." There was a mutual submission of One to the other according to God's authority that enabled them both to fulfill their individual purposes.

3. *"Authority" without true authority is no authority.* Jesus's submission to God's authority through John released Him to begin His own ministry. Yet, if He hadn't submitted, He would have had no authority for functioning in His ministry.

4. *Understanding authority is the key to life and effective living.* God's Holy Spirit dwelled in Jesus and also came upon Him at His baptism to enable Him to fulfill His calling. This would not have happened without Jesus's willingness to submit.

5. *Authority is the thread that holds the fabric of life together.* As I wrote earlier, most of the problems we are facing—whether personal, corporate, communal, or national—come from the fact that we don't understand or live according to authority that reflects the Creator's nature and purpose. Our lives are like beautiful designs that God is making on fabric that He has woven. The fabric itself is made up of threads of authority, and if we violate His authority, then the plan that He has for our lives will not unfold in His great design but instead will begin to unravel.

REPRESENTATIVES OF ULTIMATE AUTHORITY

Authority is such a vital principle because we are not authorized to function if we are not under authority. To return to the manufacturer's analogy, many companies who produce products guarantee them, but only through the proper authority—the manual and the warranty. In such cases, even though a product leaves the company's warehouse, it never leaves the company's authority. Again, not only are consumers to consult the manual to know how to use the product properly, but they are also to go only to an authorized dealer in case of any needed repairs.

Having an authorized dealer implies that the dealer is submitted to the company that delegated its authority, so that the product is still under the jurisdiction of its originator. We have "authorized dealers" in various realms of life. For instance, the CEO of an organization is like an authorized dealer because he must ultimately answer to the board of directors, to the stockholders, or to the customers.

In another example, a secretary of state represents the president of a country but also oversees ambassadors to the nations with which that country has diplomatic relations. If the system works as it was set up to, the ambassadors function under delegated authority; they represent the president, even though they are not always in direct contact with him. They are not allowed the leeway to set their own policies; they are always to be submitted to the authority of the secretary of state, who is to be submitted to the president. They are never to speak for themselves but only for the president, so they make official statements such as, "My government's position is...."

Likewise, if we are under God's authority, it is not our place to set a policy that is different from His or to speak according to our own agendas. In the same way that distance does not cancel the authority that the political ambassadors are under, our being on earth and God's being in heaven does not cancel His authority in our lives, especially since He gives us His very Spirit to dwell within us when we are restored to Him. On the contrary, it is our role to carry out His authority on earth.

> **YOUR SUCCESS IN YOUR AUTHORITY WILL DEPEND ON YOUR OWN ABILITY TO SUBMIT TO GENUINE AUTHORITY, TO LEARN, AND TO SERVE.**

Colonel Larry Donnithorne, in his book *The West Point Way of Leadership*, told how individuals become effective leaders in their own lives through a system of discipline. He wrote, "Every leader is a follower. No one commands an organization without restraints. For every leader, no matter how 'supreme,' there is always a higher authority who must be answered [whom he's responsible to]."[1]

In fact, everybody who wants to be successful must answer to somebody else. The success of a prime minister or CEO or ambassador depends largely on how well he has learned in the past to submit to authority, to learn from others, and to serve others. In the same way, your success in your authority will depend on your own ability to submit to genuine authority, to learn, and to serve. It's only when we learn submission that we can become true leaders.

Finally, as we pursue our personal authority, we must keep in mind that (1) our Ultimate Authority is God; we are to submit to Him and His purposes for us; (2) we are to "submit" to, or live according to, our inherent domains—the authority, dreams, and gifts God has given us—and not try to be someone we aren't or to succeed with improper motivations; (3) we are to submit to others' God-given authority in mutual relationship and community.

SIX

TEN PRIMARY PURPOSES OF AUTHORITY

THE ORIGINAL PLAN FOR AUTHORITY IN CREATION AND LIFE

Purpose has to do with original intent, and we have seen that authority is an inherent part of the design of humanity by its Source, the Creator God of the universe. To summarize our exploration of the meaning of true authority, and to serve as a prelude to part two of this book, in which we will examine how you can apply these truths to your personal authority, let us look at ten primary reasons why authority was established as an essential principle for our lives.

PURPOSE #1: ORDER

Authority produces and maintains order—in families, in society, in the world—because it establishes a reference for all relationships in life. When functioning according to authority, everyone knows where he is supposed to be and what he is meant to do based on the authority he has been given.

This authority must be founded on the Absolute Authority, the Creator, or else it will fall apart. *Absolute* in this sense doesn't mean controlling, abusive, or oppressive. Instead, it reflects these definitions:

1. "Independent of arbitrary standards of measurement." God's authority is stable; it doesn't change on a whim so that we are left confused or off balance. He isn't fickle or capricious. As our Ultimate Authority, God is our standard-setter. The word *ruler* was derived from *rule*, which comes from a Latin word meaning "to keep straight, direct." True authority gives you a reference, a direction in which to go.

2. "Fundamental, ultimate." There is nothing beyond or above God's principles and standards. Anything else is inferior.

3. "Perfectly embodying the nature of a thing." God's authority is inseparable from who He is—it is part of His nature.

Human beings were made for relationships and for cooperative endeavors, and God's authority provides the necessary order in which they can successfully occur.

PURPOSE #2: MAXIMUM PRODUCTIVITY

Because authority produces order, it creates an environment for maximum productivity. Previously, we looked at the analogy of the manufacturer's manual. If we follow the manufacturer's instructions for caring for a product, it will function at its highest capacity. If we violate the authorized instructions, we will impair the product's potential so that it cannot be maximized. Following inherent authority guarantees the successful functioning of the product.

In a similar way, human beings are most successful when they live according to the principle of authority. When each person comes from the reference point that everyone has personal authority—a special part to play in the whole—and each person values others' authority and contributions, then conflict, contention, friction, and confusion do not arise and drain productivity. Everyone works together for the greatest result. One definition of *productive* is "having the quality or power of producing especially in abundance." The "quality" would refer to the authority, and the "power" would refer to the ability we have each been given by the Creator to carry it out. If we violate the principle of authority, we automatically hinder our potential and effectiveness.

PURPOSE #3: PROTECTION

Authority is designed to protect its products, not to restrict them. The Creator's authority establishes the boundaries, limitations, and references that protect us from misuse, abuse, and self-destruction. When our first human parents abandoned their authority, they self-destructed, and we still experience the effects of that decision every day.

A manufacturer's manual has a list of dos and don'ts to protect the product, as well as those who relate to and deal with the product. Therefore, if we obey the instructions of our Manufacturer, if we stay in our authority, then we protect not only ourselves but also others with whom we are in relationship and with whom we deal in various realms of life.

Jesus Himself couldn't be without a covering of authority from God the Father. We must continually remind ourselves that we need to be covered by authority so that we can also protect others and keep them safe.

PURPOSE #4: PRESERVATION

Preservation is related to protection. If a manufacturer promises that his product has a lifetime guarantee if you follow certain procedures, then, if you follow them, the product should last. If you violate them, however, the product is compromised, and the guarantee is canceled.

The Creator has given promises to us, but we need to follow the corresponding conditions to be able to benefit from them. God's authority preserves the quality of our lives if we follow the instructions in His Manual, the Scriptures, for how we are to conduct ourselves. In addition, being true to the personal authority He has placed within us will safeguard His specific purposes for us. We also have God's Spirit living inside us, so we have the authority and the ability, including the perseverance, to carry out His purposes.

PURPOSE #5: REPRESENTATION THROUGH VALIDATION AND DEFENSE

Anyone who delegates part of his authority to others is responsible for representing them. We often think in terms of ambassadors representing their countries and products representing their manufacturers, but the reverse is also true. We see this reality functioning in two practical ways—through validation and defense.

> WE HAVE GOD'S SPIRIT LIVING INSIDE US, SO WE HAVE THE AUTHORITY AND THE ABILITY, INCLUDING THE PERSEVERANCE, TO CARRY OUT HIS PURPOSES.

VALIDATION

First, if you are operating under the authority of another person, that person's authority certifies the decisions and actions you take on his behalf.

Jesus continually stated that His actions were endorsed by a heavenly authority. He said, *"The very work that the Father has given me to finish, and which I am doing, testifies that the Father has sent me"* (John 5:36), and *"Do not believe me unless I do what my Father does"* (John 10:37). Jesus had peace even in regard to death because of His validated authority:

> *The reason my Father loves me is that I lay down my life—only to take it up again. No one takes it from me, but I lay it down of my own accord. I have authority to lay it down and authority to take it up again. This command I received from my Father.*   (John 10:17–18)

If you are sent somewhere under genuine authority, you can have peace because the authority is responsible for you.

In another scriptural example, the archangel Michael did not use his own authority to fight against Satan but used his words very carefully, saying, *"The Lord rebuke you!"* (Jude 1:9). Michael was acting on God's behalf but had to rebuke Satan under the authority of God's name, not his own name, for that authority to be put into effect by God.

Finally, the Roman centurion I mentioned earlier trusted in and appealed completely to the authority of God when he asked Jesus to heal his servant. He knew that Jesus's ministry was validated by the Father and that there would be no doubt that his servant would be healed. (See Matthew 8:5–13.)

DEFENSE

The second point about being represented by one's authority concerns representation by defense. If a product is defective or fails to fulfill its purpose, then the maker has to step in and solve the problem. Only the authority, or source, of the product can defend that product. Again, when certain models of Toyota cars had significant technical problems, the company's previously excellent name in the automobile industry was on the line, so the president of the company, the grandson of the founder, came to testify before the US Congress to assure the government that the company was addressing the problem. Toyota did not send a junior manager of the company to make this assurance. The president was representing not only the company but also the product; he was speaking on its behalf. In a similar way, we saw that the redemptive work of the Creator required Him to send His own Son to earth to reclaim His image in mankind.

The authority therefore represents the product. This means that if you are not under any authority, and you take action and fail, there is no one to speak for you or to protect you. But if you fail while you are under authority, your authority can help rescue you. For example, if you are on trial after being accused of a crime, it is generally recommended that you hire a lawyer to defend you rather than try to defend yourself. If you are found "defective," you need a respected authority to represent you. Many defense attorneys tell their clients not to say anything at all because it could be used against them. When you are found wanting, the authority over you is your defense.

When human beings, the "product" of the Divine Manufacturer, failed by abandoning their authority, the Manufacturer didn't discard them but came personally on their behalf to represent and defend them. Heaven didn't send an angel; instead, God the Son, whose image was on the product, came to redeem and restore humanity.

When Jesus was attacked by religious leaders who said that His testimony was not valid, He let the Father be His defense, saying,

> *"Even if I testify on my own behalf, my testimony is valid, for I know where I came from and where I am going. But you have no idea where I come from or where I am going. You judge by human standards; I pass judgment on no one. But if I do judge, my decisions are right, because I am not alone. I stand with the Father, who sent me. In your own Law it is written that the testimony of two men is valid. I am one who testifies for myself; my other witness is the Father, who sent me."* Then they asked him, *"Where is your father?"* *"You do not know me or my Father,"* Jesus replied. *"If you knew me, you would know my Father also."* (John 8:14–19)

Jesus was God in the flesh and therefore had Ultimate Authority within Himself, so He could testify on His own behalf. Even so, He directed the religious leaders to the corroborating witness of the Father, who had sent Him. Jesus always defended His words and actions by the authority of the Father. He told those who accused Him that they didn't know the true

Authority, or they would have known that His testimony was valid. *"If God were your Father, you would love me, for I came from God and now am here. I have not come on my own; but he sent me"* (John 8:42).

> ## GOD'S SPIRIT WITHIN YOU AFFIRMS THE FATHER'S WILL IN YOUR LIFE.

Once more, the key to Jesus's success was that He was under authority and had both the authorization and the power to carry out the purpose for which He came to earth. As the Father's representative, He said and did only what the Father said and did.

When you carry out your personal authority and are following the Manufacturer's Manual, the One who sent you is your defense. God's Spirit within you affirms the Father's will in your life: *"But when he, the Spirit of truth, comes, he will guide you into all truth. He will not speak on his own; he will speak only what he hears"* (John 16:13).

Jesus said, *"My Father is with me"* (John 16:32), and He told His disciples, *"Surely I am with you always"* (Matthew 28:20). A manufacturer always backs the product wherever it is sent. When you are submitted to the Ultimate Authority, you are never alone. You don't have to defend yourself. There is Someone there to defend and help you.

PURPOSE #6: SAFETY

As long as you are operating under the authority of the Ultimate Authority, you are safe. Whoever attacks you attacks the Ultimate Authority, who, through Christ, is also your Father. The Lord calls His people *"the apple of his eye"* (Zechariah 2:8). The phrase *apple of one's eye* means "one that is highly cherished."

Authority therefore becomes your sense of security. Jesus used strong words for those who would hurt anyone who belongs to the Father: *"If anyone causes one of these little ones who believe in me to sin, it would be better for him to have a large millstone hung around his neck and to be drowned in the depths of the sea"* (Matthew 18:6). That's not very safe!

It is much better to be under authority. Jesus always knew He was safe because He was not operating on His own. This did not mean He was immune to trouble and hardship, but when you are under the Ultimate Authority, you are protected so that you can complete the purpose of your personal authority. People plotted to kill Jesus on many occasions, but they could not touch Him until it was time for Him to be sacrificed on our behalf. *"They got up, drove him out of the town, and took him to the brow of the hill on which the town was built, in order to throw him down the cliff. But he walked right through the crowd and went on his way"* (Luke 4:29–30).

> ## WHEN YOU ARE UNDER THE ULTIMATE AUTHORITY, YOU ARE PROTECTED SO THAT YOU CAN COMPLETE THE PURPOSE OF YOUR PERSONAL AUTHORITY.

When you are operating under the Father's authority, you have access to His help, counsel, correction, instruction, discipline, and many other benefits that you wouldn't otherwise have. You receive foresight and hindsight—the safety of a broad vision for your life. You also have a *"hiding place"* (Psalm 32:7) in Him, a place of refuge and reference. This knowledge gives you a sense of boldness. You can have confidence because you're not on your own but have Someone protecting you.

PURPOSE #7: PROMOTION

When you operate under the Ultimate Authority, you realize that promotion does not come from other people but from God, even when you are working for and with others. Your authority and promotion are based on what you were uniquely created by God to do in concert with others. He will use other people to place you in situations in which you can carry out your unique purpose, but you are authorized by Him alone to fulfill that purpose.

Yielding to those whom God has given authority in your life while pursuing your own authority leads to advancement in responsibility. Joshua was honored by God and promoted because of his devotion to God and because of the way he was submitted to Moses's leadership. Of all the Israelites, he ended up getting the job as their next leader. We know Joshua because of his association with Moses, the same way we know about the prophet Elisha because of his association with his mentor, Elijah. Operating under authority not only preserves you but also gives you a legacy. Authority can give you a powerful life when you submit to it.

PURPOSE #8: FREEDOM

Another purpose of authority is to provide a framework and environment for total freedom. Contrary to what some people think, authority does not restrict freedom but rather ensures it. *"Now the Lord is the Spirit, and where the Spirit of the Lord is, there is freedom"* (2 Corinthians 3:17).

True freedom always exists within the context of legitimate boundaries. This is because freedom without authority, without laws and principles, turns into anarchy. One of the reasons the American Revolution was successful is that many of its leaders, such as George Washington, had "earned" authority from the citizens through their lives and accomplishments, and because many of the existing, underlying governmental structures were left essentially intact. When the royal governors left the former colonies, the American governors took their places.

PURPOSE #9: IDENTITY

Authority is the source of authenticity, and authenticity is the source of identity. Therefore, you can never know your identity without referencing your authority. Why does every manufacturer place its name on its products? For example, why does the lid of every laptop have the names of the computer's manufacturer on it so that the name can be read easily when the lid is open? It is for the purpose of reminding us continuously that the laptop's identity is connected to its source, or its authority. Any definition of that product must be in reference to its manufacturer.

> THE PURPOSE OF AUTHORITY IS TO PUT YOU IN TOUCH WITH YOUR REAL SELF AS GOD CREATED YOU.

Likewise, you cannot know who you are—your identity—apart from God, your Source. The purpose of authority is to put you in touch with your real self as He created you. Again, everyone may have an *opinion* about a product, but only the manufacturer knows its *purpose*—the what and the why of it.

PURPOSE #10: REALITY

Because authority is the source of authenticity and true identity, it is also the source of reality. You must therefore...

1. Know your authority.

2. Be true to that authority.

When you are under the Ultimate Authority and are operating in your personal authority, people can know who you really are. They can identify your gifts and abilities. This is one of the ways through which God works to fulfill your purpose in your domain. If you are not operating in your gifts, you cannot be identified and noted by other people in that way.

In addition, if you try to imitate or to "be" someone else, you have no genuine authority and will not succeed because you are not being true to the reality of who you are. You will never fulfill your *true* purpose.

CALLING AUTHENTIC PEOPLE

The world sorely lacks authentic people. Since authenticity is a key component of authority, this explains why we are in such a crisis of authority today. Some people may be actively running away from who they really are, but many others are not aware that they are living counterfeit lives. They just don't know what is within them and how to fulfill their personal authority.

In part two of this book, we will look at ways to discover and implement personal authority. What you are about to read is going to stir in you some hidden dreams that God always wanted you to fulfill. You will learn how to release them in your life and in the lives of others.

WHAT IS MY PERSONAL AUTHORITY?

SEVEN

MANIFESTING YOUR PERSONAL AUTHORITY

INHERENT PURPOSE WITH THE ABILITY TO FULFILL
THE INTENT OF THE AUTHOR

I once saw a television documentary about Carl Lewis, the nine-time Olympic gold medalist who was at one point the fastest man in the world. One segment showed Lewis with about twenty other runners lined up on a track about to race. As I watched, I observed the concept of personal authority perfectly illustrated. Lewis's performance in the race demonstrated the difference between one who is authorized and those who aren't.

When the starting gun was fired, all the other runners took off, but Lewis didn't rush. His approach to the race reminded me of King Solomon's statement, *"The race is not to the swift"* (Ecclesiastes 9:11)—especially to those who sprint too swiftly, too soon! Lewis took up a steady, cool pace down the track, and everybody else zipped past him.

The camera suddenly switched to close-up shots of the four runners in the lead. The runner in first place was straining, as if he knew, "Carl's behind me." The runner in second place was sweating, and his chest looked as if it was about to burst. I imagine that he was thinking, "I have to keep going." Meanwhile, Lewis just kept gliding along.

Suddenly, one runner dropped back, then two, then five, then ten. And then, almost all the others. The two remaining runners were killing themselves to keep going, but Lewis was still cruising. I said to myself, "Those legs were born to do this."

Lewis waited until about the last fifty yards, and then it was as if something hit him—he sprinted ahead and overtook those other runners as if they were standing still.

Then, when he crossed the finish line in first place, he didn't show off. He was humble. I liked that about him. Why didn't he show off? Because running was natural for him. He knew it was what he was born to do. He knew he was supposed to win. The crowd went crazy, but he was as cool as a cucumber.

FIVE FEATURES OF YOUR PERSONAL AUTHORITY

Lewis's performance in that race exemplified the following five features of personal authority, which you will recognize in your life, as well, as you exercise your own authority with power in your personal domain.

1. *Your personal authority is natural within you.* It is something you were intentionally authorized and gifted to do by your Creator. You were born to do it, and as you manifest your authority, you should come to realize that it is what you're meant to do.

2. *Your personal authority is valuable.* You have a gift to contribute to the world. Yet, even when you're born to do something, you may start to think that other people are rushing ahead of you in life and that you aren't keeping up in the way you should. Even right now, you may be feeling that others are leaving you way behind in success or accomplishments. But don't worry; pace yourself according to your authority, and you will arrive at the finish line at just the right time. Trying to use shortcuts to personal authority that don't reflect the Creator's purposes and ways will cause you to be unauthorized and unauthentic. You can remain at peace and continue to pace yourself when you understand who you are and the value of your life and your personal authority to your loving Creator. Jesus said, *"I have come that they may have life, and have it to the full"* (John 10:10).

> WHEN YOU ARE WORKING AT SOMETHING YOU WERE BORN TO DO, PEOPLE WILL NATURALLY BECOME AWARE OF YOU.

3. *Your personal authority is authentic.* When you are working at something you were born to do, people will naturally become aware of you. Interestingly, they may even be afraid of you. That

often happens because, if you know what you're doing, you intimidate people who are less sure of themselves just by walking into the same room they're in. You have to continue faithfully pursuing your authority, regardless of any negative reactions others may have toward you.

4. *Your personal authority flourishes in the right environment.* When you're born to do something but haven't fully entered into it, sometimes, all you need is to be in the right environment and something seems to "hit" you, and you take off. This environment is a place where you can run freely with your gifts as you follow the Creator's principles for living and for exercising authority. As the psalmist wrote, *"I run in the path of your commands, for you have set my heart free"* (Psalm 119:32). This environment also may be a place where others see your gifts, confirm that you have natural ability in your domain, and help move you forward to accomplish your goals.

5. *Your personal authority is characterized by humbleness.* When you know what you were born to do and you understand true authority, you are humble. The word *humble* comes from the Latin word *humus*, which means "earth." This brings us full circle to the principle that authority is natural. To be humble simply means to be yourself. Lewis was natural, or "earthy," in winning the race. As you exercise personal authority, you will be, too.

Where are you in terms of the above five features of personal authority in your life? Until you understand your authority, you are probably doing something unauthorized. That is why I want you to truly understand the priority, value, benefits, and necessity of identifying and exercising your inherent authority.

You have an Author, or Source, who has given you life and purpose, so you need to seriously, actively, and persistently ask yourself, "What is my natural personal authority? What am I authorized to do?" To help you answer these questions, we will first explore the value and meaning of personal authority. Then, we will look at each one of the above five features of personal authority in more depth.

THE VALUE AND MEANING OF YOUR PERSONAL AUTHORITY

GOD GAVE YOU PERSONAL AUTHORITY ACCORDING TO ORDER, PURPOSE, AND CREATIVITY

The concept of personal authority is referred to in various ways in the Scriptures, with some variations in terms depending on the translation: *call* or *calling, will of God, appointed, ordained, gift, work, ability,* and *assigned task.*

These words reveal aspects of the meaning of personal authority. For example, Jesus told a parable about a man who entrusted his money to his servants while he went away on a trip. *"To one he gave five talents of money, to another two talents, and to another one talent, each according to his ability"* (Matthew 25:15). The Greek word for *"ability"* in this verse is *dunamis,* meaning "miraculous power" or "force." This word implies that each servant had certain inherent capabilities to make something of the money entrusted to him, and that with those capabilities came a responsibility to exercise them. You, too, have capabilities and are entrusted with a personal authority to carry them out on behalf of your Creator.

Paul of Tarsus was operating in an unauthentic way when he encountered the living Jesus. We will come back to this experience in more detail in a later chapter. But at the outset of this encounter, Paul asked, *"'What shall I do, Lord?'… 'Get up,' the Lord said, 'and go into Damascus. There you will be told all that you have been assigned to do'"* (Acts 22:10). The word *"assigned"* is translated as *"appointed"* in other Bible versions. The Greek word is *tasso,* which means "to arrange in an orderly manner, i.e. assign or dispose (to a certain position or lot)—appoint, determine, ordain, set." It also means "to draw up in order, arrange." As a God of purpose, order, and creativity, the Creator has assigned or appointed each person in his rightful, authorized place to function to the fullest. He has arranged everyone in a strategic position to function smoothly with others to accomplish His purposes. Within that necessary order, He gives us extraordinary freedom to express and enjoy our individual authority.

Paul wrote to the Corinthians, *"What, after all, is Apollos? And what is Paul? Only servants, through whom you came to believe—as the Lord has assigned to each his task"* (1 Corinthians 3:5). The word translated *"assigned"* here is the Greek word *didomi,* "to give." We are each assigned or given a particular task to fulfill. If God planned intricate, interconnected functions for the physical world (such as photosynthesis) for His own purposes, what did God think about when He created you?

GOD GAVE YOU—YES, YOU!—PERMISSION AND POWER TO ACT

The concept of authority is overflowing with meaning, and that is why it is necessary to view it from many angles to fully grasp it. In earlier chapters, we defined personal authority as "the inherent gifts a person or thing possesses in order to fulfill the purpose for which that person or thing was placed on this earth." Let's explore the concepts of *authority* and *authorization* with a particular emphasis on how you can manifest your personal authority.

> WHEN GOD CREATED YOU, HE AUTOMATICALLY GAVE YOU NOT ONLY POWER BUT ALSO PERMISSION TO ACT OUT YOUR AUTHORITY; HE GAVE YOU PERMISSION TO BE YOURSELF.

The following are some definitions of authority that I have collected:

- *"Power to determine/the right to control your own destiny."* For our purposes, this definition refers to the power to be who you really are. You have the right to determine your own future based on your inherent authority from the Creator. The future is inside you. God has given you permission to be all you were born to be. That is the extent of your authority. You don't have authority to make someone else like you or to try to make yourself like someone else. You have authority only to make yourself who *you* are. That's the power within you that you need to determine, and this chapter, as well as the next several chapters, will show you how to make that determination.

- *"Delegated power or right."* You didn't generate this power, but God gave it to you in order to manifest what He put within you. He gave you the right to become what He wants you to be.

- *"Power based on right, permission to act."* When God created you, He automatically gave you not only power but also permission to act out your authority; He gave you permission to be yourself.

• *"Sanction."* This definition is related to the last one. In terms of authority, *sanction* means "explicit or official approval, permission, or ratification." *Sanction* is related to the biblical term *sanctify*, which means "to set apart for a special purpose." Therefore, God has given us sanction, or official approval, in relation to a specific position He has placed us in and from which we best function. We have been selected and set apart for a specific role.

Many people are afraid, for various reasons, to step out into their personal authority and fulfill the dreams that are within them. This is why I want you to be able to clearly understand this truth: The fact that you have been given authority means that you, personally, have the privilege and power to fulfill your life's purpose in your personal domain. You have permission to exercise the strength with which you have been endued by God. You have the right to exercise your inherent power. When you truly understand authority, you become free to be yourself.

Do you believe that authority was given to you before you were born to deliver something to the planet? We have seen that everything was created to fulfill the Author's intent. What applied to the prophet Jeremiah in this regard applies to you, as well. God told him, *"Before I formed you in the womb I knew you, before you were born I set you apart"* (Jeremiah 1:5). God chose you and set you apart for a reason.

You will manifest your authority when you have the right mindset toward it. If you want to remain or move outside of your personal authority, you will not only be frustrated or uneasy inside, but you will also miss the point of your purpose in life. Paul wrote, *"In him we were also chosen, having been predestined according to the plan of him who works out everything in conformity with the purpose of his will* ["*according to the counsel of His will*" NKJV]" (Ephesians 1:11). This means God set your destination before you were conceived, and to fulfill that destination is to be the authentic you.

Note that the above verse says God works out everything in conformity with His purposes. As His representatives, we are to do the same "working out," under the authority He has given us. Your personal authority allows you to bring things in your life into conformity with your purposes under Him. You have the power to shape your life according to your personal authority.

Let's now explore in greater depth the five features of your personal authority as you ask yourself some questions about your current life.

1. YOUR PERSONAL AUTHORITY IS NATURAL WITHIN YOU

Whatever you were born to do is natural within you; you don't have to "try" to do it. This does not mean that you won't have to work hard while fulfilling your authority, that you won't have to push yourself in certain ways to grow and accomplish your goals, or that you won't run into challenges as you pursue your personal authority. But it does mean that, generally speaking, you will feel energized, refreshed, and enthusiastic about what you are doing and will have the natural abilities to accomplish it.

You will manifest your authority only if you start with what is natural and God-directed in your life. Each person has been given gifts and a domain in which to operate them. As you yield to God and to the dream He's placed in your heart, your personal authority will emerge, and you will live with confidence and effectiveness.

LIFE WILL LOOK EASIER AND BE EASIER FOR YOU

Everything God created you to be is already inside you. This is why people who have found their personal domains make life look easy.

Not only will you make life *look* easy by exercising your personal authority, but your life will also *be* easier because you will not be fighting against unnatural or unauthorized activities or environments.

Similar to the runners who strained to keep going while Carl Lewis glided along, people who are trying to function outside of their natural territories, or domains of authority, have to struggle and work extra hard because they are not meant to do what they're doing. They may even be outwardly successful, but they're not really at rest inside; they don't have the natural lightness of spirit and enthusiasm that come from pursuing the true desires of one's heart.

YOU WILL HAVE A DEEP SENSE OF SATISFACTION

Have you ever wondered why Jesus frequently taught people using illustrations from nature? He based most of His teachings on the natural, everyday surroundings and operations that they were familiar with. For example, He referred to the lilies of the field and the birds of the air, to the catching of fish and the sowing of seeds. He continually used these illustrations as examples to show people how natural life would be when they were flowing in the Creator's purposes.

> NOT ONLY WILL YOU MAKE LIFE **LOOK** EASY BY EXERCISING YOUR PERSONAL AUTHORITY, BUT YOUR LIFE WILL ALSO **BE** EASIER BECAUSE YOU WILL NOT BE FIGHTING AGAINST UNNATURAL OR UNAUTHORIZED ACTIVITIES OR ENVIRONMENTS.

In Matthew 6:25–30, He said,

Do not worry about your life, what you will eat or drink; or about your body, what you will wear. Is not life more important than food, and the body more important than clothes? Look at the birds of the air; they do not sow or reap or store away in barns, and yet your heavenly Father feeds them. Are you not much more valuable than they? Who of you by worrying can add a single hour to his life? And why do you worry about clothes? See how the lilies of the field grow. They do not labor or spin. Yet I tell you that not even Solomon in all his splendor was dressed like one of these. If that is how God clothes the grass of the field, which is here today and tomorrow is thrown into the fire, will he not much more clothe you, O you of little faith? (Matthew 6:25–30)

It took King Solomon thirteen years to build his royal palace and to fit it with cedar, bronze, and gold. He had a huge company of workers to keep his operations in order. He accumulated gold and silver, bringing wealth to his city. He built the magnificent temple. When everything was finished, notable people from other nations, such as the Queen of Sheba, came from afar to see Solomon in his glory, with his wisdom and riches. Yet Jesus said, in effect, "This lily is here today and gone tomorrow, and its beauty is better than all the splendor of Solomon and his reign." What makes it so easy for the lily to do its work and manifest its purpose? The lily was born to be a lily.

MANY PEOPLE'S HOBBIES ARE ACTUALLY THEIR PERSONAL AUTHORITY

Trees don't *try* to grow. Birds don't *try* to fly. Fish don't *try* to swim. These abilities are natural to them. In a similar way, whatever you were built to do, you are authorized to do; it is normal for you. You can always tell what your authority is because it is fun while you're doing it—or, if not always "fun," you experience a deep sense of satisfaction from it.

On this basis, I have concluded that many people's hobbies may actually be related to their personal authority in life. They enjoy the activities they do in their spare time more than what they do on the job. This is why they can't wait to leave their workplaces at the end of the day or the week and get to their hobbies. Their hobbies are what they *really* want to do. Whereas their jobs make them feel like they are pushing a large rock up a steep hill, their hobbies make them feel like they are gliding easily downhill. Their hobbies are not difficult for them to engage in; they are exciting, pleasing, and fulfilling to do. They are natural and fun. These hobbies, therefore, reveal the true authority and gifts within these individuals.

Many people on earth are frustrated, depressed, or disillusioned *every day* because they go to jobs they are not authorized to do. They were not born to do them, and they feel—and are—out of place. I think this is sad.

Many "unauthorized" people drain others around them. You may work with some of them. They complain about the job, they complain about the boss, and they complain about you. They may even complain about the weather, how their cars are running—everything. Why? They are miserable because they haven't found themselves. Miserable people are self-hating people. Sometimes, they don't like the people around them because they are reminded of themselves—their coworkers, colleagues, or family members don't know who they are, either. In contrast, I've found that people who discover their natural authority and begin to become who they were born to be suddenly fall in love with everybody and everything around them. Things that used to bother them don't bother them anymore. They are content because they have an authentic reason for living.

WHEN YOU KNOW YOU ARE DOING SOMETHING YOU WERE NOT BORN TO DO, YOU WILL FEEL IRRITATED IN YOUR CURRENT JOB.

When you know you are doing something you were not born to do, you will feel irritated in your current job. You won't feel comfortable in it. Have you ever heard anyone say about a job, position, or environment, "This is just not me"? What do they mean by that? The job, position, or environment is locking them in. It is cramping their style. It is stopping them from being who they were meant to be.

It is frustrating to be in a place that you can't wait to retire from. Most people don't want to retire from something when they love it. Do you desire to be released from your job? Do you look forward to receiving your pension? If so, it is probably because, deep inside, you know you're not doing what you were born to do.

In addition, when you are not operating in your true territory, other people who do naturally operate in that territory will intimidate you. Remember my encounter with the shark when I was spearfishing? The shark intimidated me because he was in his natural environment, but I was not. If you are trying to do what you were not born to do, then the people who *were* born to do it will threaten you without even trying, because you will feel inadequate. Again, you will have to try extra hard to do what they're doing naturally.

To manifest your God-given authority, you first need to ask, "Am I flowing naturally in my personal domain? Or am I out of place?"

2. YOUR PERSONAL AUTHORITY IS VALUABLE

Second, your life is eternally valuable to your Creator. You have been made in His image, are loved by Him, and have been redeemed by Him. Likewise, your personal authority or assignment is immeasurably valuable to Him.

Do you know—are you *convinced* of—your value to God and to His purposes for the world?

Remember that one of the principles of authority is that the intent for which a product is designed determines the design of the product itself. The author or manufacturer determines the design, capabilities, qualities, and characteristics of the product. All of these are in keeping with the purpose for which the product is created. Therefore, the author is also the originator of the *value* and *worth* of the product.

I want to give you an indication of how awesome you really are through the truths presented in Psalm 139. This psalm, written by King David, helps us to better understand the value of our unique personal authority. The reason God gave up His Son Jesus Christ to die for you is that He knows the treasure within you. The authority that He put inside you is so valuable that He didn't want you to go to your grave without manifesting it. We cannot allow the cemetery to be the burial place of the treasure God has put in our lives. The earth needs your purpose, your authority, and your gift!

> ## THE EARTH NEEDS YOUR PURPOSE, YOUR AUTHORITY, AND YOUR GIFT.

YOU ARE WONDERFULLY MADE

Psalm 139:13 says, *"For you created my inmost being."* God created your inner "circuits," your components; He caused you to be a vital being, made in His image, and gave you purpose.

"You knit me together in my mother's womb" (verse 13). God not only created your inmost being, but He also created your body. After you were conceived, He knitted or wove you in your mother's womb, according to His own design for your life.

"I praise you because I am fearfully and wonderfully made; your works are wonderful, I know that full well" (verse 14). You are "fearfully" made. This refers to a positive fear, such as reverence or awe. You are "wonderfully" made. The Hebrew word translated *"wonderfully"* means "to distinguish," to "put a difference," or "to be distinct." God made you unique.

You may feel that you are not perfect, but all of your physical characteristics are in God's plan. When you look in the mirror, your first statement should be, "Wonderful!" because you are wonderfully made. Your temperament, your personality, your stature, your face, your skin color, even your family heritage are all used by God for your personal authority. Why? Because your purpose required that you be who and what you are.

The prophet Isaiah declared, *"O LORD, you are our Father. We are the clay, you are the potter; we are all the work of your hand"* (Isaiah 64:8). He also said, *"Does the clay say to the potter, 'What are you making?'"* (Isaiah 45:9). Let us not therefore reject what God has done. Let us not speak against what God calls good. We shouldn't compare what God calls good to what men call good, because men don't know what good is. God made you beautiful.

YOU HAVE A SPECIAL PURPOSE FOR YOUR LIFE

"My frame was not hidden from you when I was made in the secret place. When I was woven together in the depths of the earth, your eyes saw my unformed body" (Psalm 139:15–16). This means that your whole structure, your body, was not hidden from God when you were made in the *"secret place."* God's eye is on pregnant women and on their unborn children. This is why we have to be careful about our concept of when a fertilized egg becomes a human being. As soon as the egg and sperm unite, God releases an eternal spirit to take up residence in that "house." I believe that God does not allow a sperm and an egg to unite unless He has a reason and a purpose for that human being. Regardless of the circumstances surrounding that conception, it is a result of *preconception.* God has already preconceived in His mind that He wants something accomplished on earth. He has something He wants to accomplish through you, and so He created you to do it.

You are not a mistake. Every time a male discharges sperm, about five hundred million sperm are released. All five hundred million sperm dash toward the egg, but only one makes it. Four hundred and ninety-nine million potential humans did not make it to the egg, because what is needed on earth required you. That is why I believe there is an awesome sense of destiny deep inside every human being. There is a cry that says, "I was born to do something. I don't know what it is, but there is something I was meant to do!"

Where does that cry come from? It comes from beyond your intellect and beyond your emotions. It comes from a place so far within you that the Bible calls it *"the deep"*: *"Deep calls to deep"* (Psalm 42:7). And what is your deep calling out to? It is God. Only God can answer your cry. The cry can be satisfied only in God because nobody knows a product like the one who made it. No one knows the material like the author. Nobody knows the reason why something was made better than the one who created it.

Beyond a doubt, this planet needs the personal authority you're carrying within you. The same is true about every other human being. It is a tragedy whenever someone dies through a drug overdose or a suicide or another type of abuse to his own body. God weeps because those people never discovered who they truly were.

Likewise, when an unborn baby is aborted, all of heaven weeps because earth will never receive the awesome gift that God has sent through that child. Do you ever wonder what would have happened if Mary, the mother of Jesus, had had an abortion? In that manger lay a child who carried within Him the salvation of the world. Or, what would have happened if Moses's mother hadn't protected him and had allowed Pharaoh's soldiers to kill him? In that basket drifting along the Nile was a child who carried within him the leadership of the nation of Israel and the writing of the first five books of the Bible.

Every day, I walk with a sense of awesome responsibility, knowing that I have to do what I was born to do before I die. And so do you. You were not born just to make a living. You were born to give a unique aspect of life to this planet, to make a contribution. That area is your authority; that's the domain in which you exercise leadership.

YOU ARE A "BESTSELLER" WAITING TO BE READ

"All the days ordained for me were written in your book before one of them came to be" (Psalm 139:16). Before you were conceived, God "finished" your life. What you were meant to do was ordained and "written" before the day you were born. This means that you are a bestseller waiting to be read by life. Everything that you are supposed to be and do and accomplish is already written in this "book" God has written as your Author. You are already predestined to reveal to the world the hidden thoughts and plans of God, which He has placed within you.

YOU ARE ALREADY PREDESTINED TO REVEAL TO THE WORLD THE HIDDEN THOUGHTS AND PLANS OF GOD, WHICH HE HAS PLACED WITHIN YOU.

"How precious to me are your thoughts, O God! How vast is the sum of them! Were I to count them, they would outnumber the grains of sand" (Psalm 139:17–18). I believe David was saying, in effect, "When I think about what You have done in my life, and about the plans for me You wrote in Your book, the knowledge is absolutely priceless to me, though I am not capable of analyzing all of Your amazing thoughts!" God's thoughts about you are so awesome that your attempt to understand them would be like trying to count the grains of sand on the seashore—an impossibility. What God thinks about us is so remarkable that nobody could calculate or comprehend it.

Think about some of the people you grew up with. Aren't there some people you thought would never make it in life but who now have successful businesses? There are people whom society had evaluated and declared would never be any good to anyone, and yet, after a while, God did a miracle in their lives. They got in touch with their own personal authority and their gifts, and they became tremendous assets to society. I find these types of results amazing. This is why the Scriptures say that God's thoughts about us are so awesome that we can't analyze them. To manifest your God-given authority, you should never write yourself off but rather discover what God has written about you.

3. YOUR PERSONAL AUTHORITY IS AUTHENTIC

God created everybody with a domain of authority, and that domain is where you manifest your true self. The Author's goal for you is to be authentic, and you are authentic when you become what you were designed to be. I have met thousands of unauthorized people over the years who were doing something they were not born and "wired" to do, and they were filled with frustration.

Many people live their lives, die, and are buried without ever having really "shown up" on earth because they were never authentic. They live for sixty, seventy, eighty, or more years, but nobody ever "sees" them— they never witness the manifestation of who these people really are on the inside. They see mere impressions of other people that they have put on like veneers. If you compare yourself with others and feel inferior to them to the point that you try to imitate them; when you try to talk like other people, look like other people, and do things like other people, you are not being authentic.

To be authentic means to manifest one's true self and to fully exercise one's gifts. Are you authentic? Have you recognized what is unauthentic about yourself and shed the veneer from your life?

It's a paradox that while certain people are intimidated by or resent people who are authentic, there is also nothing in the world that attracts some people more than a person who is authentic. Authentic people draw others who see something fresh and confident in them, and who sense acceptance from them because they are no longer in competition with others.

Tell yourself, "I will be authentic before I die. As I pursue my inherent authority, other people are going to be able to see who I truly am. Right now, I'm still wearing other people's images, but living according to my authority in my personal domain will remove the veneer and let what is inside be revealed."

Once more, to be authentic is simply to be what you are naturally. Have you ever heard someone exclaim, "Look! Do you see that bird? It's *flying*!"? No. Birds fly overhead every day, so that we often don't even notice them. Birds are authorized to fly, and they are authentic when they are doing what they were meant to do.

WHEN YOU FIND WHAT YOU WERE BORN TO DO AND FUNCTION IN IT, IT IS SO NATURAL THAT IT IS NOT "SECOND NATURE" BUT "FIRST NATURE."

Likewise, personal authority is inherent, natural, and right. When you find what you were born to do and function in it, it is so natural that it is not "second nature" but "first nature."

Perhaps, when you see people in their natural domains, or functioning in their strengths, you sometimes think, "I wish I could play the piano like that. I wish I could write like that. I wish I could speak like that. I wish I could paint like that. I wish, I wish…." You must stop wishing and discover your own territory. That is the way to be authentic. That is the way to manifest your personal authority.

4. YOUR PERSONAL AUTHORITY FLOURISHES IN THE RIGHT ENVIRONMENT

Seeds become trees because that potential is naturally within them. All they need is the right environment and the right nutrients. Likewise, manifesting your personal authority requires you to nurture the right environment for it. Paying attention to this aspect of authority will allow you to flourish and to maximize your effectiveness.

CREATE YOUR OPTIMUM ENVIRONMENT

You create the right environment by removing what is distracting and superfluous to your authority and replacing it with what will build you up in it. For example, if you want to develop your gift for making furniture but spend all your time watching old television programs, you will not fulfill your potential in life. Instead, you can visit and observe other furniture makers at their craft, do research on furniture design, find a space where you can work, and so on.

You can also create the right environment by seeking the support and encouragement of those who know you and will affirm your gifting, and by gaining additional knowledge, training, and skills that will help you to optimize your abilities.

In addition, your personal authority will often *create* an environment in which it can thrive as you operate in your personal domain. A colleague told me that during a business trip, she was in an airport going from one gate to another for a connecting flight when she saw a women's restroom with a sign outside that read, "This restroom was cleaned by Valerie." When she walked inside, she heard Valerie singing cheerfully, "This is a good day. It's what you make of it"—"it" referring to life. Valerie greeted every woman who entered with a cheery, "Welcome to Valerie's happy restroom!" The place was sparkling, and so was Valerie's personality. In the rushed, tired, and harried world of a busy airport, she lifted people's spirits while providing a much-needed service. She created her own positive environment, and she oversaw that large restroom with true authority!

People who have discovered their personal authority and have created an optimum environment for it will work at it even if they don't get paid. When you are doing what you were born to do, you don't need external motivation to work long hours. People have to tell you when it's the lunch hour or when it's time to go home. When you find your real work, you want to stay with it all day and all night. The right authority and the right environment give you powerful motivation and satisfaction.

THE "WRONG" ENVIRONMENT CAN BE YOUR "PRE-OCCUPATION"

People who are in jobs or circumstances that are not related to their personal authority don't really have occupations; they have *pre*-occupations. When you find your true vocation, you will not be "pre-occupied" but "occupied"—interested, absorbed, and engaged with your purpose. It would be a terrible thing never to proceed beyond your pre-occupation.

YOU CAN EASE YOUR JOB FRUSTRATION BY FOCUSING ON WHAT IT CAN PREPARE YOU FOR—ON THE KNOWLEDGE, EXPERIENCE, AND SKILLS YOU ARE GAINING THROUGH IT.

However, I believe that the Creator, in His wisdom, will sometimes allow us to be "pre-occupied" in certain jobs for a time in order to gain experience and skills that we will be able to use later in our true occupations. In this way, your pre-occupation is your job, but your occupation is your real work.

Most people don't go to work. They simply go to a job. If you are in a job that is not aligned with your purpose, then consider it to be only temporary. Your managers and coworkers don't know who you really are inside, but God does. Every position in life is only temporary until you reach the point where you are in a position to manifest your true self.

If your present job is a pre-occupation, don't just resign without having any specific plans. You can ease your job frustration by focusing on what it can prepare you for—on the knowledge, experience, and skills you are gaining through it. You can go to your place of employment telling yourself, "I'm going to discover my authority, my assignment, and then relate this job to my true work, learning everything I can here that will help me to move further along toward where I want to go."

PATIENTLY AWAIT YOUR MANIFESTATION

One other point to keep in mind is that you may be a "late bloomer." It takes some people a little longer than others to manifest their latent gifts and skills, for various reasons. It may be that the combined experiences of your life, and not just your "pre-occupations," are preparing you for the time when you will find yourself in the right environment, among the right people, and then your personal authority will take off. Again, this will be an environment where you can run freely with your gifts, and, most likely, your progress will be exponential because you have been preparing for this moment for quite a while. Therefore, if you are still nurturing the knowledge and skills that will enable you to fully manifest your personal authority, then be patient with yourself and your circumstances and thank your Creator for authorizing His perfect timing in your life.

5. YOUR PERSONAL AUTHORITY IS CHARACTERIZED BY HUMBLENESS

People who know and manifest their personal authority are not arrogant about their accomplishments; they don't throw their success in other people's faces, as if they are superior. While they enjoy their work, they are humble about it because they know they didn't create themselves but were given their gifts by God.

When you are operating in your personal authority, you will experience great personal fulfillment and the joy of working in your domain. There is nothing wrong with this. It is natural to enjoy what you are meant to do! But those who keep their personal authority in perspective don't show off. Like Carl Lewis, they are down-to-earth. In addition, they are able to submit to others' authority in their realms because they recognize that valuable gifts have been given to all.

ARE YOU MAXIMIZING YOURSELF? THE FOUR FOUNDATIONAL PRINCIPLES AND YOU

In chapter one, I listed four foundational principles for understanding authority and entering into the power of your personal domain, which we have been exploring in this book. Let us now consider them in light of your specific personal authority.

The Principle of the Author. The only one who knows the true and original purpose and function of a product is the author. Are you connected to the Author of life, so that you can discover the purpose and authority He has placed deep within you? This is the first and most important step to manifesting your personal authority. Authenticity begins with being connected to the Creator God through Jesus Christ, the Authorized Dealer, and desiring to live according to His established principles and standards. He *is* Reality. Jesus said, *"I am the way and the truth and the life. No one comes to the Father except through me"* (John 14:6).

It won't do much good to pursue personal authority if you are only half committed to the One in whose image you are created, the One who deeply loves you and has placed wonderful gifts and dreams within you. Even if you were to exercise certain inherent gifts and be successful from an outward perspective, you wouldn't be truly reflecting all that He has placed within you and all that He could do with those gifts if they were used for His purposes and to honor Him. As Paul wrote, *"Now to him who is able to do immeasurably more than all we ask or imagine, according to his power that is at work within us"* (Ephesians 3:20).

Once you know you are connected to the Creator, stay connected to Him by reading His Word and by talking with Him, which is also called praying. As you talk with Him, ask Him to make your personal authority clear to you. He made you, and He knows what He put inside you to do for your generation. *"We are God's workmanship, created in Christ Jesus to do good works, which God **prepared in advance** for us to do"* (Ephesians 2:10). Then, anticipate His answer, recommit to Him everything that He has placed inside you, and see what happens!

> **WHEN YOU DISCOVER WHAT YOU WERE CREATED TO BE, GOD EXPECTS YOU TO USE THAT DISCOVERY TO MAXIMIZE YOURSELF.**

The Principle of Authorization. Authorization is the legitimate transfer of power to a representative to be used specifically for the purpose for which it was delegated. The one who receives the delegated power is consciously aware that he does not personally own it.

The Author put something within you that He wants to see manifested on the earth. Your personal authority is the authorization that the Creator has given you to represent His image, desires, ideas, and purposes in the world. You were born with the authority to execute a specific assignment, and only you can do it the way you were born to do it. When you discover what you were created to be, then God expects you to use that discovery to maximize yourself. Your personal authority is to be offered back to Him with gratitude.

The power, or backing, for this authority is the unique blend of inherent gifts, abilities, and perspectives that you possess in order to fulfill the purpose for which you were created. Through the restoration provided by the Authorized Dealer, the Creator has also given us His own Spirit to live within us and enable us to carry out our purposes. This is the ultimate gift of His representation in our lives, and we need to follow the guidance of His Spirit within us.

Authorization is therefore the lawful right and freedom given by the Author to His creation to exercise and manifest the ability or power He caused it to possess. Do you have the mindset that your gifts and abilities are authorized by the Creator to be used to fulfill His purposes in the world? Until we exchange the idea of selfish ambition for selfless service, we will not be able to truly manifest our personal authority.

The Principle of Authenticity. Inherent authority is found in one's purpose, or assignment, in the world. You may find that you have more than one assignment at different times of your life within the same domain or related domains. You must know your area or areas of authority and thus discover your authentic self so that you can be faithful to fulfill what you are authorized to do. How well do you know your area or areas of authority? If you are well acquainted with your personal domain, are you being faithful to operate within it? What might be hindering you from this, and how can you address it?

The Principle of Authority. An author naturally incorporates into the making of his product the capacity—or, the authority and the power—to perform, to produce, and to fulfill its purpose. You were born with delegated authority. Your authority is the divine gift, assignment, passion, and contribution that you were placed on this earth to deliver to humanity. No one can steal it, prevent it, devalue it, or stop it unless you let them. How will you serve your gift to the world?

THE PRINCIPLE OF LIFE

The principle of life for every human being is to reconnect to the Author, discover his personal authority, become authentic, and fulfill what he is authorized to do.

I hope you will take these truths about manifesting your personal authority to heart. For me, this knowledge came about by a process of reconnecting with the Creator, studying His Word, experiencing life, reading a multitude of books, and talking with many people. I want to make this process easier for you, and that is why I have written this book. I want you to discover the freedom and joy of operating in your personal domain. Therefore, we will next explore the benefits you will receive from exercising your God-given authority.

EIGHT

BENEFITS TO LIVING IN YOUR PERSONAL AUTHORITY

THE FREEDOM TO BE WHO YOU WERE CREATED TO BE

In this chapter, I provide an overview of the tremendous benefits you experience as you exercise your personal authority, which allows you the freedom to be who you were created to be. Then, in the next chapter, I show how you can discover your personal authority to ensure that you begin receiving these benefits.

YOU ARE AN ORIGINAL

Everybody was born an original, but most people end up being copies. The world has so many duplicates that it's hard to find an original walking around. The "normal" people are the copies.

When you manifest your personal authority, you are not just a variation of someone else. You know who you truly are, and that is the key to your originality. There's only one of you, and you make the most of it, expressing your unique design. You put into effect your God-given vision and goals for your life, even though they may be different from those of the people around you.

YOU KNOW YOUR INTRINSIC VALUE

While many people struggle to find a sense of personal significance for their lives, you understand that your significance comes from your inherent personal authority and from the love of the One who made you. Because you are aware of your intrinsic value, your life is filled with hope and purpose. You don't succumb to uncertainty about your worth because you recognize that you are of tremendous importance to your generation, and this insulates you from any arrows of undue criticism and negativity that may come your way.

YOU EXPERIENCE PERSONAL FULFILLMENT

As you live according to your personal authority, you experience the contentment and gratification that come from serving the world through your natural gifts and inherent purpose. You have the certainty that you aren't wasting your life but are using your time, talents, experience, and energy in the best ways possible.

YOU HAVE GENUINE CONFIDENCE

Because you know you are authorized by your Creator, you move forward with confidence so that you are able to fulfill what you were born to accomplish on earth. You have courage, take risks, and express your creativity, but you never "experiment" with your life. You have a specific reason for living, and you purposefully pursue it.

In addition, you don't wonder if what you are pursuing is going to work; you know it is going to work because you are meant to do it. First, you are confident in your inherent natural abilities. Even if what you are trying to do fails twenty times, you know it will eventually have to succeed. You interpret failure as only a temporary school that teaches you lessons in character, skill, and perspective. You never quit; you only rest before you begin again.

Moreover, you are confident that the resources you need will be available. Why? You believe that everybody is supposed to be prosperous—having more than enough for himself—through the exercise of his gifts, so that his resources can be reinvested in his purpose and also given to those who are in need: "*One man gives freely, yet gains even more; another withholds unduly, but comes to poverty. A generous man will prosper; he who refreshes others will himself be refreshed*" (Proverbs 11:24–25).

YOU ARE FREE FROM COMPETITION WITH OTHERS

By exercising your personal authority, you establish yourself as unique and genuine, and this reality counteracts any momentary thought that you have to compete with others to confirm your own worth and place in the world. Because you know who you are, you can't be easily manipulated by those who want to use you. You aren't looking to boost your ego, beat out the competition, or put anyone else down. You want only to manifest who you truly are in fulfillment of your God-given purpose.

> **BY EXERCISING YOUR PERSONAL AUTHORITY, YOU ESTABLISH YOURSELF AS UNIQUE AND GENUINE.**

Likewise, you are not intimidated by others. No one can threaten your true authority—even though some people may try to—because you're not trying to outrun them; you're just being yourself.

You also know that if you try through manipulation or force to compel other people to conform to *your* ideas for them, you will be working against the Creator's purposes. You have learned that the Creator wants you to awaken to your own ability and calling and to keep out of others' business so that you can eliminate any perceived need to be in open or subtle rivalry with them. As you do this, it enables you to work according to your own authority.

YOU ARE FREE FROM COMPARING YOURSELF WITH OTHERS

Because you recognize that you are distinct from all others in your authority, you don't compare yourself with anyone else. You don't keep checking your progress in life in relation to others and judging whether they are ahead of you or behind you, and you don't compare the results of your work against theirs.

You may learn new skills and techniques from observing other people who have gifts and abilities that are similar to yours so that you can grow in effectiveness in your personal domain. But this observation is not for the purpose of comparison; it is a form of mentorship. You are blessed as you exercise personal authority because you don't feel a need to mold other people to be like you, and you don't feel a need to mimic other people in order to measure up to them. Your style, your focus, your perspective remain yours. You know you have an audience of One, your Creator, and that He is cheering you on.

YOU ARE FREE FROM JEALOUSY

Since you know your intrinsic value and distinctness and are free from competition and comparison, you don't feel jealous of others. If other people can do certain things better than you can, this doesn't make you feel second-rate. Why not? Again, it isn't any of your business. You can do things that other people cannot do. You understand that, according to the way the Creator designed the world, everyone's authority complements everyone else's authority, and that problems begin when people feel others have something that is greater than they have but that they *should* have.

You never lose the genuine you for the sake of jealousy because you know it is the only "you" that has real authority. No one else can do what you were born to do the same way that you can, with your personality, perspectives, and experience. You recognize that being jealous of someone who was born to do something you can't do, or who was born to do it in a different measure than you were, is a total waste of time. Instead, you tap into your own authority and get to work!

YOU DON'T HAVE TO BE AFRAID

Because you know you were born to do something specific and are trusting in your ability to fulfill it, you are not afraid of failing or of anyone who may criticize you or attempt to prevent you from doing it. You have such conviction about your calling that you move forward with anticipation and purpose, no matter what.

As a person operating under authorization, you find that fulfilling your personal authority is enjoyable and not anxiety-producing. Even with the inevitable pressures, struggles, and responsibilities of life, you sleep well at night because these difficulties ultimately aren't your problem. You are functioning under the delegated authority of your Creator, and He will make a way for you to do what you are meant to do. Your job is to do what you were designed to do, and the Authority above you is responsible for everything else, including the results of your efforts.

YOU HAVE INTERNAL MOTIVATION AND PASSION

Your authority automatically produces in you a passion for life because it operates in the midst of your deepest desires and vision for the future.

This gives you tremendous internal motivation to act on your purpose and gifts and to see your vision become a reality. As you function in your personal domain, you exhibit qualities of a self-starter. You don't wait for someone to prompt you to use your gifts or to work toward your goals; instead, you can't wait to get up in the morning and continue working on them.

Your internal motivation and passion also foster a persevering attitude within you. No matter how long it takes to develop your natural abilities, put your plans into action, or see results, you keep going and keep believing and keep moving forward.

YOU ARE AUTHENTIC

The combination of all the above makes you *authentic*, which means you express your true self, reflecting your dreams, ideas, and creativity. You know yourself well and consistently act on that knowledge, using your gifts to manifest the treasure that God has hidden in your inner being and wants you to serve to the world. And, you *maintain* your authenticity, because you are aware that it is vital for exercising true authority and keeping it effective.

Are you ready to receive all the above benefits in your life? In the next chapter, we will look at some specific and practical questions that will help you to confirm your own personal authority.

NINE

TWELVE KEYS TO DISCOVERING PERSONAL AUTHORITY

TO EXERCISE PERSONAL AUTHORITY, YOU MUST KNOW YOURSELF

Billions of people use the social networking platform Facebook. They share photos of themselves and their loved ones, updates on their lives, articles that interest them, videos they find funny, events they're participating in, products they support, and much more. Yet, with all that information, I wonder how many of those billions still do not truly know themselves and the personal authority God has placed within them. The world is filled with unauthentic people doing the unauthorized. They may be sincere and well-meaning in their endeavors, but one can be sincere and unauthentic at the same time.

I encourage you to take the time to make sure you truly know yourself, because it is impossible to exercise personal authority until you do. Since the Creator has placed your authority inside you, to be exercised through the guidance and power of His Spirit who resides within you, you will learn much about yourself by examining your thoughts, ideas, and personal passions.

Your personal authority can be described using various terms, such as your life's *vision* or *purpose*, your *realm of leadership*, and your *gifting*. It can be identified through your *natural desires* and what you sense as your *inherent assignment* in life. All these words are helpful for understanding the concept of personal authority as it manifests itself in various ways in your life.

DEVELOP A PERSONAL AUTHORITY PROFILE

This chapter includes questions for you to reflect on and answer in what I believe will be a fun and inspiring exercise for you. Thinking about these questions is going to awaken in you some hidden dreams. You will be drawing from your inner desires and passions and imagining possibilities generated from ideas that reside deep within your heart. In this way, you can move from just thinking about personal authority or wishing you could exercise it to actually operating in it.

To summarize your "research," I suggest that you develop a Personal Authority Profile. A sample profile is included in the back of this book. This profile should generally be reserved for yourself to help you understand your authority. People can run into problems when they start consulting other people to discover themselves because they may succumb to another person's opinion instead of pursuing what is truly authentic about them. You have to protect yourself from that. On the other hand, you may want to show your profile to your spouse or one or two close friends because sometimes others who know us well can help us to see aspects of ourselves that we are not able to see, such as gifts, talents, and interests that we may take for granted or abilities we may have forgotten that we exercised in the past. They may say, "Remember when you loved doing _____ as a child?" or "I recall how good you were at _____." Use discretion and don't share too much until you have come to many of your own conclusions, so that you won't be unduly influenced by others. Then, share your findings with two or three others, if you wish.

HOW WELL DO YOU KNOW YOURSELF?

Ask yourself the following twelve key questions, taking time to remember the past, to evaluate your current gifts, abilities, and preferences, and to envision the future. Record your conclusions in a notebook or on your computer after you use the sample profile form to discover your personal authority. Also consider what might be preventing you from fully realizing your personal authority—or realizing it in the first place—such as fear, complacency, and so forth, and use the suggestions in this book for overcoming them.

Here, then, are twelve keys to discovering your authority. The following questions are meant to help you to hone in on your personal domain. Some of the questions are similar, but their purpose is to confirm what you were designed to do in life. If you give totally different answers to each question, then you will need to continue refining your answers. You also may not have a clear response to every question, but focus on the ones that you do have specific answers to.

KEY #1: WHAT IS MY DEEPEST DESIRE?

Write down what you profoundly feel you would like to do with your life using your gifts, and what you would like to do to impact humanity in your lifetime. These will not be things that you have a general or passing "interest" in but rather a *deep yearning or aspiration to do.*

> ## IT IS TOO EASY TO SPREAD OURSELVES THIN AND THEN NEVER FULFILL OUR PURPOSES.

Through the years, you may find two or three things that you are meant to do in different seasons of your life, but you have to distinguish between what you *might* like to do and what you feel you *must* do. It is too easy to spread ourselves thin and then never fulfill our purposes. Remember that although you may experience stages in your life in which you engage in various endeavors, and though you may manifest your personal authority in several ways using one or more gifts, these manifestations will be centered around a particular area or theme that reflects God's specific purposes for you.

KEY #2: WHAT AM I TRULY PASSIONATE ABOUT?

What do you really care about? What gifts and abilities do you especially enjoy using? Once you find the answers to these essential questions, you can tap into your passion to help fulfill your personal authority.

God set each one of us apart and said, "You were born for this assignment. You have the authority to be free within this domain of life." Again, authority is the freedom to be who you are. Authority doesn't restrict; it releases. Authority doesn't hinder you; it helps you. Authority doesn't stop you; it provides momentum and access. Authority is the most awesome experience of freedom anyone can have. It is incredibly satisfying to be doing what you know you were born to do, and to be doing it without limit.

Jesus stated, *"With God all things are possible"* (Matthew 19:26). He was saying, in effect, "With God, all things you were called to do are possible." Nothing is impossible if you were born to do it. It may take twenty, forty, or even sixty years, but you will get it done. Think of Noah, who was born to build the ark so that he and his whole family would be safe when the earth was destroyed by the great flood. No one could build a boat better than Noah did! He built a huge structure that would house him and his family, as well as all the animals they took with them, and that would be completely watertight—and it worked! (See Genesis 6:5–8:22.)

I imagine that people laughed at him, because the ark took him nearly one hundred years to build, and it had never rained on the earth prior to this time. They probably criticized him, abandoned him as a friend, and talked about him behind his back. If he had built the ark during our times, he would have been the brunt of mockery on all the television talk shows and Internet blogs. Pictures of him and his ark would have been on the front pages of the major newspapers. The media would have said he was crazy, demented, nuts. But despite the immense challenges, Noah kept on building.

When someone is authentic, when he is passionate about his purpose, he can't be stopped; he won't be discouraged for long. No matter what people throw at him, he still says the same thing: "I'm going to do it."

What do *you* have that kind of passion about?

KEY #3: WHAT MAKES ME ANGRY?

There is constructive anger, and there is destructive anger. Most of us think of the destructive kind when the word *anger* is mentioned. Yet some anger is legitimate, such as anger directed at the wrongs in this world. Paul wrote, *"'In your anger do not sin': Do not let the sun go down while you are still angry, and do not give the devil a foothold"* (Ephesians 4:26–27). He was quoting Psalm 4:4, which reads, *"In your anger do not sin; when you are on your beds, search your hearts and be silent."*

> **WHEN SOMEONE IS AUTHENTIC, WHEN HE IS PASSIONATE ABOUT HIS PURPOSE, HE CAN'T BE STOPPED; HE WON'T BE DISCOURAGED FOR LONG.**

Anger can be legitimate, but misdirected anger makes us vulnerable to being tripped up by the devil and weakens our authority. For example, when Cain became angry because God accepted his brother's offering but not his, God told him, *"Why are you angry? Why is your face downcast? If you do what is right, will you not be accepted? But if you do not do what is right, sin is crouching at your door; it desires to have you, but you must master it"* (Genesis 4:6–7).

In another example, Moses desired that his people be released from the oppression of slavery in Egypt, but he took matters into his own hands and killed an Egyptian overseer who was abusing an Israelite. As a result, he had to flee the country for forty years until he was ready to follow God's way of setting the people free. (See Exodus 2:11–15, 23–3:22.)

Anger that is selfishly or rashly motivated is destructive, but anger that is based on a desire for people to be treated right, that is based on compassion for others, and that is grieved by injustices is constructive if it leads to positive action to remedy the problems instead of being allowed to fester into resentment, bitterness, unforgiveness, or violence against the perpetrators. *"Do not repay anyone evil for evil. Be careful to do what is right in the eyes of everybody"* (Romans 12:17).

What is it in life that makes you angry enough to take action on behalf of those who are mistreated, abused, or oppressed? What plans do you have that could alleviate the suffering of others? What ideas do you have for communicating positive values and mindsets to people? The answers to these questions will lead to your personal authority.

KEY #4: WHAT IDEAS ARE PERSISTENT IN MY HEART AND MIND?

Is there something specific you would like to accomplish? What recurring dreams do you have for your life? I believe that the thoughts, ideas, plans, and dreams that remain consistent within you were put there by your Creator. We will talk about timing in a later chapter, but you should realize that your consistent thoughts and dreams can come to pass even if they don't manifest right away.

I often refer to Key #4 as "the idea that never leaves you." Perhaps you have become preoccupied with other things, but this idea always returns to your thoughts. It is a passion that won't subside, a persistent desire or tug at your heart.

Joseph had God-given dreams of being put in a position of authority over his family. Not understanding at first that this position was for the purpose of helping his family survive rather than for feeding his ego, he went through a series of extremely humbling experiences—including being sold into slavery and being imprisoned because of a wrongful accusation—before he was ready to fulfill his personal authority in life. He eventually became the second most powerful ruler of Egypt under the pharaoh and saved the lives of his family during a time of severe famine. (See Genesis 37, 39–47.)

What long-standing aspiration do you have? What vision, idea, or dream is tugging at your heart today? Is your motivation for doing it positive or selfish? Are you willing to do it to honor God and build up others?

KEY #5: WHAT DO I CONSTANTLY IMAGINE MYSELF DOING?

What do you imagine yourself becoming? What do you *really* want to do that you may not have told anyone else about?

It may be something you think about while you're at your workplace and wish you could be doing instead of your current job. It may be something you see others doing, and you say to yourself, "I'd like to do something like that! Only I would do it in this way...." Perhaps it is something you lie awake at night and imagine yourself building, writing, drawing, constructing, or performing. You may have dreamed about doing this thing ever since you were a child.

Ask yourself, "What would I prefer to be or to do? What gifts or skills would I use and develop in order to be or do this?"

KEY #6: WHAT DO I WANT TO DO FOR HUMANITY?

What do you wish you could accomplish for humanity? Is it the creation of a new invention or a groundbreaking medicine? Do you want to fix a specific problem or bring about a certain reform in society? Do you want to provide a haven where people can obtain much-needed rest and relaxation in the midst of their busy lives? You might not desire to build a physical structure, such as an architect or building contractor would, but you may want to build up the social structures of your nation, and that may be the gifting and area of your personal domain.

Key #6 could also take the form of these questions: "What kind of impact would I like to have on my community?" or "What do I want to pass along to the next generation?" or even "What would I like to be remembered for?"

What positive thing do you have a passion to leave as a heritage to those who will come after you in life?

KEY #7: WHAT WOULD BRING ME THE GREATEST FULFILLMENT?

To answer this question, begin by thinking about your activities and accomplishments in the past—at your school, at your job, with your favorite hobby, or with any other involvements. Pinpoint three endeavors or achievements that have given you the greatest satisfaction and fulfillment in life so far. What is it about these things that gave you satisfaction and fulfillment? Are you currently involved in these activities? Why or why not? Would similar activities, projects, or endeavors bring you the same measure of personal pleasure? If so, what might they be?

Try to evaluate what motivates and gratifies you the most in life, and then imagine the possibilities of how you could incorporate it into your life as your vocation or life focus.

KEY #8: WHAT WOULD I DO FOR NO MONEY OR OTHER COMPENSATION?

Is there something you would find so rewarding that you would do it even if you weren't paid for it and received no other type of compensation, even the thanks or praise of others?

Perhaps you are already doing something like it on a volunteer basis at a nonprofit organization, at your church, or as your hobby. What is it, and what is the nature of it? For example, does it involve working with children? Teens? Adults? Helping people recover from addictions? Spending time with elderly people in nursing homes? Fundraising for medical research? Teaching people to read? Visiting veterans in the hospital? Does it involve community projects, such as planting gardens, recycling, cleaning up graffiti, and so forth? Do you like to volunteer at your local library or a nearby historic site? Or, do you enjoy music or another art form?

THE VERY THING THAT YOU COULD DO FOR NO MONEY USUALLY BECOMES THE ENDEAVOR THAT WILL PAY YOU.

Your answers to the above questions may well determine your area of authority, especially since we have seen that many people are much happier working at their hobbies than at their jobs, so that their hobbies reflect their true purposes in life.

The Key #8 question leads to a paradox, however. The very thing that you could do for no money usually becomes the endeavor that will pay you. You do it so naturally and become so good at it that it attracts compensation from people who recognize its value. Or, you are so fulfilled in doing it that you would be infinitely happier taking a job related to that area than you would be at your current job, even though the current job pays more.

The issue is attaining quality of life and fulfilling your true contribution to your generation. Would you rather be paid a little more and experience lifelong frustration and dissatisfaction, leading to mental and physical stress and nagging feelings that your life isn't counting for anything? Or, would you rather accomplish your purpose, serve others, and live a happier, healthier, and more balanced life? I believe that by living in their personal authority, many people would solve their mental health, physical, or relational problems.

Therefore, ask yourself what activities you are currently receiving satisfaction from that you aren't being paid for, what you are so dedicated to that you would continue to do it even if you stopped receiving money for it, and what you would do for no compensation at all.

KEY #9: WHAT WOULD I RATHER BE DOING?

Are you are always thinking about something else you'd rather be doing than what you are currently involved in? That "something else" is probably your area of authority. As long as you continue to think you would rather be doing something else, then you shouldn't be doing what you're presently doing. It's not a difficult thing to figure out.

Another way to look at this question is based on our earlier discussion about our personal authority being our true home, habitation, or abode. Ask yourself, "What would I feel 'at home' doing? What seems natural and comfortable to me?"

When you find your authority, you don't really go to a job; you go "home." In fact, many people who are functioning in their authority physically work at home because their authority is connected with who they are and their entire lifestyle. If people are happy to leave their jobs, they're not at home in them. And when they don't feel at home, they end up being competitive with others. They fight for resources they perceive to be scarce, thinking there are not enough positions, assets, or praise to go around. In contrast, a person who knows and exercises his own authority compares himself only with himself and knows that everything he needs will be provided. He periodically reviews his life by asking himself, "Am I doing what I should be doing to fulfill my authority?"

People who are causing problems in their workplace perhaps need to be relocated to a different department or area of the company that they are better suited for. Or, perhaps they need a totally different environment. If you are not functioning in your true position of authority, you can destroy an organization through complaining and conflict. Finding and living in your authority protects you and others because, as we have seen, authority brings order and peace.

You are at home when you are working in your authority and gifting. What would you rather be doing with your life? What makes you feel most at home when you are doing it?

KEY #10: WHAT WOULD I DO IF I KNEW I COULD NOT FAIL?

If you could do anything in the world and know that it would succeed, what would you do?

First, eliminate superficial answers to this question! Some of those would be winning the lottery, getting back at everyone who has ever insulted you, and so forth. Instead, this question is designed to help you to eliminate the fear and doubt that can crowd into your mind and block your thoughts when you begin to think about what you would really like to do in life. Forget the fear and doubt and consider nothing to be impossible.

What endeavor, enterprise, creative work, project, or plan would you engage in if it were risk-free? If it would be a success, no matter what obstacles tried to prevent it? If money were no object? If you didn't worry that you had the wrong background, the wrong looks, the wrong job experiences, or whatever else you would normally think of as a roadblock?

I encourage you to take extra time on this question. Fear can be a powerful inhibitor to thinking clearly, and it may take you a little while to get past any feelings of fear so that you can think and dream without hindrance. Then, when you are able to write down your answer, evaluate it in light of your other answers and what you are beginning to learn about your personal authority.

KEY #11: WHAT IS THE MOST IMPORTANT THING I COULD DO WITH MY LIFE?

Discovering personal authority usually comes when we evaluate what is most important to us in life. This is often not what is most pressing on our calendars or what would make us look the most successful in the eyes of others, but what is truly the most significant contribution we could make, along with the best choice of lifestyle that is prioritized to reflect our foundational values and beliefs.

> DISCOVERING PERSONAL AUTHORITY USUALLY COMES WHEN WE EVALUATE WHAT IS MOST IMPORTANT TO US IN LIFE.

Another way of putting this key question is, "What will I wish I had done when I look back on my life?" or "What will I regret not having done when it comes time for me to die and meet my Creator?"

You therefore have to consider what, *above all other things*, is the most significant thing you could do with your life, what you want to occur in your life, and how you want to live your life.

KEY #12: WHAT ENDEAVOR OR ACTIVITY WOULD BEST CONNECT ME TO MY CREATOR?

An essential final question to ask yourself is what vocation would keep you connected to the Creator and faithful to His authority, laws, and life principles. Personal authority comes from God and would never involve any activity that is contrary to His nature and ways.

First, of course, anything illegal or immoral would not be a legitimate domain for personal authority.

Second, personal authority won't be found in endeavors that are pursued selfishly or for the purpose of boosting one's ego or showing off.

> *Who is wise and understanding among you? Let him show it by his good life, by deeds done in the humility that comes from wisdom. But if you harbor bitter envy and selfish ambition in your hearts, do not boast about it or deny the truth. Such "wisdom" does not come down from heaven but is earthly, unspiritual, of the devil. For where you have envy and selfish ambition, there you find disorder and every evil practice. But the wisdom that comes from heaven is first of all pure; then peace-loving, considerate, submissive, full of mercy and good fruit, impartial and sincere.* (James 3:13–17)

Working in your personal domain will promote the "fruit of the Spirit" in your life: *"The fruit of the Spirit is love, joy, peace, patience, kindness, goodness, faithfulness, gentleness and self-control"* (Galatians 5:22–23). God-given authority is always a positive force; it helps or builds up humanity in some way.

Third, there are certain activities and areas of life that you will know are not the domain of your personal authority because they consistently get you into some kind of trouble—whether that trouble is overt or involves bad attitudes or an unhealthy or unproductive lifestyle. We must seriously ask ourselves, "What types of activities and areas present unhealthy temptations to me? In contrast, what activities and endeavors draw me closest to God and His ways when I engage in them?" The answers to these questions will not be the same for every person. We all need to adhere to the clear principles of Scripture. Yet each person also has his own areas of weakness about which he must be on guard. There may not be anything intrinsically wrong with a certain activity, but if you always feel pulled away from God because of it, then something about it isn't right for you. *"Each one is tempted when, by his own evil desire, he is dragged away and enticed. Then, after desire has conceived, it gives birth to sin; and sin, when it is full-grown, gives birth to death"* (James 1:14–15).

Your personal authority will be positive and uplifting to you. Through it, you will be able to honor the Creator who made you and reflect aspects of His character and purposes.

SUMMARIZE YOUR FINDINGS

The above twelve questions are worth taking the time to think about and answer for yourself so that you can move forward with your authority. When you have fully answered the above questions, asking God to guide you in them, and you feel that your answers have revealed your personal authority, write a summary statement of what you believe you were put on this earth to do.

Then, answer the questions for each of the following headings:

- *Documenting Your Personal Authority*: In what specific ways have I exercised this authority in the past? How can I build on this in the future?

- *Exercising and Refining Your Personal Authority*: In what ways will I develop and apply my personal authority now that I know what it is?

- *Releasing Your Personal Authority*: Who has the knowledge, skills, and commitment to help me to release my authority? (For more information on this, see chapter 11.)

Print your summary statement and/or your full profile, as well as a list of the benefits to living in your personal authority, and tape them where you will see them often to help you to focus on living in your personal domain on a daily basis.

> ## GOD WANTS ALL OF US TO BE ACTIVE PARTICIPANTS IN HIS PURPOSES ON EARTH THROUGH OUR PERSONAL AUTHORITY.

God wants all of us to be active participants in His purposes on earth through our personal authority. The Scriptures are the only book that says God created us to have dominion over and to rule the earth. The Bible is the only book that says about Jesus, *"You...have redeemed us to God by Your blood out of every tribe and tongue and people and nation, and have made us kings and priests to our God; and we shall reign on the earth"* (Revelation 5:9–10 NKJV).

A king is someone who is authorized to rule. There is a domain of life in which you were born to rule. You'll never be fulfilled until you discover that area, and you'll always be trying hard and struggling in some way until you find it. But when you do find it, working in it will seem like operating a well-oiled machine. All of a sudden, you'll connect with life. That ability is what Jesus came to reclaim for you.

Will you determine to be authentic? Will you seek to discover, by the help of God's Holy Spirit, who you truly are? I am excited at what you will find when you answer the twelve key questions in this chapter.

TEN

IGNITING YOUR PERSONAL AUTHORITY

THE PATH TO EXERCISING YOUR INBORN LEADERSHIP

Michael Jordan was a phenomenal basketball player who played for the Chicago Bulls. Many consider him to be the greatest basketball player in the history of the sport. In game two of the 1986 playoffs, Jordan threw sixty-three points against Larry Bird and the Boston Celtics, a single-game scoring record for the playoffs that still holds at the time of this writing.[1] It almost seemed as if he didn't even have to *look* at the basket to make the shots. It was in his blood. When he came down the court and jumped to shoot, he was like a rolling "mean machine." He was born to do it.

Yet, in late 1993, when he was still only thirty years old, he announced his retirement from basketball. Shortly afterward, he signed a baseball contract with the Chicago White Sox. Here was a man who was extraordinarily gifted in basketball deciding to play baseball.

The most awkward thing I ever saw was Michael Jordan with a baseball bat. Even the uniforms seemed wrong on him. He was so tall (six feet six inches) that his jersey rode up high. While he apparently worked very hard at baseball and learned all he could, it just didn't seem the right fit to me. Then, after about a year in baseball, he left and returned to the NBA, where he continued his extraordinary basketball career.[2]

Michael Jordan's experience is instructive to personal authority because even when you know your gifting, you can lose focus and move into a realm outside your natural domain.

MOST PEOPLE ARE LIVING UNAUTHORIZED LIVES

The domain of your personal authority is where you are authorized to function by inherent purpose. When you are in your area of authority, it's as if an instinct takes over, much like Michael Jordan's basketball playing.

Or, it's like a reflex. It is an unforced, almost unconscious, part of your nature. You don't have to work it up.

Therefore, one of the greatest mysteries to me is the fact that most people are living unauthorized lives. They've never asked themselves (or they have failed to continue to ask themselves) concerning their jobs or other activities, "Was I created to do this?" We have seen that personal authority is the legal right and freedom given by the Author to human beings (and other living things) to manifest the special ability and power He caused them to have. Manifesting what is within him is what gives a person authenticity. To be authentic means (1) to be (or become) oneself, (2) to manifest one's true self, and (3) to be true to oneself.

In this chapter, I want to present seven important guidelines that will help you to ignite and to *continue* manifesting the personal authority within you.

GUIDELINE #1: STAY IN YOUR OWN AREA OF GIFTING

First, in order to function in your personal authority, you have to stay in your own area of gifting. To stay there, you have to know what is *not* right for you as much as you know what *is* right for you. Time is too precious to waste on the wrong things.

Because Michael Jordan was away from basketball for over a year, he had to spend months working to recondition himself so that he could return to the top form he'd previously had. Although he still had amazing natural talent, he'd lost the sharp edge on his precision and skills. He'd lost his sensitivity to the game. I saw Jordan play his first three games after returning to basketball, and the opposing players seemed to run all over him because they had never stopped playing and were still at the peak of their abilities.

> YOUR DOMAIN OF AUTHORITY IS WHERE YOU CAN
> PROSPER AND WORK WITH JOY.

This is what happens when you move out of your personal authority. When you leave your inherent gift for something else, those with similar gifts who keep using them will remain sharp. And when you return to your gift, you'll have to work to "catch up" to them. You have to make sure you stay in your conditioning and your area of skill.

Your domain of authority is where you can prosper and work with joy. As we have seen, even though it will include discipline and effort, it will seem easy to you in many respects because you were built for it. Paul of Tarsus wrote, *"Brothers, each man, as responsible to God, should remain in the situation ["state" NKJV; "condition" NASB] God called him to"* (1 Corinthians 7:24). For the word *situation*, we might also substitute the word *position* or *gift*. This verse is saying, in effect, "Stay in the authority the Creator has given to you. This is your responsibility to Him."

GUIDELINE #2: DON'T ALLOW OTHERS TO PRESSURE YOU INTO A DIFFERENT AREA OF AUTHORITY

In order to stay in your own area of authority, you must not allow other people to pressure you into doing something that isn't right for you according to your inherent purpose. If you give in to them, you won't be able to be truly authentic. Paul encouraged his readers in first-century Rome—as well as us today—to find their unique domains and to stay in them by not conforming to false ideas or yielding to the pressure to follow a path contrary to the Creator's established principles and laws.

> *Do not conform [be molded] any longer to the pattern of this world, but be transformed by the renewing of your mind. Then you will be able to test and approve what God's will is—his good, pleasing and perfect will. For by the grace given me I say to every one of you: Do not think of yourself more highly than you ought, but rather think of yourself with sober judgment, in accordance with the measure of faith God has given you. Just as each of us has one body with many members, and these members do not all have the same function, so in Christ we who are many form one body, and each member belongs to all the others. We have different gifts, according to the grace given us. If a man's gift is prophesying, let him use it in proportion to his faith. If it is serving, let him serve; if it is teaching, let him teach; if it is encouraging, let him encourage; if it is contributing to the needs of others, let him give generously; if it is leadership, let him govern diligently; if it is showing mercy, let him do it cheerfully.* (Romans 12:2–8)

Paul was talking about discovering your own personal gifting from God. When he wrote about *"different gifts, according to the grace given us,"* he was referring to the authorized abilities that we have been given by our Creator. Jesus equated our understanding of authority with faith (see Luke 7:8–10), so the *"measure of faith"* Paul mentioned above can be seen as our understanding of and full acceptance of the authority God has given us.

MOVE AGAINST THE FLOW OF UNAUTHORIZED OPINION

What does it mean for you to keep from being molded to the pattern of the *"world"* in terms of your personal authority? It means not to follow the standard perspectives and conventions of the general culture around you, through which (sometimes well-meaning) relatives, friends, educators, unauthorized authority figures, and others will often pressure you to conform to what they want you to be and do, or to what they think is important and worth pursuing in life, rather than your God-given dreams and ideas. The world's mind is often already made up about us, and we have to work against the flow of that opinion if it is contrary to our personal authority.

Trying to be what you weren't born to be is likely the most frustrating experience you could have. Did you ever have a teacher say to you, "You'd make a good _____," and you felt pressured to pursue a certain vocation, even though it was the last thing you wanted to do? Or, sometimes, parents will say to their children, "I always wanted to be a _____, but I never was able to, so you're going to become one." The children have no interest in these occupations, but they go into them because their parents want them to. For example, a father may tell his son, "I always wanted to be a lawyer but didn't have the money. I worked my hands to the bone in the factory, so, no matter what you say, you're going to be a lawyer. You're going to be what I always dreamed of being."

WHEN A PERSON CEASES TO BE AUTHENTIC JUST SO THAT HE CAN BE ACCEPTED, HE HAS BROKEN FAITH WITH WHO THE CREATOR HAS MADE HIM TO BE.

What a tragedy it is that we have such a large mass of unauthentic people in the world. We cannot follow the dreams of others but must instead follow the dreams the Creator has implanted within us. Therefore, when you attend school or go to your business or organization, don't try to be "accepted." You are too unique to be accepted as one of the crowd. That doesn't mean that we should try to offend others, but if offense comes by the fact that we are being authentic, we have to realize that this sometimes comes with the territory. When a person ceases to be authentic just so that he can be accepted, he has broken faith with who the Creator has made him to be. No one should compromise who he is in order to gain acceptance from anybody else. You are not like anybody else. You are authentic. Authority is the right and the power to be and to become who *you* are.

Sometimes, people don't try to steer you toward a different direction in life but seem to dismiss your worth or capabilities outright. Don't accept this rejection of who you are and the purpose for which the Creator has made you. Paul wrote, "*We speak of God's secret wisdom, a wisdom that has been hidden and that God destined for our glory before time began*" (1 Corinthians 2:7). There is a "*secret wisdom*" that is in God. In the context of your personal authority, there is something God destined for you to become, for you to accomplish, that was hidden in Him before the world began. And it's a secret. Why? Because only God knows what He created you to do.

Human beings need God in order to discover and fulfill their purpose for living. It is not, as some believe, because we should be "religious." Religion is a sad reason to come to God. God wants you restored to Him so you can have a relationship with Him, and so He won't lose what He put in you to manifest on the earth. Jesus's coming to earth and dying on the cross for you is a measure of the treasure that is inside of you.

Yet it's very difficult to become what you were born to be when you are around people who are "toxic" toward you. By their negativity and criticism, they damage your environment for developing your gifts and ideas, and they thwart your pursuit of your dreams. Certain environments are just not good soil for the seed of your authority. If your mother keeps telling you that you are nothing and will never amount to anything, and your father keeps saying he wishes you'd never been born, the chances are slim that you will fulfill your purpose. You often have to remove yourself as much as possible from that type of environment if you're going to become who you were born to be.

Sometimes, God will take us away from our familiar environments because the people who grew up with us believe they know everything about us, even though they don't. People who know our pasts can interfere with our futures. They enjoy feeding us information about our former mistakes and failures. They may even actively try to stop us from becoming what we were born to be. However, all they know is what we've shown them so far.

It's interesting to note that, in certain biblical accounts, when God called a person for a particular purpose, He told or caused him to leave his home and go elsewhere so he could have the training and experience he would need to fulfill his calling. For example, Abram was called away from his homeland so that a new nation could be born. (See Genesis 12:1–4.) Joseph was separated from his family so that he could mature and become a wise ruler. (See Genesis 37:23–28; 50:18–21.)

You should never go into the future looking in the rearview mirror. Instead, look at your dream, based on your authority. Take your eyes off your past and look at the vision and the assignment that God has put in your life.

"None of the rulers of this age understood it" (1 Corinthians 2:8). Applying this idea to our God-given authority, we might phrase it in this way: "None of the authorities of this world, whether teachers, employers, parents, or other relatives, understand this wisdom that is destined for you, this treasure." People don't always understand the wisdom of God, especially if they are not in relationship with Him. This is one of the reasons why, when others tell us that we can't do something, we tend to rebel against what they are saying. We know, deep inside, that they're not qualified to tell us our limitations.

It is true that some people can give us good advice and help us to understand the gifts within us and what we do best. Moreover, in chapter 11, we will see that others also can help to release our authority. Yet nobody has a right to tell you what you cannot do if God has placed it within you to accomplish.

> **NOBODY HAS A RIGHT TO TELL YOU WHAT YOU CANNOT DO IF GOD HAS PLACED IT WITHIN YOU TO ACCOMPLISH.**

For example, a person may tell someone else, "I don't think you're good at such and such." That may or may not be the case. That person may not yet have fully accessed his authority. He may be a late-budding artist or teacher or engineer. We don't really know who others are on the inside. Perhaps, ten years ago, people wrote you off concerning something, and now you're doing exactly what they told you that you couldn't do. People develop physically, spiritually, emotionally, mentally, and psychologically at different rates, and they even begin to manifest their true authority at different times. It's important for all of us to seek to discover who we were created to be so we can be developing ourselves toward those ends.

A young man gave a testimony in my church saying that he had been a "hard drug addict." Then, he added, "Look what God has done." Therefore, in spite of any present conditions, don't give up on yourself. And don't give up on your children's futures. Don't cancel your hope for your son if he is using drugs. Don't reject your daughter if she is pregnant out of wedlock. Within your children are treasures that God gave His Son to reclaim. That is why we must continue to tell others the good news from the Manufacturer that everyone has personal authority within him, that he is valued and unique in the Manufacturer's eyes, and that he can be restored to the Manufacturer by the gift of the Authorized Dealer.

Paul paraphrased Isaiah 64:4, saying, *"No eye has seen, no ear has heard, no mind has conceived what God has prepared for those who love him"* (1 Corinthians 2:9). I believe he was indicating that no one has seen the real you yet! People may size you up and dismiss you, tell you that you're a nobody, that you're just a waste of time and a miserable irritation to them. They may express negativity all the time. Yet the Scriptures say that those people can't see, hear, or imagine what God has in mind for you.

Many people's ears hear things about others that are only part of the story. For instance, someone may tell you, "Have you heard? So-and-so is pregnant." You can answer, "Yes, I heard, but according to the Word of God, ears have not heard the rest of her story yet. The rest of her story will come after she discovers and lives in her personal authority."

You need to affirm this truth for your own life: "Whatever I am now is only temporary. What you see is not what you get. Only God has the last word on me!"

Remember that...

+ Moses was a murderer—temporarily. (See, for example, Exodus 2:11–15; 3:1–10.)

+ Rahab was a prostitute—temporarily. (See, for example, Joshua 2; 6:17–25.)

+ Gideon was a coward—temporarily. (See, for example, Judges 6:11–7:25.)

+ Paul of Tarsus was a killer—temporarily. (See, for example, Acts 7:55–8:3; 9:1–22.)

You haven't read the end of your story yet, so don't close the book. People may have written you off, or you may have jumped some pages in your book. For example, perhaps you were supposed to be married in chapter 7 of the book of your life, but you got married in chapter 3 and got divorced in chapter 5. Now, you think, This is it. There's nothing left for me. God is saying, "No, you just got married to the wrong person in the wrong chapter." Let me tell you, if you got married in the wrong chapter, you will need a lot of grace. But God still has good plans for your life, and you can still live according to your authority. Or, maybe you were supposed to complete your education in chapter 8 but you dropped out in chapter 4. Get back on course. Return to school and finish your studies, even if you have to go to classes with much younger students. Don't worry about them. Just get on with your dream and say, "I have to learn this so I can do what I was born to do." If you need to, get a tutor or other assistance so that you can regain what you lost while you were out of school. God will give you back what belongs to you. Or, perhaps you were supposed to start your own business in chapter 13, but you tried to start it in chapter 7, and the business failed, and you had to get a regular job again. Setbacks don't necessarily mean that the dreams weren't from God. Yet, you need to pursue His dreams in His timing. You were just attempting to fulfill them in the wrong chapters of your life.

KEEP A STEADY AND PURPOSEFUL PACE

Don't try to rush anything. Remember Carl Lewis, and keep yourself to a steady pace as you run in the path of your authority. If you are about to complete chapter 5 of your life, move on to chapter 6 next and then chapter 7 instead of concentrating on chapter 10. You need to plan for the future, but don't try to live there before it arrives. Stop thinking about what you don't have yet and work your way to your ultimate purpose.

We read 1 Corinthians 2:9, which says, *"No eye has seen, no ear has heard, no mind has conceived what God has prepared for those who love him,"* but verse 10 is the clincher; this is a wonderful revelation from our Creator. It begins, *"But God…."* Remember, your teachers don't really know you, your employer doesn't really know you, the government officials don't really know you, and even your family doesn't really know you. *"But God"* does. Why? Because God is the *"author and finisher of our faith"* (Hebrews 12:2 NKJV, KJV).

"But God has revealed it to us by his Spirit" (1 Corinthians 2:10). The only way to know the truth about yourself is by a revelation from God's Spirit. You are so awesome that you need to be explained by God. No human can explain you. God Himself has to do this. Jesus asked His disciples,

> *"Who do people say the Son of Man [Jesus] is?" They replied, "Some say John the Baptist; others say Elijah; and still others, Jeremiah or one of the prophets." "But what about you?" he asked. "Who do you say I am?" Simon Peter answered, "You are the Christ, the Son of the living God." Jesus replied, "Blessed are you, Simon son of Jonah, for this was not revealed to you by man, but by my Father in heaven. And I tell you that you are Peter, and on this rock I will build my church, and the gates of Hades will not overcome it. I will give you the keys of the kingdom of heaven; whatever you bind on earth will be bound in heaven, and whatever you loose on earth will be loosed in heaven."*
>
> (Matthew 16:13–19)

Jesus told Peter, in effect, "Peter, you just got information! No one can know Me unless the Father reveals it to him. And let Me tell you something about your personal authority. You will be a leader in My church, and I give you the keys of the kingdom of heaven."

YOU ARE SO AWESOME THAT YOU NEED TO BE EXPLAINED BY GOD. NO HUMAN CAN EXPLAIN YOU.

What is inside you is so tremendous that only God has the details. This is why you shouldn't allow yourself or others to limit you based on your past behavior or circumstances. You are greater than what you've done. Nobody really knows you except the One who created you, and only God's Spirit can reveal to you the details of His plan for you.

Then, 1 Corinthians 2:10–14 says,

The Spirit searches all things, even the deep things of God. For who among men knows the thoughts of a man except the man's spirit within him? In the same way no one knows the thoughts of God except the Spirit of God. We have not received the spirit of the world but the Spirit who is from God, that we may understand what God has freely given us [including what He has authorized us to be and do]. This is what we speak, not in words taught us by human wisdom but in words taught by the Spirit, expressing spiritual truths in spiritual words. The man without the Spirit does not accept the things that come from the Spirit of God, for they are foolishness to him, and he cannot understand them, because they are spiritually discerned.

Again, when you start telling people about the dream God has put in your heart, sometimes those who don't have His Spirit will call it foolishness. On this basis, it is possible that you can measure the validity of your dream by how many people say it is ridiculous. If everybody says it's possible, perhaps it isn't from Him. Yet when people start telling you that you cannot do it, that it's impossible, that it's foolish, that you don't have the intelligence for it, or that you don't have the connections for it, then it just might be from God.

God will always give you a dream that requires His help to accomplish. That's why it will always be impossible for you to do it by yourself. His assignments for us will always demand His assistance so that we realize they are from Him. Personal authority is not the same as self-authority; our authority does not come from us, even though it is in us. It has been *placed* within us by the Creator. *"Let him who boasts boast in the Lord"* (1 Corinthians 1:31).

No matter what people have told you in the past, therefore, plug into God's authority in your life. Submit to the Author of your salvation and discover the dream He has placed in your heart. Remember that you are authorized to accomplish your purpose in life, and that nobody else can do it in exactly the way that you can. Your personality is designed for your authority. Everything about you is perfect for what you were created to do.

> **YOUR PERSONALITY IS DESIGNED FOR YOUR AUTHORITY. EVERYTHING ABOUT YOU IS PERFECT FOR WHAT YOU WERE CREATED TO DO.**

You may have picked up many habits, concepts, and ideas from other people about what your life should be. You may have learned to imitate other people. But from this day forward, you can determine to be authentic. Let your desire be to manifest yourself. The Creator will not allow you to get lost in the crowd. You are important, essential, original.

GUARD AGAINST PURELY EMOTIONAL DECISIONS

We have emotional investments in our relationships with our family members, friends, and mentors, and it is not always easy to separate ourselves from these emotional ties, when necessary, in order to be faithful to our personal purposes. For example, Michael Jordan has indicated that a main reason he pursued baseball was that his late father—who had been murdered just months before Michael announced his retirement from basketball—had encouraged him to follow his childhood dream of becoming a Major League Baseball player. His beloved father's advice, combined with the emotional strain of having tragically lost his father, apparently led him into an area that was not his special gifting.[3] These types of influences are understandably powerful in our lives, and we have to be careful to assess why we are doing what we do.

EVALUATE WHETHER YOU ARE BEING TRUE TO YOURSELF

Too often, we look at other people's experiences and situations as our guide but fail to look in the mirror and ask ourselves, "Am I being true to myself, as the Creator made me? Is this me? Is this who I really want to be?" Again, most of us have become what other people have expected us to be. We are afraid to be who we really are because we don't want to rock the boat. We are so busy trying to fit in that we have no time to stand out. And we're so committed to pleasing everybody else that we never please our Creator or ourselves. It's no wonder Paul said, *"Do not conform any longer to the pattern of this world, but be transformed by the renewing of your mind"* (Romans 12:2).

Paul's caution to us is important because if we do not conform to these pressures but are transformed by renewing our thinking according to our authority, then our authority and the way we are to carry it out will be confirmed to us—*"then you will be able to test and approve what God's will is—his good, pleasing and perfect will"* (verse 2). We will know what we were born to be and to do. Don't allow society's thinking—or your own thoughts based on society's thinking—to pressure you into determining what your personal domain should be according to its values rather than the Creator's.

GUIDELINE #3: KNOW THE STRENGTH OF YOUR OWN AUTHORITY

EVERYONE'S GIFT IS NEEDED

To keep from being unduly persuaded by others, you must know and trust in the strength of your own authority. Paul wrote, *"We have different gifts, according to the grace given us"* (Romans 12:6). We all have different gifts according to the grace—the abilities, the talents—that we have been given. Different gifts do not all have the same function, and we need to recognize and enjoy our particular gifts.

"Just as each of us has one body with many members, and these members do not all have the same function, so in Christ we who are many form one body, and each member belongs to all the others" (verses 4–5). Everyone has a specific authority, an area of gifting, and that authority is needed by everybody

else. If we don't find our areas and fulfill them, then we are causing weaknesses or "sicknesses" in the "body"; we are hindering the welfare of our generation. We are actually having a negative impact on the community. If we (1) all belong to each other, and (2) all have different gifts, that means that the other members of the community need our gifts, and that we need theirs.

Suppose you had a toothache. Would you go to your car mechanic to get it checked out? A mechanic does have various tools, including pliers, and if you wanted to go that route, I'm sure he'd fix you up! No, the reason you sit back and close your eyes and trust a dentist is that you respect the diplomas hanging on his wall. You believe he has the education and training that qualify him to work on your teeth. You wouldn't want to be sitting in a dental chair awaiting a root canal and have the dentist come in and say, "Now, let's see, I've never done this before. What should I do first?" At that point, it's definitely time to leave—through the window!

"Do not think of yourself more highly than you ought, but rather think of yourself with sober judgment, in accordance with the measure of faith God has given you" (Romans 12:3). Paul was saying that we should think of ourselves according to the gifts God has given us and not get carried away trying to accomplish or establish something we're not designed for. We're not to wander into others' territories just because we think we would enjoy their assignments more. In this sense, "thinking of ourselves more highly than we ought" refers to thinking of ourselves in a different manner from how we should, thinking of ourselves in terms of something that is not right for the domain of authority we have been called to.

Did you know that you cannot find your gift by attending high school or college? It isn't there. Instead, you bring it with you because it's *in* you. Education cannot give you a gift; it can only help you refine it. If you're in college and you don't know your gift, you're probably going to be changing majors every other month. In Proverbs 18:16, Solomon told us, in effect, that our gifts make room for us, prosper us, and bring us before notable people. It's your gift—not your education, not your job—that brings you before influential people. It's your gift that prospers you. If you want to be truly successful in life, you have to find your area of authority and its accompanying gift or gifts. Then, you need to make a point to recognize the strength of that authority, stay with it, and develop it.

> **IF YOU WANT TO BE TRULY SUCCESSFUL IN LIFE, YOU HAVE TO FIND YOUR AREA OF AUTHORITY AND ITS ACCOMPANYING GIFT OR GIFTS.**

Let your mind be renewed by God's Word, and then you will be transformed into what God's perfect will is for you and your life. You won't think of yourself more—or less—highly than you should, but you'll think of yourself in just the *right* way—according to your authority.

"DIFFERENT" ISN'T A VALUE JUDGMENT

"*We have different gifts*" (Romans 12:6). I hope it is clear to you that the term "*different gifts*" does not mean that some personal authority gifts are more important than others—*different* just means "different." This point is crucial, because some people believe that if their gifts aren't up-front where everybody can see them, then they must be inferior. They think that the person who is always conspicuous is the one who is the most valuable. Yet just because you're not out front doesn't mean you're not important.

In another of his writings, Paul said that some of the most important parts of the body are hidden. (See 1 Corinthians 12:22–24.) Consider how the human body functions. Your heart is never seen, yet it circulates blood throughout your body and keeps you alive. If your heart were to become visible outside your body, then, unless you were on an operating table having surgery, you would likely be dead! Likewise, when people are out of place from their authority, they can "kill" the community.

> *If the whole body were an eye, where would the sense of hearing be? If the whole body were an ear, where would the sense of smell be? But in fact God has arranged the parts in the body, every one of them, just as he wanted them to be. If they were all one part, where would the body be? As it is, there are many parts, but one body.*
>
> (1 Corinthians 12:17–20)

When you discover your gift, you might find that it functions more in the background, but if you're not operating in it, then those who need your gift will lack something vital.

GUIDELINE #4: TRUST IN YOUR INHERENT GIFTING

Once you know your authority and recognize its uniqueness and the important contribution it brings to others, you have to trust it. Trusting in your inherent gifting will allow you to fulfill your authority and not become sidetracked.

Many of us have been living in an "illegal" manner. Instead of trusting in our gifting, we're trying to do something else. For example, some people are attempting to undertake business ventures that they weren't born to do. These ventures are going to be harmful for them. By the time they have failed at them many times and life has beaten them up, they should figure out that these endeavors are not their calling and go back to operating in their real gifts.

It is true that the pursuit of any genuine calling will involve some setbacks and require perseverance, but this is not what I'm referring to. I'm talking about when people keep running after something that isn't right for them and blaming either their circumstances, other people, or the attacks of the devil for their problems. But neither their circumstances, nor others, nor the devil is responsible for the barriers to what they're trying to do if their ventures are not related to their personal domains of authority. People who try to do things they weren't born to do will cause heartache for themselves and others. They will frustrate everyone around them, and they will become the problem.

> PEOPLE WHO TRY TO DO THINGS THEY WEREN'T BORN TO DO WILL CAUSE HEARTACHE FOR THEMSELVES AND OTHERS.

Not everyone is gifted to run his own business. Some people are better suited to having a job with a steady salary rather than one that requires taking risks involving capital or overseeing other people. Certain people are called to hold things together but not to initiate them. Holding things together is just as essential as starting them. Every bolt needs a nut, but there are a lot of nuts running around with nothing to be bolted on to. They say, "I want to do this and I want to do that," and they know they can't do those things, but they keep trying, anyway. Years later, they're still in debt trying to figure out how to get their "authority" to work.

In addition, a person can be talented, skilled, and experienced in something but still be unauthorized, because authority has a specific assignment or assignments, as well as a particular realm, connected with it. Again, you wouldn't let your car mechanic operate on your body. It doesn't matter how many certificates he has on the wall; he may have gone to ten schools for training in car mechanics and be the best in the country, but you wouldn't say, "You were so good at fixing the engine in my car, why don't you open me up and do surgery on me, too?" His skills are useless for surgery. Similarly, authority is specific. It comes down to this question: "What was I really born to do?"

We must also realize that when we are functioning outside our authority, we may be causing someone else to be out of order, too, because we're in his place. In this way, we may be gifted, talented, and skilled but also disruptive and even detrimental.

The world is filled with many active but unauthorized people. You need to find the place where you flourish and trust in your inherent gifting. How do you flourish? Again, Paul wrote, "*We have different gifts, according to the grace given us*" (Romans 12:6). Note that he said that your gift comes with grace. The word translated as "*grace*" in this passage is the Greek word *charis*, which refers to "the divine influence upon the heart, and its reflection in the life; including gratitude." God's influence has given us the ability to do certain things. So, if you are built to be an apple tree and you're trying to bring forth oranges, you're going to be frustrated because that ability isn't built into you. God gives grace for the gift and power for the purpose. When David was chosen by God to be king of Israel and was anointed by God's representative, the prophet Samuel, "*from that day on the Spirit of the LORD came upon David in power*" (1 Samuel 16:13). David received both the authority of kingship *and* the enabling power by his anointing. Whatever God gives you to do, He graces you to do. Remember, authority is equal to its power.

In relation to exercising personal gifts, Paul said things such as, *"If it is serving, let him serve; if it is teaching, let him teach; if it is encouraging, let him encourage; if it is contributing to the needs of others, let him give generously; if it is leadership, let him govern diligently"* (Romans 12:7–8). Notice how he kept saying *"let him."* When a person has a gift, we, as his counterparts, must trust in his ability and allow him to do it. We shouldn't prevent him from exercising his gift by making him feel guilty about doing it or forcing him to do something else instead. In other words, we need to let the gift give. We need to allow the person to be himself.

"If it is contributing to the needs of others, let him give generously" (Romans 12:8). Giving is actually a gift in itself. Some people have the ability to make a lot of money, and they do so in order to give abundantly to others. Some people just love to give and are always giving. Without thinking, they will give you their own houses and go live in the street, only to realize afterward, "I just gave my house away!" Other people have to try hard to give; they have to pray for the willingness to do it. Some people seem to need a special revelation from God to give. Everybody has a different gift, a different strength.

Paul mentioned "encouraging" as a specific gift, as well. Some people were born just to cheer others up and affirm them. Every time they're around, they say things that make you feel good about yourself. Maybe Paul was thinking of his fellow traveler and partner Barnabas, who was designed to encourage. When those who belonged to the brand-new church in Jerusalem were afraid of Paul because he was known as a persecutor, Barnabas encouraged everybody and assured them, in effect, "This guy's okay. He has reconnected with the Creator and is living in his true authority now." And they accepted Paul because Barnabas encouraged them in it. (See Acts 9:26–27.)

One of Jesus's twelve disciples, Andrew, was also an encourager. There's no book in the Scriptures entitled "the book of Andrew," though there are two books named after his brother Peter. Yet Andrew was the one who first introduced Peter to Jesus. (See John 1:35–42.) Jesus got Peter in order, and Peter became one of the principal leaders of the fledgling church. Yet Andrew gets the credit for encouraging Peter to meet Jesus in the first place. Everyone has a vital role. Let me therefore encourage you not to be a counterfeit but to trust in and exercise your unique gift. There are too many counterfeits in the world today.

GUIDELINE #5: DON'T APOLOGIZE FOR YOUR AUTHORITY

To be authentic in our authority, we must also learn to accept and be comfortable with the gifts and perspectives God has given us. Some people are always apologizing for being themselves. The remedy for this improper mindset comes from a verse we looked at earlier: *"Do not think of yourself more highly than you ought"* (Romans 12:3). Again, what is the other side to this statement? Once you find out how you ought to think about yourself—as you learn God's Word, as you gain knowledge about who He created you to be, and as you are transformed by the renewing of your mind—then think *that* way. *"Think of yourself with sober judgment, in accordance with the measure of faith God has given you"* (verse 3). You're to think about yourself with clearheaded honesty—not with intimidation or fear about what others will think or say—about who you really have been created to be. If you therefore happen to be very good at something, and you know it, you can say, "Guess what? I'm good at this." That isn't pride or boasting, even though some people may perceive it that way. You're just thinking in the way that you ought to think about yourself, and, by manifesting your gift, you allow others the opportunity to blend it with their gifts for the corporate good.

GUIDELINE #6: EVALUATE YOURSELF ONLY BY YOURSELF

DON'T EVALUATE YOURSELF BY SOMEONE ELSE'S AUTHORITY

As we think of ourselves *"with sober judgment, in accordance with the measure of faith God has given"* (Romans 12:3), we need to evaluate how we are fulfilling our purposes in life in relation to what the Creator has designed us to do. We are not to use other measures, such as the standards of other people's gifts or false authority. There are many people who are proud of accomplishments that God is likely disappointed in because they have been sidetracked from their true purposes. There may be things you have done that you think are great, yet God is saying, in effect, "Based on your authority, this doesn't come close to My purposes for you."

This is one reason why you shouldn't allow other people to tell you how "great" you are. Only the Creator knows how great you *could* be. When you receive plaques, awards, or accolades from others, you have to consider those honors according to a higher perspective. They could be dangerous to you if you start to think that you have already "arrived" and fulfilled your purpose when you actually have more to do. Believing such tributes can also be limiting if they reflect things you have accomplished based on a counterfeit authority rather than your true authority. They can cause you to veer further off course from where you should be based on your inherent gifts. A lot of people want to be things they're not authorized to be, and they "think more highly of themselves" than they should.

THERE ARE MANY PEOPLE WHO ARE PROUD OF ACCOMPLISHMENTS THAT GOD IS LIKELY DISAPPOINTED IN BECAUSE THEY HAVE BEEN SIDETRACKED FROM THEIR TRUE PURPOSES.

EVALUATE YOURSELF BY YOUR OWN CAPACITY AND POTENTIAL

If you are not sidetracked but are currently pursuing your personal authority, you need to evaluate your progress in relation to where you would be if you were truly applying yourself and being purposeful in fulfilling it. For example, if your car has the capacity to travel at a speed of 150 miles per hour, but you never go over 65 miles per hour, that doesn't cancel the car's ability to travel 150 miles per hour. Perhaps you are going 65 and pass another person on the road who is going only 50. The other person may be impressed and say, "Wow, isn't he speedy?" and you may be feeling pretty accomplished. But when you compare yourself with your own "speedometer"—your capacity, your potential—you may actually be doing rather poorly.

When my son and daughter were younger and still in school, I sat them down for a talk because each of them had a grade on the latest report card that was lower than what they were capable of. My wife and I had worked hard with them in their studies and knew their abilities. I asked my daughter, "Are you pleased with this?" She said no but added, "But many children received grades similar to this." I said, "Let's forget about the other children. Are you pleased with this?" "No, Daddy." "Okay. What do you think you were capable of getting in this class?" She said, "I could have gotten a ninety-five." I said, "Good. So, why didn't you get it?" And she had to literally judge herself. She said, "Because I didn't try hard enough." I said, "You see, you don't need a teacher's report card. You are your own report card. If eighty percent of the class got the grade that's on this report card, and you got one mark higher than eighty percent, then you may appear to have done well. But if you compare yourself to what you should have gotten, you have fallen short. You can always find somebody whom you are better than. But the person you have to 'beat' is yourself."

Have you ever stood before a crowd and performed something, and the crowd cheered, but when you went offstage, you were upset? I've had this experience a number of times. Why do we feel this way? Because we were not comparing ourselves against the people's reaction but against what we knew we were capable of.

EVALUATE YOURSELF BY YOUR CREATOR'S PURPOSE FOR YOU

When we are born, we come onto the stage called earth, and our audience is an audience of One. We were created to "perform" for that single audience. He is the Manufacturer of the entire world, the Author of all creation. He built everything to fulfill what it was designed to do. And God expects pleasure from all these things. *"Thou hast created all things, and for thy pleasure they are and were created"* (Revelation 4:11 KJV). The entire creation was designed to please God. The only thing God is having trouble with is human beings! Every fruit tree knows what fruit it should yield, but somehow we humans keep becoming things God never intended. And I believe God is too frequently saying, "This is not what I wanted. How did I get this product when I built that one?"

> THE ENTIRE CREATION WAS DESIGNED TO PLEASE GOD. THE ONLY THING GOD IS HAVING TROUBLE WITH IS HUMAN BEINGS!

That is why our number one goal should not be to please other people but to please the Author who created us. As Paul wrote,

We, however, will not boast beyond proper limits, but will confine our boasting to the field God has assigned to us, a field that reaches even to you.... Neither do we go beyond our limits by boasting of work done by others.... For we do not want to boast about work already done in another man's territory. But, "Let him who boasts boast in the Lord." For it is not the one who commends himself who is approved, but the one whom the Lord commends. (2 Corinthians 10:13, 15–18)

Remember that authority is *from* the Author and *for* the Author. Authority is fulfilled when the Author is pleased. This is critical to God. Until He says, "Well done," we don't quit trying. Until He says, "Good and faithful servant," we have not made it. (See, for example, Matthew 25:14–29.) Everybody else is just applauding. Only God knows when the show is over. Only He has the right to say when you have succeeded or failed. So, the pleasure of the Author is the goal of the authorized.

Paul emphasized, "*Who are you to judge someone else's servant? To his own master he stands or falls. And he will stand, for the Lord is able to make him stand*" (Romans 14:4). The Author knows what He gave you and what He authorized you to become. And "[you] *will stand, for the Lord is able to make [you] stand.*"

GUIDELINE #7: IF YOU STRAY FROM YOUR AUTHORITY, SIMPLY SUBMIT TO AUTHORITY AGAIN

If you knew and exercised your personal authority at one time but have strayed away from it, the first thing you should do is submit to your authority again so that your gifting can be renewed within you. You should (1) submit to your Creator, (2) submit to the personal authority, dream, and gifts He's placed inside you to help guide your life instead of trying to be someone else, and (3) submit to others in community and relationship as everyone serves his gifts for the benefit of all involved.

We see this process illustrated in the life of Paul. He was operating under a false authority rather than God's authority by persecuting God's own people—the followers of Jesus—in Jerusalem. Then, "*still breathing out murderous threats*" (Acts 9:1) against Jesus's disciples, he went to Damascus, under the sanction of the unauthorized religious leadership, to take prisoner any of Jesus's followers who were there. However, after

Paul encountered the risen Jesus on the road to Damascus, his entire outlook changed, and he came under the true authority of God. Once he did so, God sent a man named Ananias to him, despite Ananias's initial fear, because He wanted to encourage Paul in his new assignment in life, his true authority:

> *"Lord," Ananias answered, "I have heard many reports about this man and all the harm he has done to your saints in Jerusalem. And he has come here with authority from the chief priests to arrest all who call on your name." But the Lord said to Ananias, "Go! This man is my chosen instrument to carry my name before the Gentiles and their kings and before the people of Israel."*   (Acts 9:13–15)

Paul reported later that Jesus had told him during their encounter on the Damascus road, *"It is hard for you to kick against the goads"* (Acts 26:14). A *goad* is defined as "something that pains as if by pricking," such as a thorn, or a "sting" or a "sharp point." You get the idea. However, in a figurative sense, it can refer to a "divine impulse." This seems to imply that, deep down, Paul knew he was operating under a false authority and was therefore fighting against the "divine impulse" within him, or the pricks of his conscience, that called him to true authority. This inner conflict was apparently emotionally and mentally painful for Paul. Remember that when you are not operating according to your authority, it takes extra effort to work. It's not natural. Things end up being twice as difficult, or taking twice as long, or needing twice as much attention because you're not built for them.

In contrast, as we have seen, when you are authorized to do something, you have also been empowered to perform it. Once Paul understood his true authority and was living according to it, he *"grew more and more powerful"* (Acts 9:22) in carrying out his life's assignment.

Whatever your gift is, that's where your power is. You have the authority to be yourself because you are gifted to be yourself.

ARE YOU WHO YOU REALLY WANT TO BE?

Are you who you really want to be in life? If not, then you had better leave who you have been trying to be and start moving toward who you really want to be, because *that's* the real you. That's what you're supposed to manifest. That's what other people need to receive from you. That's being authentic.

When you discover your true self, you will suddenly become distinctive. Not exclusive, just distinctive. Yes, you need other people, but you don't want to *be* anybody else. Others will learn from you, but they will never become you, and vice versa.

The Creator is looking for people who will become who He created them to be. What He put in you may be buried under the influence of other people's counterfeit perspectives, counterfeit lifestyles, or counterfeit ideas and opinions about you, as well as your own uncertainty and misunderstanding about your purpose. As a result, God can't see the reflection of Himself that He put within you, and He can't witness the manifestation of His ideas through you.

Will you become all you were created to be? Igniting your personal authority through these seven guidelines will allow you to experience the reality and the power of living according to your personal domain.

ELEVEN

THE INTERDEPENDENT NATURE OF AUTHORITY

THE BENEFITS AND RESPONSIBILITIES OF MENTORSHIP, DELEGATION, AND SUBMISSION

Authority is a team effort rather than a solo activity. Although each individual has a personal authority, the nature of authority is such that people's purposes are interrelated and function interdependently in corporate life. It is a foundational principle that we need each other's authority to fulfill our own authority.

EVERY PERSON ON EARTH YIELDS TO AUTHORITY

In chapter 5, we saw that nothing the Creator made can exist without submission to some authority because, by its nature, authority involves both dependence and interdependence. First, everything depends on the Creator to exist because everything in life flows from Him and is maintained by Him. Second, the lives of living things are naturally interwoven for their existence and growth. Third, we all need to submit to the personal authority of others in order to function in life, and we all naturally yield to others' authority. I used the everyday example of submission in which we trust the dentist's authority to safely and effectively work on our teeth. There are hundreds of other examples, such as needing to stop at red lights or yield to other cars when we are driving. Much of common courtesy is actually a form of submission to others for their benefit.

Although interdependence is a natural state of life, the give-and-take of genuine authority has often been lacking. Misuse and abuse of authority have given rise to misconceptions about leaders and followers and the characteristics of submission, causing people to steer clear of situations in which they feel they are "taking orders" from others. Compounding this mindset is the fact that many people have felt overwhelmed by circumstances in their lives that have made them feel powerless.

Again, because many of our parents, teachers, employers, and other authority figures did not understand authority and misused it in relation to us, we are afraid to submit to others and therefore find it difficult to release our own true authority. Consequently, many of us have dreams, goals, and gifts trapped inside us.

Despite their past experiences, those who resist genuine submission and the concept of delegation rob themselves of the benefits and opportunities connected with interdependent relationships. They unfortunately restrict themselves from experiencing God's purpose and will for their lives by their attitudes about what they perceive as "authority."

A TIME TO DELEGATE, A TIME TO SUBMIT

At various times in your life, you will be called upon to delegate to others based on your authority. At other times, you will be called to submit to others based on their authority. This is just a part of life. It is not something you need to be uncomfortable about, whether you are on the giving or receiving side.

Some people are as uncomfortable about directing others as they are about taking orders because they don't want to feel as if they are "bossing others around." Not wanting to exercise false authority is a commendable attitude, and their concern would be valid if delegating were the same thing as acting like a tyrant or having the "boss spirit." It is not. Instead, delegation is a natural aspect of legitimate authority. We need to recognize this truth, because the role of directing and mentoring others may be an integral part of fulfilling our own personal authority. Therefore, understanding true delegation and true submission will free all of us to experience the Creator's purposes and plans for our lives.

> UNDERSTANDING TRUE DELEGATION AND TRUE SUBMISSION WILL FREE ALL OF US TO EXPERIENCE THE CREATOR'S PURPOSES AND PLANS FOR OUR LIVES.

As we survey the topics of delegation, mentorship, and submission in this chapter, let us keep in mind the following foundational points:

1. Our Ultimate Authority is God; we are to submit to Him and His purposes for us.

2. We "submit" to or live according to our inherent domains—the authority, dreams, and gifts God has given us—instead of trying to be someone we aren't or to succeed with improper motivations.

3. We submit to others' God-given authority in relationship and community.

4. To function properly either in the role of delegator or delegatee, it is vital that we clearly know our own self-worth. We must know that we are of great value to God and that He has given us special gifts and abilities to contribute to corporate life, or we may be overly influenced by other people's opinions or demands and be unable to fulfill our authority.

Let us now look at what it means to delegate authority and submit to authority, as well as the responsibilities and benefits connected with each role.

PRINCIPLES FOR DELEGATORS AND DELEGATEES

We were all created in the image of God, and He Himself is a delegator. He has delegated authority to each of us for our individual purposes and pleasure in life. God *"richly provides us with everything for our enjoyment"* (1 Timothy 6:17). Similarly, part of God's delegation of authority is to give people the ability to release the authority of others through mentorship and the pursuit of common goals.

THE AUTHORITY YOU HAVE RECEIVED FROM GOD WAS BESTOWED ON YOU TO SHARE WITH OTHERS TO ACHIEVE POSITIVE RESULTS.

Human delegation is therefore the transfer of authority. It is taking the permission you have from the Creator to use power and sharing it with someone else. Delegation gives the other person the right to function in that authority.

The following are essential principles for delegated authority.

AUTHORITY IS LEGITIMATE ONLY IF IT HAS BEEN DELEGATED

Unless authority has been given to you, you don't have it. It cannot be seized and still be legitimate. Authority is given for specific reasons and purposes, and these can't be carried out if someone is unauthorized. This is why all authority must come from God as the Ultimate Authority, and why any authority we administer as human beings must be God-given, as well.

AUTHORITY IS GIVEN SO THAT IT CAN BE SHARED

Authority is not given to be kept but to be distributed. The authority you have received from God was bestowed on you to share with others to achieve positive results. While this principle is true for anyone in his personal authority—all gifts and abilities have been given to benefit not only ourselves but also others—it is especially applicable to those who have areas of oversight or power to delegate to others. Delegation of authority is the transfer of legitimate power to enable others to exercise or operate in their authority. Perhaps the highest form of delegation is that which empowers people to empower still others for the benefit of all. Anyone who hoards his authority and refuses to delegate it is violating a natural principle of authority. Like the manna that was hoarded by the Israelites, authority that is not used for its intent becomes corrupt. (See Exodus 16:13–20.)

Jesus Christ perfectly exemplified the principle of shared authority. He always delegated His authority for the purpose of benefiting others. As God's Son, the Word made flesh, He seems to have progressively received authority from the Father. But whatever authority He received, He always used and delegated in service to others. Here are some examples:

- Jesus's obedience up to the time of and including His baptism by John brought His Father's affirmation: *"This is my Son, whom I love; with him I am well pleased"* (Matthew 3:17). He was one in purpose with the Father.

- After Jesus overcame the temptations of the devil, He *"returned to Galilee in the power of the Spirit"* (Luke 4:14). He was given both authority and power for His ministry.

+ Jesus manifested that authority and power: *"Jesus went throughout Galilee, teaching in their synagogues, preaching the good news of the kingdom, and healing every disease and sickness among the people"* (Matthew 4:23).

+ After Jesus had demonstrated that He had the power and authority of the Father, He delegated it to His disciples: *"He called his twelve disciples to him and gave them authority to drive out evil spirits and to heal every disease and sickness"* (Matthew 10:1).

+ Jesus delegated authority to still more of His followers: *"After this the Lord appointed seventy-two others and sent them two by two ahead of him to every town and place where he was about to go"* (Luke 10:1).

+ Through His obedient life and sacrificial death, Jesus qualified for *"all authority."* After His resurrection, He said to His followers, *"All authority in heaven and on earth has been given to me. Therefore go and make disciples of all nations, baptizing them in the name of the Father and of the Son and of the Holy Spirit, and teaching them to obey everything I have commanded you. And surely I am with you always, to the very end of the age"* (Matthew 28:18–20). Note that in response to all authority being given to Him, He told His disciples, *"Therefore go."* He immediately delegated His authority. He didn't control, hoard, or sell it. He didn't say, "All authority has been given to Me; therefore, I will use it all Myself." He distributed it.

+ Jesus promised additional authority to His followers: *"To him who overcomes and does my will to the end, I will give authority over the nations"* (Revelation 2:26).

Jesus was constantly transferring authority to fulfill His purpose, to release the purposes of others, and to benefit the community and the world at large. We who have been given authority are to do the same.

Authority, whether it is personal or corporate, is always to be used to serve, benefit, or improve others. Paul wrote of *"the authority the Lord gave us for building you up rather than pulling you down"* (2 Corinthians 10:8). If someone is a legitimate authority, it shows by how much his authority benefits people's lives. If someone in a position of authority doesn't help others, he is not exercising genuine authority but merely power.

> IF SOMEONE IS A LEGITIMATE AUTHORITY, IT SHOWS BY HOW MUCH HIS AUTHORITY BENEFITS PEOPLE'S LIVES.

AUTHORITY SHOULD NOT BE DELEGATED BASED ON FAVORITISM

Delegation of authority should not be motivated by partiality or favoritism. This is in keeping with the nature of our Creator. *"God does not show favoritism but accepts men from every nation who fear him and do what is right"* (Acts 10:34–35). Paul wrote to his mentee, Timothy, *"Do nothing out of favoritism"* (1 Timothy 5:21). And we read in the book of James,

> *My brothers, as believers in our glorious Lord Jesus Christ, don't show favoritism. Suppose a man comes into your meeting wearing a gold ring and fine clothes, and a poor man in shabby clothes also comes in. If you show special attention to the man wearing fine clothes and say, "Here's a good seat for you," but say to the poor man, "You stand there" or "Sit on the floor by my feet," have you not discriminated among yourselves and become judges with evil thoughts?... But if you show favoritism, you sin and are convicted by the law as lawbreakers.*
>
> (James 2:1–4, 9)

You don't give authority just because you like someone but because his unique gifts, talents, and personality correspond with the tasks or supervision that needs to be delegated for a certain project. In this way, you are being responsible for the authority that was delegated to you.

AUTHORITY SHOULD NOT BE GIVEN TO THE UNTESTED

Authority and its accompanying power should never be delegated to someone who is immature or someone who is a novice in the area of oversight. Instead, delegated power must be invested in increments and installed as a result of trust that the delegatee has earned over time. Before delegating authority, therefore, you should first evaluate a person's maturity by learning how that person has functioned under authority in the past. Does the person work well with others, or is he always fighting direction and openly or subtly contentious? A person cannot receive from an authority he doesn't submit to.

The one receiving the authority must also allow the delegator to lead and support him. Paul wrote, "*If* [a person's gift] *is leadership, let him govern diligently*" (Romans 12:8). In other words, let the person whom God called to be the visionary or overseer *be* the visionary or overseer. The delegatee shouldn't give him a hard time. If the delegator is forced to become something he's not because of the resistance of those whom he's trying to delegate to, it is going to cause problems for the whole organization. Let him remain in his authority.

Those who are untested in regard to submission make potentially dangerous leaders. Why? We come to trust someone as a result of assessing that person's attitude toward power, fame, popularity, pride, and so forth. An improper attitude in any of these areas is dangerous for someone in a position of leadership and must be dealt with before that person is given authority. We have witnessed the tragic outcomes in nations throughout the world after someone has been thrust into authority or has seized a leadership role for which he was not qualified.

Remember that Jesus Himself was tested and proven trustworthy in three areas before He began to fully embark on His life's purpose. These tests occurred during His temptation by the devil in the desert right after He was baptized by John. (See Matthew 4:1–11.) Anyone in leadership must pass these same tests:

1. *The appetites test.* This test includes drink, food, and sex. The devil wanted Jesus to gratify His hunger more than any other considerations, including His relationship with God the Father. A person must be able to manage his physical desires before being given authority and power.

2. *The fame and popularity test.* When the devil challenged Jesus to jump off the pinnacle of the temple, the courtyard below was filled with a quarter of a million people who had come to Jerusalem for the Passover feast. The whole point of this test was to see if He would desire instant fame rather than be obedient toward God and receive "all authority" at the right time, after His sacrifice and resurrection. (See Matthew 28:18.) If a person hasn't passed the test of popularity and desire for instant fame, he shouldn't be trusted with authority.

3. *The power test.* The devil told Jesus that if He would worship him, he would give Him all the power of the kingdoms of the world. No one should be given power until he doesn't desire power for its own sake.

> ## A PERSON MUST BE ABLE TO MANAGE HIS PHYSICAL DESIRES BEFORE BEING GIVEN AUTHORITY AND POWER.

The three qualifications established by God, therefore, for one to be trusted with exercising authority, as well as delegating it to others, are control over one's appetites, a willingness to go through the process of submission and obedience to earn trust and respect rather than seeking instant fame, and a desire to serve rather than a desire to wield power.

Note that even though Jesus had already been affirmed by God the Father as His Son because of Jesus's submission and obedience, God still tested Him. After passing the tests, *"Jesus returned to Galilee in the power of the Spirit"* (Luke 4:14). He received the empowerment of increased authority. And He never used His authority for personal gain, for destroying anyone else—including His enemies—or for fame. He used it for the redemption, advancement, development, and protection of other people. Jesus is our clear example that the ultimate purpose of authority and power is *service*—serving the interests and needs of others. It is never self-serving. Such an attitude toward one's authority is so crucial that the testing is necessary.

True success in life, therefore, requires submission to legitimate authority. The spirit of genuine submission and humbleness will always bring favor with God. Likewise, a person's success as a delegator will depend on his own ability to submit to genuine authority, to learn from it, and to serve. It's only when we learn submission that we can become true leaders. We can decide whether we want to succeed or fail in God's eyes by our attitudes toward authority.

DELEGATED AUTHORITY MUST BE PRECEDED BY PREPARATION

Before you delegate authority to someone, you must prepare and train him. The delegatee first needs to be taught the true purpose and responsibility of authority. People must be prepared to receive power since the use of power is the highest form of responsibility. Until a person understands the danger of power, as well as its benefits, he should never be given authority. This is why a prerequisite for using the power of authority is the quality of humility. Humility is a consciousness of one's vulnerability. You cannot fully trust a person who doesn't know his own weaknesses or is unwilling to counteract or compensate for them. The delegatee also needs to be trained in the various aspects of his future oversight responsibilities.

An essential role of someone in a position to delegate authority, then, is to know when a person is ready to receive authority. Authority must not be delegated prematurely.

> A PREREQUISITE FOR USING THE POWER OF AUTHORITY IS THE QUALITY OF HUMILITY. HUMILITY IS A CONSCIOUSNESS OF ONE'S VULNERABILITY.

DELEGATED AUTHORITY SHOULD NOT BE ABANDONED

Authority and power should be delegated in installments and never abandoned. The delegator continues to be answerable for them even after sharing them with someone else.

Authority is always responsible for the authority it delegates. When Jesus gave authority to His disciples, He did leave not them on their own to figure out what they were supposed to do next. He said, "*I will not leave you as orphans; I will come to you*" (John 14:18), and "*Surely I am with you always, to the very end of the age*" (Matthew 28:20).

Those to whom you delegate authority may be in charge of various areas, but you are still responsible for those areas in the end. This is why you need to monitor, assess, and regulate delegated authority on a consistent basis. Delegation always has an accountability factor. If I delegate authority to someone, I must remain conscious of the fact that what I gave that person was on loan to me, as well. So, even though I delegate authority, I am using borrowed power. Again, everyone under authority is answerable to the Ultimate Authority.

DELEGATED AUTHORITY IS ALWAYS DELEGATED AUTHORITY

Likewise, if authority has been delegated to you, it isn't a license for you to begin to function totally on your own. Always remember that your authority is a trust that has been given to you and that you are responsible to the one who gave it. To put it simply, authority is synonymous with responsibility. The need to report to your delegator is built-in. We can respond constructively to the authority of others as we recognize their own inherent God-given authority.

DELEGATED AUTHORITY SHOULD BE AUTHENTIC

A delegator should never attempt to force a delegatee to violate or neglect his personal domain of authority and thus be rendered unauthentic. In other words, we shouldn't make people operate in domains that are not natural for them; we shouldn't expect orange trees to yield apples. A person is given gifts by His Creator to be used *"in proportion to his faith"* (Romans 12:6), so a leader needs to allow people to use their true gifts. Let people be themselves, not images of your own making. The benefit will be happier, more productive delegatees instead of complaining, contentious ones.

DELEGATED AUTHORITY IS PROTECTED BY THE DELEGATOR

Just as the Creator supports and protects us as the recipients of His authority, the person who delegates authority is responsible for protecting the one to whom he delegates it. The delegatee should be allowed to carry out the authority he has been granted. However, he must also be given the assurance that he may, when needed, refer to or appeal to the delegator, who should make it a priority to offer assistance, wisdom, direction, and encouragement. If problems arise, they are ultimately the delegator's responsibility.

DELEGATED AUTHORITY CAN BE RECALLED

The one who is in authority should never be afraid to recall delegated authority when necessary. Authority is a privilege and not a right. It is permission to use someone else's power. Someone who is functioning outside of his delegated authority is illegal and cannot be fully trusted. Jesus told a parable in which a rich man discovered that his manager had squandered his resources, and he told him, *"You cannot be manager any longer"* (Luke 16:2). Even though the manager ended up redeeming himself in the eyes of his employer, Jesus was telling us that authority can be withdrawn for misuse. If someone disappoints, he can be *dis*-appointed.

Since delegated authority is always borrowed, the person who distributes it is responsible for how, when, and to whom that authority is delegated, and he will have to give an account for it. Sometimes, the delegator has to remove someone from a position of authority for the very reason that he is accountable before God and it's the responsible thing for him to do for the protection and benefit of all those involved.

There were a number of times in the history of Israel when the people were misrepresenting God as their Source to such a degree that they, in a sense, had to be temporarily recalled until they returned wholeheartedly to Him and to their assignment of revealing His nature and purposes to the world. Even during their periods of "recall," God was working in the lives of individual Israelites to continue His purposes, but the nation was not functioning as it was intended to.

To return to an earlier example, if I am the leader of a nation and give you authority as an ambassador to another nation, then the power, or backing, to carry out your assignment comes with it. What gives it authorization is the fact that I gave it to you. And you have to use that authorization for the specific reason it was given, or it's a misuse of power. In this case, I can recall you from that other nation and hold you accountable for your lack of representation. If you change your attitude, I may send you back to finish your assignment. If you refuse to represent my policies, I can take away your assignment and give it to another who will carry it out.

BENEFITS OF GENUINE SUBMISSION

When it is our position to submit to the authority of others, how should we think about our role? Again, submission is a voluntary and natural act as part of the interdependent nature of authority. It is not the same thing as surrender, in which a person succumbs to another through manipulation and fear.

Genuine submission is one person's willing and conscious yielding to another person's God-given personal authority. The Scriptures say that Jesus was "*faithful to the one who appointed him*" and that He was honored for submitting to His life's mission, even to the point of paying the ultimate sacrifice for us.

> [You] *who share in the heavenly calling, fix your thoughts on Jesus, the apostle and high priest whom we confess. He was faithful to the one who appointed him, just as Moses was faithful in all God's house. Jesus has been found worthy of greater honor than Moses, just as the builder of a house has greater honor than the house itself. For every house is built by someone, but God is the builder of everything.*
> (Hebrews 3:1–4)

> *Let us fix our eyes on Jesus, the author and perfecter of our faith, who for the joy set before him endured the cross, scorning its shame, and sat down at the right hand of the throne of God.* (Hebrews 12:2)

The first Adam did not submit to God, but Jesus, the "*last Adam*" (1 Corinthians 15:45), did. We are to focus on Him as the "*author and perfecter*" of our faith and authority. He is qualified to be the Author and Perfecter because He submitted completely to the authority of God the Father.

Let's return to the scene of Jesus's baptism in order to highlight the benefits of submission to God and those to whom He has delegated authority. Remember that Jesus submitted to John in accordance with the authority John had received from God to baptize.

GENUINE SUBMISSION IS ONE PERSON'S WILLING AND CONSCIOUS YIELDING TO ANOTHER PERSON'S GOD-GIVEN PERSONAL AUTHORITY.

> *As soon as Jesus was baptized, he went up out of the water. At that moment heaven was opened, and he saw the Spirit of God descending like a dove and lighting on him. And a voice from heaven said, "This is my Son, whom I love; with him I am well pleased." Then Jesus was led*

by the Spirit into the desert to be tempted by the devil.

(Matthew 3:16–4:1)

From this account, we can glean these benefits of genuine and faithful submission:

* Heaven, or the presence and resources of God, opens over your life. You have access to the privileges of true relationship and connection with Him.

* You are "introduced" to others by God Himself. You don't need to scramble for self-promotion, because God will bring promotion to you as you faithfully follow in His ways.

* You are confirmed by God Himself. God the Father called Jesus *"my Son, whom I love,"* and as we pattern our lives off Jesus, we will be affirmed in a similar way as a member of God's family. Jesus said, *"Whoever does the will of my Father in heaven is my brother and sister"* (Matthew 12:50).

* You receive a special anointing of God's Spirit available only to those under submission.

* You become prepared and equipped by God's Spirit for tests and trials.

* You sometimes receive greater honor than the person to whom you submit. As God in the flesh, Jesus was greater than John the Baptist and all other people, although the manifestation of this greatness depended on His submission to authority. As you submit to earthly authority, you may also find yourself becoming "greater" in influence or accomplishments than the one you submit to. This is not always the case, and it would not mean that you have greater value than the other person. It would mean that your personal authority naturally extends to a wider or deeper domain in life.

Do the above benefits change your perspective on submission?

ENTERING INTO A MENTOR-MENTEE RELATIONSHIP

The give-and-take of authority and submission may best be exemplified by the mentor-mentee relationship. A mentor is someone who invests his time, energy, and genuine interest in the life of another for the purpose of enabling that person to fulfill his personal authority. The mentee may initiate the relationship, and he voluntarily submits for the sake of learning and growing as a person.

> IF YOU ARE WISE, YOU MAKE A CAREFUL SEARCH FOR A MENTOR WHO IS VERY EFFECTIVE IN A DOMAIN THAT IS LIKE YOURS.

I mentioned earlier that when you know who you are in your God-given authority, the first thing you look for is the authority that God has placed in your life to benefit and protect you and to release your own authority. If you are wise, you make a careful search for someone who is very effective in a domain that is like yours and, after prayerful consideration, ask to enter into a mentoring relationship with him or her. (It is usually best, for a number of reasons, for men to have male mentors and for women to have female mentors.) This person may be a family member, a civic leader, a leader in your church, or a member of an organization in which you are involved.

Unfortunately, people rarely will go to others and ask to be in such a relationship in order to learn what they know and to see firsthand how they function in their authority. Yet it is the people who have the humbleness of heart to seek a mentor-mentee relationship, rather than those who try to push or manipulate their way to the "top," who become true leaders.

EXAMPLES OF MENTORSHIP

A famous example of mentorship is found in the Scriptures and involves the prophets Elijah and Elisha. God had told Elijah that Elisha was his authorized successor.

> [The Lord said,] "Anoint Elisha son of Shaphat from Abel Meholah to succeed you as prophet."… So Elijah went from there and found Elisha son of Shaphat. He was plowing with twelve yoke of oxen, and he himself was driving the twelfth pair. Elijah went up to him and threw his cloak around him.…Then [Elisha] set out to follow Elijah and became his attendant.   (1 Kings 19:16, 19, 21)

Elijah's cloak, or mantle, was the symbol of his prophethood, and by putting it around Elisha, he was demonstrating that he would pass along his authority to Elisha.

Note Elisha's attitude. He wasn't like most people, who want the position before they have earned the necessary qualifications and gained experience. He was willing to become Elijah's full-time attendant and to observe him as he fulfilled his calling as a prophet. He was not afraid to submit his life to Elijah for fear of having his life ruled and controlled by Elijah or his own future forfeited. That kind of fear comes from misunderstanding authority, which, in its true form, releases and frees a person to fulfill his purpose.

The greatest example of a mentor is Jesus Christ, who mentored the small group of twelve men from among His disciples whom He had chosen to train as His apostles, or those who would have special authority in establishing His church on earth after He returned to God the Father. The word *apostle* comes from the Greek word meaning "a delegate; specifically an ambassador of the Gospel; officially a commissioner of Christ" or "a messenger, one sent on a mission." Jesus trained and then delegated authority to these men, who would be ambassadors and messengers of Jesus's mission to bring the kingdom of God to earth. Their mentorship relationship would last for three and a half years, until Jesus's death and resurrection.

These men submitted to the mentoring of their Master Teacher. They spent large amounts of time with Jesus, observed His way of life firsthand, and endeavored to imitate it. They were able to ask Him questions and benefit from His knowledge and wisdom for the purpose of personal transformation. He asked them questions and tested them to see if they understood who He was and the truths and principles He was teaching. (See, for example, John 6:5–13.)

SELECTING A MENTOR: ASSESSING ATTITUDES AND QUALITIES

Mentorship should not be entered into lightly. When deciding whom to approach as a potential mentor, and even when you are considering taking a job, joining a church, or aligning yourself with an organization or individual who can influence you and the direction of your life, refer to the following checklist first. It will save you time and help keep you from heartache and even abuse.

Submit yourself only to someone…

+ who loves you.

+ who will receive no personal gain from your submission.

+ who is committed to your success more than you are.

+ who has passed the three crucial tests of (1) the appetites, (2) fame and popularity, and (3) power.

+ who is secure in his leadership and ability.

+ who is or has been where you want to go.

+ who has access to those whom you need to know.

+ who is willing to teach you everything he knows.

KEY CHARACTERISTICS OF MENTORSHIP

What will being a mentee or delegatee mean for you? The following is a list of the general characteristics and benefits of mentor-mentee relationships and delegated authority:

- *Identification/Identity*: the association of yourself and your name with the respected authority

- *Accountability*: follow-up of your delegated authority and actions and evaluation of your progress

- *Responsibility*: a solemn trust to carry out and show evidence of the delegated authority

- *Credibility*: authorization to work on the authority's behalf and, in some cases, to succeed him

- *Representation*: the authority's endorsement and certification of the decisions and actions you take on his behalf, as well as the benefit of his defense and help on your behalf

- *Counsel/Advice*: the knowledge and wisdom of the respected authority gained from years of experience and study

- *Protection*: the safety of being able to appeal to the decisions and problem-solving responsibilities of the authority

- *Physical Resources*: the supplies and support needed to carry out your authority

- *Personnel*: access to people, through the respected authority, who can assist you to accomplish your responsibility and fulfill your personal calling

A PERSON WITH GENUINE AUTHORITY CAN OPEN DOORS FOR YOU

As you can see, when you submit to an authority, you identify with him and receive many benefits from your relationship, including credibility. This is where the power of mentoring comes in. In fact, a person in authority can transfer to you in a very short time what it took him an entire lifetime to achieve.

> WHEN YOU SUBMIT TO AN AUTHORITY, YOU IDENTIFY WITH HIM AND RECEIVE MANY BENEFITS FROM YOUR RELATIONSHIP, INCLUDING CREDIBILITY.

Consider the case of Moses and Joshua. Shortly before Moses died, he transferred leadership of Israel to Joshua, under God's guidance. None of the people argued about it or nominated someone else for the job; Joshua was accepted as Moses's successor. *"Now Joshua son of Nun was filled with the spirit of wisdom because Moses had laid his hands on him. So the Israelites listened to him and did what the* LORD *had commanded Moses"* (Deuteronomy 34:9). In effect, Moses transferred forty years of leadership to Joshua in about forty seconds. Similarly, Elijah's anointing as a prophet of God was transferred to Elisha when it came time for Elijah to leave this earth. This transfer was represented by the symbolic act of Elisha receiving Elijah's mantle, or cloak. In fact, Elisha desired and received a double portion of Elijah's anointing. Other prophets recognized this anointing and said, *"The spirit of Elijah is resting on Elisha"* (2 Kings 2:15).

Many people believe that submission means restriction, so they compete with authority or try to make themselves look equal to someone in an authority role. Frankly, the dumbest thing you can do is to compete with true authority. Submission to authority opens doors that you don't have to push. A person with genuine authority can help you progress quickly in accomplishing something that could take you ten years to achieve on your own.

Again, when you submit to authority, you receive everything the person can give you—friendships, resources, experiences, the lessons learned from his failures, and access to influence and fruitful environments. John the Baptist had many followers as he prepared the people for the coming of the Authorized Dealer, the Messiah. People went to him *"from Jerusalem and all Judea and the whole region of the Jordan"* (Matthew 3:5). So many people came that he had a massive campaign. Jesus could have thought, "I'm going to attract some of John's crowd and start My own ministry with them." Instead, He submitted, and John's followers legitimately became His.

> *John saw Jesus coming toward him and said, "Look, the Lamb of God, who takes away the sin of the world! This is the one I meant when I said, 'A man who comes after me has surpassed me because he was before me.'. . . I have seen and I testify that this is the Son of God." The next day John was there again with two of his disciples. When he saw Jesus passing by, he said, "Look, the Lamb of God!" When the two disciples heard him say this, they followed Jesus.*
>
> (John 1:29–30, 34–37)

If you submit to and receive from one who has true authority, you eventually will receive his credibility. John willingly transferred his whole school of followers to Jesus. He stated, *"The reason I came baptizing with water was that he might be revealed to Israel"* (verse 31). Jesus rightfully "inherited" John's followers at the outset of His ministry, and some of them became His closest disciples. John's former disciples were already in tune with the message that they needed to align their lives with the Creator God and that the kingdom of God was coming to earth.

Jesus didn't have to strive or promote Himself to accomplish the purpose for which He had come. As He followed God the Father's ways, God provided for Him. Many people are working too hard because they haven't entered into submission and received its benefits. Submission reduces stress, saves time, and eliminates work. When you submit in a genuine way, you work smarter, not harder.

"NO TRESPASSING!"

When people truly understand authority, delegation, and submission, life runs much more smoothly for them, and their relationships are characterized by order and peace. They function in their areas of personal authority, respect others' authority, and don't trespass on the authority of those around them. In this way, both harmony and effectiveness are achieved.

> MANY PEOPLE ARE WORKING TOO HARD BECAUSE THEY HAVEN'T ENTERED INTO SUBMISSION AND RECEIVED ITS BENEFITS.

Part of the Lord's Prayer is, *"Forgive us our debts, as we also have forgiven our debtors"* (Matthew 6:12). This could also be phrased, "Forgive us our trespasses, as we also have forgiven those who trespass against us." Could the greatest Example of authority have been calling our attention to the need to stay in our realms of authority and not trespass on others' authority or interfere with their personal callings?

The only way to fully experience God's plan for your life is to understand the interdependence of your personal authority with the personal authority of others and to carry out that interdependence through mentorship, delegation, and submission.

TWELVE

HOW TO THRIVE UNDER AUTHORITY (BOTH POSITIVE AND NEGATIVE)

REMAINING TRUE TO YOUR AUTHORITY WHILE RESPECTING THE AUTHORITY OF OTHERS

Having talked about the benefits and responsibilities of mentorship, delegation, and submission, we still need to address certain needs and issues that arise within these relationships. It is sometimes difficult to know how to blend or balance authority and submission, especially when we find ourselves in circumstances where those who are in positions of authority don't understand true authority or don't practice its principles. While we should never willingly enter into an authority relationship with someone who isn't submitted to anyone else or who misuses authority, there may be times when we find ourselves in such a relationship in our families, our jobs, or other situations in life.

The following general guidelines will help you to respond positively to, and even thrive under, both genuine authority and false or uninformed authority. Note that your personal situations must be considered individually, with careful thought and prayer to the Ultimate Authority, as the following points cannot address every circumstance you may encounter. The main thing to remember is that you can remain true to your personal authority while respecting the authority and positions of others.

STUDY THE FORMAL ORGANIZATIONAL STRUCTURE OF THE GROUP

Study the formal organizational structure of the family, community, or business you are a part of. This will help you to understand the relative positions and interrelationships of all the members. It will answer the question of who, officially, is your immediate authority, and whom you can appeal to in relation to a problem or need. It will also clarify those who are the immediate authorities of all others in the group, especially if they differ from your immediate authority.

If you happen to be in the senior position of authority, then remember that your ultimate authority is your Creator and that you are responsible to Him for all the members of the group. In addition, you should have one or two people or a small group to whom you make yourself accountable, for your own protection and safety as a leader. You need to be able to discuss your role and responsibilities as a senior authority with those who can help you remain true to the Creator's principles and ways.

STUDY THE INFORMAL STRUCTURES OF THE GROUP

Next, study the informal structures of authority within the family, community, or business. Even though certain formal structures and procedures are usually in place, individuals often interact with one another in "unofficial" ways according to their personalities, relationships, and past experiences or histories. If you learn both the official and unofficial structures, you will gain a better understanding of how authority, delegation, mentorship, and submission actually function in your group.

For example, in a family, although the role of the parents is to teach, train, and supervise all the children, the children relate to their parents in different ways according to their ages, temperaments, styles of learning, and so forth. Even though their parents may want to treat them exactly the same, the fact that each child has a singular makeup makes this difficult at times, if not impossible. Different approaches will be needed with different children in terms of teaching, correcting, and nurturing the unique character of each relationship.

In another example, someone working in the warehouse of a company may not have immediate access to the CEO on a job-flow chart, but because he has worked there for thirty years and has been there since the business was established, the CEO may seek him out directly for information or advice rather than making the request through his supervisors.

As you make your study of the organization, be sure to assess your own formal and informal relationships in the group so that you are fully aware of how you interact with others on an official and unofficial basis. Having a knowledge of both of these structures will help you to receive the support you need, make good and efficient decisions, participate in the life of the group, and accomplish your assignments, goals, and objectives in accordance with your personal authority.

IDENTIFY THOSE WHO POSSESS EARNED AUTHORITY AND INFLUENCE

Third, identify the individuals who possess "earned" authority and influence within the formal and informal structures of the organization. A person who has earned authority has knowledge, wisdom, experience, and skills that others in the group recognize and respect, so that people go to him for key information and assistance that will help the family, community, or business to solve problems and to run smoothly overall. An individual with earned authority might be the founder of an organization, someone promoted to manager from within the staff of a company, a president emeritus, a grandmother or grandfather, or a long-term employee. Note that these individuals may or may not be in a visible role; they may have a quiet role that functions in the background but wields great influence on the group as a whole.

REFER TO YOUR IMMEDIATE AUTHORITY FIRST, ESPECIALLY WHEN IN DOUBT

If you have a concern or a problem that needs to be addressed, always refer to your immediate authority first, such as a parent, a committee chairman, a teacher, a supervisor, a director, or a CEO. You should follow the same course when you are in doubt about who you should go to regarding a question or situation—the immediate authority is where you begin.

In a case where the issue *is* your immediate authority, you may be tempted to go above him to address the problem. However, this is usually a poor move because it will undermine personal responsibility and positive interaction in the relationship.

Please note that in special circumstances, such as issues of physical abuse or sexual harassment that involve your immediate authority, you should appeal to someone who will treat the problem with confidentiality and seriousness. Most workplaces have established procedures to protect employees in these cases and to provide a neutral third party for employees to talk with, such as a human resources director. If the abuse or harassment is coming from a family member, you should contact a respected pastor, family counselor, or women's shelter.

Generally, though, by going to your immediate authority with an issue, you will follow the proper order. You will likely incite a lack of trust in both your direct authority and any authority above him if you immediately go over his head. As uncomfortable as the interaction might be, go to the supervisor, director, chairman, or parent first and explain clearly and respectfully what the issue is.

For example, if you are having difficulty getting your work done at your job because of something the supervisor is doing, or because of some practice in your department, tell him what is hampering you. I suggest that if you do not receive a helpful response, you should go back to the supervisor two more times. You should document these conversations in some form. If you still do not receive a positive response, then you should go to the next level. This would be the one who is your supervisor's immediate authority. You want the authority above your supervisor to know that you have followed the proper order in addressing the problem before coming to him. The company may deal with the supervisor when you explain the situation, but any such action is under their domain and is not yours to try to accomplish in some other way.

Going to your supervisor or your supervisor's immediate authority is not something to do lightly. Don't go to your supervisor over trivial matters or go to the next level of authority because you have a grudge against your supervisor. Instead, make appeals about matters that truly hinder you from being able to perform your job.

NEVER BYPASS, OVERSTEP, OR IGNORE YOUR IMMEDIATE AUTHORITY

Similarly, never bypass, overstep, or ignore your immediate authority when it comes to other interactions in your family, community, or business. Always follow the lines of designated authority.

For example, Jesus told His disciples, "*The Father will give you **whatever you ask in my name***" (John 15:16). Jesus has all authority, and for His disciples to ask in His name maintains the power as well as the order of true authority.

In the case of Joseph, the pharaoh gave him authority over all Egypt by giving him his own signet ring. Yet even though Joseph had great latitude in ruling and was second in command, he still had to answer to the pharaoh. (See Genesis 41:40–42.)

> FOLLOWING DESIGNATED AUTHORITY WILL HONOR GOD, AND HE WILL REWARD YOU FOR YOUR WORK.

A practical example of this guideline in the workplace would be to channel all communication—ideas, suggestions, and so forth—through your supervisor in an email or memo so that it's clear to others that this is how you operate. Let it go up the line. The first person in authority has the decision of whether or not to communicate the idea or suggestion. If you document your communication, the supervisor is the one who will answer for it if an idea is not passed along.

It's possible that he may take credit for something you suggested. In that case, be honest if you are asked about it, but otherwise entrust it to God to work out rather than going around complaining about it. Peter's advice to first-century slaves seems to apply here: *"Submit yourselves to your masters with all respect, not only to those who are good and considerate, but also to those who are harsh. For it is commendable if a man bears up under the pain of unjust suffering because he is conscious of God"* (1 Peter 2:18–19). Following designated authority will honor God, and He will reward you for your work. (See Colossians 3:23–24.)

SUBMIT TO THE POSITION OF AUTHORITY AND NOT NECESSARILY THE PERSON

This guideline addresses how to respond to illegitimate authority. If you need to operate under someone who doesn't understand or accept true authority, recognize that you are submitting to the position that has been delegated to him from those higher than he. The office is more important than the officer in this case.

However, if you are asked to do something that would violate God's principles, you cannot, of course, participate. You should follow the example of Daniel as he lived as an exile in Babylon, in an environment of idol worship under the kings Nebuchadnezzar and Darius. For example, when a royal decree was issued that all the people had to worship only King Darius for a period of thirty days, Daniel kept praying only to God and, as a result, was thrown in a lions' den. God protected him, and his life was spared. Yet, as a testimony to Daniel's respect for authority, when Darius came to see if he had survived, Daniel did not say to him out of anger and resentment, "O king, go to blazes!" Instead, he greeted him with an energetic, "*O king, live forever!*" (Daniel 6:21) and explained how God had rescued him and that he was innocent of offending the king. (See Daniel 6.)

The eleventh chapter of Hebrews gives a list of people who served God even in the midst of dire circumstances. Some were miraculously delivered, while others were mocked, physically abused, imprisoned, or even killed. All of them were noted for their faith. Regardless of whether they were delivered or not, they all received God's commendation and reward for staying true to Him and His ways.

Serve the position, if not the person, whenever possible, and serve God at all times.

MAKE AN UNAUTHORIZED AUTHORITY ACCOUNTABLE TO YOUR CONVICTIONS

If an unauthorized authority asks you to do something that you cannot in good conscience do, and if he is not accountable to anyone else, then you must make him accountable to your own convictions.

What does this mean? You can sometimes work under an authority figure who is contrary to your ideals and principles and end up influencing that person because you are confident in your own personal authority and because it is stronger than that person's public authority. In the above example, Daniel did not succumb to idol worship, and those around him— including the king—had to deal with his convictions. The king's other advisers had manipulated Darius to make the decree because they were jealous of Daniel. His principles, wisdom, and work ethic had given him such favor with the king that he was about to be made second in command, and they thought that hitting him in the area of his own convictions would cause his downfall. (See Daniel 6:3–9.) Instead, the opposite happened. Though Darius couldn't revoke his decree, he was relieved to find that

Daniel had been saved from the lions, and he not only promoted Daniel but honored Daniel's God, as well. Those who opposed Daniel received the punishment they had sought for him. (See Daniel 6:10–28.)

Similarly, Joseph knew God as his reference in life and therefore was established in ethics and morals and understood righteous boundaries, but he seemed to be able to work with anyone in an authority role. Even after being sold into slavery, he served those over him honorably—his first Egyptian master, Potiphar; the prison warden who oversaw him after he was falsely accused by Potiphar's wife; and the pharaoh.

When Potiphar's wife tried to seduce Joseph, he refused to compromise his principles, and so she told lies that resulted in his imprisonment. Then, even after Pharaoh's cupbearer, who had been jailed with him, was restored to his role after Joseph interpreted his dream but promptly forgot about his promise to help Joseph, Joseph kept trusting God to deliver him from prison. After two years, when the pharaoh had a troubling dream, the cupbearer remembered Joseph, and Joseph not only was freed but was made second in command in Egypt. (See Genesis 39:1–41:44.)

Daniel and Joseph cooperated with unauthorized authority figures as much as possible, but they never compromised their relationships with God.

One of the keys to keeping this balance is a principle I highlighted earlier: when you are operating under your personal authority and know that your Ultimate Authority is God, you are no longer threatened by anyone, and you don't need anything from anyone else in order to feel valuable or safe; therefore, no one can manipulate or coerce you into doing something you don't want to do.

> DANIEL AND JOSEPH COOPERATED WITH UNAUTHORIZED AUTHORITY FIGURES AS MUCH AS POSSIBLE, BUT THEY NEVER COMPROMISED THEIR RELATIONSHIPS WITH GOD.

In other scriptural examples, even under the threat of death, Esther, at her uncle Mordecai's urging, was willing to risk her own life before King Xerxes to save her people from death. (See the book of Esther.) Daniel was not afraid to appeal to King Nebuchadnezzar, who had ordered all the king's advisers put to death, including Daniel and his friends, or to ask God for the interpretation of the king's troubling dream. (See Daniel 2.) When Daniel's friends Shadrach, Meshach, and Abednego were threatened with death in a fiery furnace if they didn't worship the golden idol that King Nebuchadnezzar had made, they refused, saying,

> *O Nebuchadnezzar, we do not need to defend ourselves before you in this matter. If we are thrown into the blazing furnace, the God we serve is able to save us from it, and he will rescue us from your hand, O king. But even if he does not, we want you to know, O king, that we will not serve your gods or worship the image of gold you have set up.*
>
> (Daniel 3:16–18)

Again, the king had to respond to the convictions of Shadrach, Meshach, and Abednego, which they were willing to die for. God protected them from the furnace so that they not only survived the fire but also didn't even have the smell of smoke on their clothes. (See verses 22–30.)

In your interactions in family, community, and business settings, you hopefully will never face anything as dire as Daniel and his friends, Joseph, or Esther did! However, their experiences illustrate that you can remain true to your principles and your personal authority while still serving unauthorized authority as you honor God in your life.

DISCOURAGE COMPLAINING AND THE DEFAMATION OF AUTHORITY

If others in your family, community, or company are grumbling and complaining about authority—either authorized or unauthorized authority—do your best to discourage or dilute this attitude by promoting positive conversation and peace among members of the group. We read in the book of Hebrews,

> *No discipline seems pleasant at the time, but painful. Later on, however, it produces a harvest of righteousness and peace for those who have been trained by it. Therefore, strengthen your feeble arms and weak knees. "Make level paths for your feet," so that the lame may not be disabled, but rather healed. **Make every effort to live in peace with all men** and to be holy; without holiness no one will see the Lord. See*

*to it that no one misses the grace of God and that **no bitter root grows up to cause trouble and defile many.*** (Hebrews 12:11–15)

Even though circumstances may not be pleasant and may even be unfair, again, encourage respect for the office if not the person. This must be done with tact and patience, but you can often defuse a gripe session or negative situation by offering constructive, practical alternatives to complaining and by steering the conversation toward more positive topics. You can also discuss going through the proper channels to try to correct the problem, as described above.

ENCOURAGE OTHERS TO RESPECT AUTHORITY BY YOUR OWN EXAMPLE

What are you demonstrating about your own attitude toward authority in the various realms of corporate life you are involved in? It's important not just to discourage *others'* complaints about authority but also to encourage members of the organization to respect authority by your own example. You will always be tempted to talk negatively to others about certain people in the group or about the organization itself in regard to people's attitudes, policies, and so forth, but resist this temptation. Paul wrote,

> *Do not let any unwholesome talk come out of your mouths, but only what is helpful for building others up according to their needs, that it may benefit those who listen.* (Ephesians 4:29)

Commit your concerns to your Ultimate Authority and let Him lead and guide you:

> *Do not be anxious about anything, but in everything, by prayer and petition, with thanksgiving, present your requests to God. And the peace of God, which transcends all understanding, will guard your hearts and your minds in Christ Jesus. Finally, brothers, whatever is true, whatever is noble, whatever is right, whatever is pure, whatever is lovely, whatever is admirable—if anything is excellent or praiseworthy—think about such things.* (Philippians 4:6–8)

REMEMBER THAT SUBMISSION TO AUTHORITY IS AN ESTABLISHED PRINCIPLE

To thrive under authority, we need to remember that both delegating and submitting to established authority are built into creation and life. Primarily, you submit to authority not for the purpose of protecting your relationship with that authority but rather preserving your higher relationship with the Creator, who established authority and desires that we live in it for the sake of peace and order. Like Jesus, we need to obey God to fulfill *"all righteousness"* (Matthew 3:15), which means "all right standing, or positioning."

> *Whatever you do, work at it with all your heart, as working for the Lord, not for men, since you know that you will receive an inheritance from the Lord as a reward. It is the Lord Christ you are serving.*
> (Colossians 3:23–24)

THIRTEEN

TWELVE PRINCIPLES OF AUTHORITY IN RELATION TO YOUR CALLING

UNDERSTANDING THE SCOPE OF YOUR AUTHORITY AND DOMAIN

"The honor of your presence is requested...."

When you receive correspondence in the mail that begins with those words, you know you are being invited to a special event—a wedding, a milestone anniversary celebration, a birthday party, or another significant occasion. If such an invitation were to come from a head of state, it would be regarded as a particular honor. To enter into your authority is to accept the honor of a gracious invitation from the Sovereign of the universe to join with Him in fulfilling a significant purpose in the world.

In conveying the meaning of personal authority in preceding chapters, I have sometimes referred to it using additional terms, such as *assignment*, *life mission* or *vision*, *vocation*, *work*, *occupation*, and *calling*. The Greek word *kletos*, which is translated as "calling" in various places in the Scriptures, has the meaning of "invited." The word *calling* is defined in *Merriam-Webster's Collegiate Dictionary* (eleventh edition) as "a strong inner impulse toward a particular course of action especially when accompanied by conviction of divine influence."

These concepts provide a good description of personal authority. We were created with an inherent "impulse," or motivation, to pursue a particular purpose in life in service to others, and we have been invited to fulfill that purpose by God Himself.

I have summarized the authority of our calling in twelve principles, and as we move to part three of this book, I want to highlight them so that you may be sure about the scope of your personal authority and domain. These principles summarize the nature of your own personal authority so that you can identify, understand, and take action to fulfill your calling with the conviction that God has given it to you to serve your generation.

> ### YOUR CONNECTEDNESS TO THE CREATOR UNITES YOU WITH ALL OTHERS WHO ARE RESTORED TO HIM.

PRINCIPLE #1: AUTHORITY IS GENERAL

Human beings were given dominion, or a general authority over the earth, at creation (see Genesis 1:26), though they abandoned this authority. When you reconnect to your Creator through the Authorized Dealer, Jesus Christ, you are restored to this authority, and you are also given another general authority. It is to act on the Creator's behalf in communicating to the world the opportunity for all people to be restored and reconnected to Him and to receive the benefits of coming under His eternal warranty and discovering their own personal authority. (See, for example, Matthew 28:18–20.)

Your connectedness to the Creator unites you with all others who are restored to Him. It is essential to understand that you have common purposes together with them, as those reconciled to the Creator, even as you exercise your personal authority. Paul wrote,

> *Make every effort to keep the unity of the Spirit through the bond of peace. There is one body and one Spirit—just as you were called to one hope when you were called—one Lord, one faith, one baptism; one God and Father of all, who is over all and through all and in all.*
>
> (Ephesians 4:3–6)

PRINCIPLE #2: AUTHORITY IS SPECIFIC

In Ephesians 4, we saw that there is one body, Spirit, Lord, faith, baptism, and God and Father of us all, who is the Ultimate Authority and who unites us. The next verse in that passage, however, begins with *"But"*: *"But to each one of us grace has been given as Christ apportioned it"* (verse 7). There is individual grace (divine influence, or divine invitation) *within the context* of our oneness with others that enables us to carry out our specific callings. "Each one should use whatever gift he has received to serve others, faithfully administering God's grace in its various forms" (1 Peter 4:10).

Paul wrote about his own authority in a way that we can all take to heart:

> I press on to take hold of that for which Christ Jesus took hold of me. Brothers, I do not consider myself yet to have taken hold of it. But one thing I do: Forgetting what is behind and straining toward what is ahead, I press on toward the goal to win the prize for which God has called me heavenward in Christ Jesus. (Philippians 3:12–14)

PRINCIPLE #3: AUTHORITY IS COMMUNITY BASED

Authority is characteristically community based and interdependent. We all have something to bring to a community that will contribute to its life, no matter in what realm that community exists. We are meant to use our authorized power within such communities as we fulfill our unique callings.

> Just as each of us has one body with many members, and these members do not all have the same function, so in Christ we who are many form one body, and each member belongs to all the others. We have different gifts, according to the grace given us. (Romans 12:4–6)

> What then shall we say, brothers? When you come together, everyone has a hymn, or a word of instruction, a revelation, a tongue or an interpretation. All of these must be done for the strengthening of the church. (1 Corinthians 14:26)

PRINCIPLE #4: AUTHORITY IS CENTRAL

True authority is central to your nature as God created you; it is an integral part of your personality and gifts. It is not something you have to put on as an addendum to who you really are, and it will not seem forced or uncomfortable to exercise but instead natural. Because of this, personal authority is liberating to the one who enters into it.

For you created my inmost being; you knit me together in my mother's womb. I praise you because I am fearfully and wonderfully made; your works are wonderful, I know that full well. My frame was not hidden from you when I was made in the secret place. When I was woven together in the depths of the earth, your eyes saw my unformed body. All the days ordained for me were written in your book before one of them came to be. (Psalm 139:13–16)

PRINCIPLE #5: AUTHORITY IS EQUIPPED

When God called Moses to lead the Israelites out of slavery in Egypt, Moses said, *"O Lord, I have never been eloquent, neither in the past nor since you have spoken to your servant. I am slow of speech and tongue"* (Exodus 4:10). Moses didn't realize that power came with the authority he had just been given.

The LORD said to [Moses], "Who gave man his mouth? Who makes him deaf or mute? Who gives him sight or makes him blind? Is it not I, the LORD? Now go; I will help you speak and will teach you what to say." (Exodus 4:11–12)

God had told Moses, *"I am sending you to Pharaoh"* (Exodus 3:10), so Moses wasn't going to Pharaoh on his own merits but under the authority of God.

Like Moses, most of us don't recognize the natural power of our personal domains, and we also don't realize that our Creator stands by us to enable us to fulfill the authority He has given us. The book of Hebrews encourages us, *"Let us hold unswervingly to the hope we profess, for he who promised is faithful"* (Hebrews 10:23).

> ## WHEN YOU FUNCTION UNDER GOD'S AUTHORITY,
> ## ALL HIS RESOURCES ARE ON YOUR SIDE.

When you operate in the authority of your calling, you are automatically equipped for it because God is faithful to supply what you need. You are "self-sufficient" in the sense that you were born with a purpose, and you have built-in abilities that God assigned to you to fulfill it. Moreover, when you function under God's authority, all His resources are on your side, as well, just as they were for Moses.

PRINCIPLE #6: AUTHORITY IS SELF-FULFILLING

The gifts that the Creator has planted within you will grow and be fruitful as you trust in the power of what He has given you and commit its use to Him. God says,

I am watching to see that my word is fulfilled. (Jeremiah 1:12)

As the heavens are higher than the earth, so are my ways higher than your ways and my thoughts than your thoughts. As the rain and the snow come down from heaven, and do not return to it without watering the earth and making it bud and flourish, so that it yields seed for the sower and bread for the eater, so is my word that goes out from my mouth: It will not return to me empty, but will accomplish what I desire and achieve the purpose for which I sent it. (Isaiah 55:9–11)

PRINCIPLE #7: AUTHORITY CAN LIE UNDISCOVERED OR DORMANT

Even though personal authority is self-fulfilling, it can remain undiscovered or hidden inside us—sometimes for a lifetime—unless we awaken to its reality in our lives and put it into the context of a restored relationship with our Creator. This is one of the reasons that Paul wrote to the first-century Ephesians,

I pray also that the eyes of your heart may be enlightened in order that you may know the hope to which he has called you, the riches of his glorious inheritance in the saints, and his incomparably great power for us who believe. (Ephesians 1:18–19)

Authority will also lie dormant within us if we ignore, neglect, or reject it. Paul wrote to Timothy, "*I remind you to fan into flame the gift of God, which is in you through the laying on of my hands*" (2 Timothy 1:6), and Jesus told this parable about the gifts and calling that are entrusted to us by God:

[The kingdom of heaven] *will be like a man going on a journey, who called his servants and entrusted his property to them. To one he gave five talents of money, to another two talents, and to another one talent, each according to his ability. Then he went on his journey. The man who had received the five talents went at once and put his money to work and gained five more. So also, the one with the two talents gained two more.* **But the man who had received the one talent went off, dug a hole in the ground and hid his master's money.**

(Matthew 25:14–18)

The parable continues with the master returning and the servants who had been entrusted the five talents and the two talents presenting their doubled talents to him. He replies to each, "*Well done, good and faithful servant! You have been faithful with a few things; I will put you in charge of many things. Come and share your master's happiness!*" (verses 21, 23). Then, the servant with the one talent—who we are told buried it out of fear (see verses 24–25)—came and gave it back to the master, having obtained no increase in the property.

His master replied, "You wicked, lazy servant! So you knew that I harvest where I have not sown and gather where I have not scattered seed? Well then, you should have put my money on deposit with the bankers, so that when I returned I would have received it back with interest. Take the talent from him and give it to the one who has the ten talents. For everyone who has will be given more, and he will have an abundance. Whoever does not have, even what he has will be taken from him."

(Matthew 25:26–29)

We do not need to fear having nothing to show for ourselves to our Creator if we invest in and exercise our natural gifts and talents and then wait expectantly in faith for the results.

In addition, when we use what we have been given for the sake of others, it is multiplied back to us: "*Give, and it will be given to you. A good measure, pressed down, shaken together and running over, will be poured into your lap. For with the measure you use, it will be measured to you*" (Luke 6:38).

PRINCIPLE #8: AUTHORITY IS REFINED WITH USE

Just as we need to put our gifts to work in the first place, we need to refine them by continual use, training, and development so that they can be optimally effective.

We constantly pray for you, that our God may count you worthy of his calling, and that by his power he may fulfill every good purpose of yours and every act prompted by your faith.   (2 Thessalonians 1:11)

Do not merely listen to the word, and so deceive yourselves. Do what it says. Anyone who listens to the word but does not do what it says is like a man who looks at his face in a mirror and, after looking at himself, goes away and immediately forgets what he looks like. But the man who looks intently into the perfect law that gives freedom, and continues to do this, not forgetting what he has heard, but doing it—he will be blessed in what he does.   (James 1:22–25)

> **PERSONAL AUTHORITY IS A PERMANENT PART OF OUR NATURE; IT DOESN'T GO AWAY.**

PRINCIPLE #9: AUTHORITY IS PERMANENT

Personal authority is a permanent part of our nature; it doesn't go away, "*for God's gifts and his call are irrevocable*" (Romans 11:29). Our authority may be recalled for misuse, but our essential makeup and gifts remain. If we realign our lives with God, He will restore us and renew our calls. "*We know that in all things God works for the good of those who love him, who have been called according to his purpose*" (Romans 8:28).

This principle is the reason why the same ideas and dreams keep coming back to us throughout our lives. We must realize that our personal authority is connected to our identity and reflects our true purpose so that we will seek to pursue what we are called to do in life.

PRINCIPLE #10: AUTHORITY IS GOD'S PERFECT WILL

Human beings were both created and restored with the purpose of authority, which tells us that authority is God's perfect will for us. I didn't understand authority for many years, yet as I studied its principles, I began to appreciate that authority was the best thing God ever gave us, for many reasons. I have presented a number of those reasons in this book—authority gives us purpose, protection, fulfillment, motivation, a place in life, order, peace, and much more.

> *His divine power has given us everything we need for life and godliness through our knowledge of him who called us by his own glory and goodness.*   (2 Peter 1:3)

The more we learn about our inherent authority and exercise it in our lives, the more we come to understand how important it is in relation to God's will for us.

> *Do not conform any longer to the pattern of this world, but be transformed by the renewing of your mind. Then you will be able to test and approve what God's will is—his good, pleasing and perfect will.*   (Romans 12:2)

PRINCIPLE #11: AUTHORITY REQUIRES PERSONAL SUBMISSION TO GOD

Each of us must submit to God and allow Him to unfold His purposes for our lives as we exercise personal authority. Focusing on what is happening in another person's life rather than on what He has given us and how He is leading us will always pull us off track. Jesus's disciple Peter started to do this, but Jesus's response to him was, *"You must follow me"*:

> [Jesus] *said to* [Peter], *"Follow me!" Peter turned and saw that the disciple whom Jesus loved was following them. (This was the one who had leaned back against Jesus at the supper and had said, "Lord, who is going to betray you?") When Peter saw him, he asked, "Lord, what about him?" Jesus answered, "If I want him to remain alive until I return, what is that to you? You must follow me."*   (John 21:19–22)

Principle eleven sheds additional light on principles one and two, which are that authority is general and authority is specific. Even though we all have general calls to authority in relation to creation and restoration, each of us must individually follow the Authorized Dealer as we obey the Word of God and follow the leading of the Spirit of God in order to fulfill the Manufacturer's specific purposes for us.

> *All Scripture is God-breathed and is useful for teaching, rebuking, correcting and training in righteousness, so that the man of God may be thoroughly equipped for every good work.* (2 Timothy 3:16–17)

> [Jesus said,] *"I have much more to say to you, more than you can now bear. But when he, the Spirit of truth, comes, he will guide you into all truth. He will not speak on his own; he will speak only what he hears, and he will tell you what is yet to come. He will bring glory to me by taking from what is mine and making it known to you. All that belongs to the Father is mine. That is why I said the Spirit will take from what is mine and make it known to you."* (John 16:12–15)

PRINCIPLE #12: AUTHORITY HAS A TIME FOR MATURE ADMINISTRATION

King Solomon wrote, *"There is a time for everything, and a season for every activity under heaven"* (Ecclesiastes 3:1). There is a time for everything, and there will be a time for the mature administration of your personal authority.

The Scriptures say that when Jesus came to earth to fulfill His calling to restore human beings to their Creator, it was at just the right time:

> *But when the time had fully come* ["the fullness of the time had come" NKJV], *God sent his Son, born of a woman, born under law, to redeem those under law, that we might receive the full rights of sons.* (Galatians 4:4–5)

The timing of authority is a significant principle for us to keep in mind. We need to be sensitive to the ways in which God is working in our lives. We don't fully know the amount and type of preparation we may need for the mature administration of our authority, but we do know that the

Scriptures teach the importance of our training, testing, and incremental growth, which lead to maturity and usefulness for God. We therefore have to be continually preparing to exercise our authority by developing our character, gifts, and skills so that we will be ready when God opens doors of opportunity for us.

> In a large house there are articles not only of gold and silver, but also of wood and clay; some are for noble purposes and some for ignoble. If a man cleanses himself from the latter, he will be an instrument for noble purposes, made holy, useful to the Master and prepared to do any good work. (2 Timothy 2:20–21)

> Whoever can be trusted with very little can also be trusted with much, and whoever is dishonest with very little will also be dishonest with much. So if you have not been trustworthy in handling worldly wealth, who will trust you with true riches? And if you have not been trustworthy with someone else's property, who will give you property of your own? (Luke 16:10–12)

When those doors of opportunity open, you may find that you continually operate in your authority, or you may have periods when you pull back and regroup or rest before mobilizing again. But as you prepare yourself and your gifts, and as you stay connected to your Creator, you will know when it is time to get active and administer your authority. It will be for you "the fullness of time."

PART THREE

RESTORING TRUE AUTHORITY IN THE WORLD

FOURTEEN

KEYS TO REESTABLISHING LEGITIMATE AUTHORITY ON EARTH

PROMOTING CORPORATE DEVELOPMENT THROUGH FREEDOM AND ACCOUNTABILITY

Imagine that you live in a nation ruled by a harsh dictator. The government of your native country has controlled every aspect of your life for as long as you can remember, and you have now been assigned to a forced labor camp. Your soul is crying out for freedom, and, in desperation, you join with several others who have planned an escape from the camp. After successfully escaping, you arrange to be smuggled out of the country. You travel in a small boat across the ocean for weeks with little food and water in search of a better life in a country that gives rights to its citizens and also defends them. Finally, you reach its shores. Now, all you need is someone in a position of authority in that country to grant permission for you to enter and build a better life. You need legal status to live there.

Unexpectedly, you are greeted on the shores of the new country by your older brother! He had traversed the dangerous seas a few years before you, and he had been in contact with those who were smuggling people out of your native country. Knowing you were coming, he had already made arrangements for you to receive asylum in the new land.

Your brother now lives in a community with members of your extended family whom he also enabled to gain freedom, and who now help him free others, as well. You are overjoyed as you enter your new life in the company of a loving, supportive family.

WELCOMING PEOPLE TO A NEW "COUNTRY"

People across the world who are living under false authority in its various forms are like citizens of an oppressive nation. Jesus Christ is their "older Brother" who has gone ahead and prepared the way for them to enter a new country, the kingdom of God, which is characterized by peace, order, and freedom, and where every person's value and significance are recognized. "*Those God foreknew he also predestined to be conformed to the likeness of his Son, that he might be the firstborn among many brothers*" (Romans 8:29).

When we have gained an understanding of genuine authority and have entered into its freedom, we become a part of our older Brother's community in the kingdom of God on earth and can participate in helping to reestablish legitimate authority in the world. We are responsible for seeking to enable others to enter into a new way of life in which they can be free of the restrictions and abuse of false authority and can exercise their full personal authority in the context of their interactions and relationships with others. In this way, we are called to welcome people to a new "country."

Let us look briefly at the oppressive "nation" that people need to be set free from, and then we will look at twelve keys for helping to release them from false authority.

THE STEADY EROSION OF AUTHORITY

The false authority that we experience in the world today is both a long-standing issue—stemming from our first parents' abandonment of authority—and the result of a slow, steady erosion of authority during the twentieth century.

The principles established by the Creator have been recaptured and implemented in societies, to varying degrees, during periods of human history, and a hundred years ago, people had a much clearer understanding of true authority and a corresponding respect for it.

GENUINE AUTHORITY IS STILL OUR ONLY HOPE FOR THIS PLANET.

Nations and cultures were certainly not living according to the Creator's principles in *all* aspects of life. There were numerous social ills and injustices in the previous hundred years, as there are today. Authority structures were misused by individuals who operated within them, resulting in forms of oppression and the abuse of human dignity through systems that reduced people to subhuman status, forced people into servitude, and robbed them of their freedom. The twentieth century may have been the bloodiest on record, with its wars, ethnic "cleansing," and the annihilation of millions by dictators and tyrants.

I stand against any and all misuse of authority that abuses, dehumanizes, and destroys people. The purpose of this book is to help rescue authority from this dark history and from potential future abuses. As I wrote earlier, many people throughout the world have abandoned the concept of authority, partly as a result of these outrages and their consequences. Yet *genuine* authority is still our only hope for this planet. It therefore needs to be our focus and priority in rebuilding the broken lives and struggling nations of our world.

A RECOGNITION OF THE ESSENCE OF AUTHORITY IN FORMER YEARS

Even with the misuse and abuse of authority in the recent past, there was still among many people in various nations a general understanding and acceptance of the essence of true authority and its supporting structures in society, such as the family, the government, the church, and business. Historically, the established role of authority in these realms was much clearer, and there was therefore more order and harmony. For example, there were certain expectations and boundaries in regard to having children in the context of marriage and an agreement that the marital union should be esteemed and protected. People generally showed more respect for their leaders and coworkers on their jobs. Young people were taught to esteem the elderly, and value was placed on age and wisdom. There was a respect for sacred institutions. More honor was given to those who contributed their lives to the development of society than to celebrities, those who are often just "famous for being famous."

Community and governing institutions were also more respected. This respect for civic and public offices was held not only by citizens and constituents, but also by the ones who held the positions. For example, one didn't hear as much about mayors, pastors, and other leaders getting into moral or ethical trouble because they honored the trust they had been given by their positions.

Of course, there were exceptions to this general attitude toward authority by people who flaunted and abused their positions and got away with it because they were never caught or it was never made public. But as a general rule, people valued and respected the role of authority in their lives.

DISMISSAL OF AUTHORITY IN CONTEMPORARY SOCIETY

As we have seen, in today's world, there is a general confusion about and dismissal of authority, and that ignorance about authority has led to disordered lives. For instance, fathers, mothers, and children aren't incorporating the principles of authority into family life. As a result, many parents are abdicating their roles as the senior authority in the family, many husbands and wives are not sure who is responsible for what, and many children do not esteem their parents. Another outcome is that few parameters are taught to the children, so that children themselves are having children, and the offspring of these unauthorized parents are not prepared to pass along any clear concept of what authority looks like.

In the realm of government, scores of citizens have little respect for their national leaders or esteem for their national symbols. Self-serving "politicians," rather than statesmen, are prevalent. Many politicians pursue positions of authority not to empower others by serving their constituencies but rather to use their power to secure and preserve personal advantages.

In the realm of the church, some religious leaders have allowed their physical passions to overrule their responsibilities to the point where certain priests and preachers have used their authority to abuse, manipulate, and, in some cases, destroy the lives of the parishioners entrusted to their oversight.

In the realm of business, a pursuit of greed and speculation rather than honest enterprise has led some executives and their corporations into shaky or illegal practices that have sometimes caused the downfall of both executives and institutions. Some labor union leaders have also abused their positions of authority and the trust their members have placed in them to bring about just and equitable working conditions; they have used members' dues for their own agendas while weakening legitimate companies—in some cases, putting them out of business and their members out of their jobs.

A RISE IN INDIVIDUALISM

One of the factors contributing to the dismissal and erosion of authority throughout the world is the increasing popularity of the idea of individualism, which is often promoted through the political system of democracy. A pursuit of democracy has captured the minds of many people in nations around the world, and this has led to life-affirming freedoms and benefits for people who have long suffered under the oppression of false authority under communism, dictatorships, and colonialism.

While there have been many positive results from the spread of democracy, people's concept of this political system often focuses on the idea of individualism to the point where they feel they are not answerable to anyone for anything, and that no one can tell them what to do. The abandonment of false authority was necessary, but it seems that many people have abandoned all authority along with it. An overemphasis on individualism can cripple people's potential by causing them to seek power alone rather than genuine authority. At its extreme, an attitude of individualism ignores the reality that human beings are meant to live in community, in the various forms we have been discussing, and to contribute their strengths and gifts to one another. Significantly, it can also write off the necessity of personal responsibility and the give-and-take of established authority and submission that allows life to operate smoothly and brings order and peace in a nation.

Also contributing to the erosion of authority in our nations are changes in social mores, which have moved away from the Manufacturer's original design. Again, an attitude of "I can do anything I want, and you can't tell me what to do" has superseded a basic understanding of the value of living according to the Creator's principles and laws. The trend today, allegedly in support of people's individual rights, seems to be a dedication to eradicating foundational authority. Yet, this is the only thing that can *renew* and *preserve* our contemporary society.

For example, such a perspective can infringe on family life in a case where, if your thirteen-year-old daughter becomes pregnant, she has a right to withhold this information from you, and you have no authority in her life in this situation. Instead, the state, through the public school she attends, has the authority and influence over her. In this and other ways, parents have lost their authority to other authorities that are operating under false principles. Under such circumstances, do we wonder why society has continued to disintegrate? The question is, what kind of authority will be promoted in society—a false or a genuine one?

IGNORANCE OF TRUE AUTHORITY IS THE FATHER OF ANARCHY.

Ignorance of true authority is the father of anarchy. A society without authority is no longer a true society because a society is made up of social relationships, and social relationships need the framework of authority to function in a healthy and effective way.

This is why the principles of genuine authority must be clearly communicated to people in all nations. People need to understand the benefits of personal and corporate authority for their own lives, as well as the lives of others. True authority in a society brings a necessary structure, peace, and fruitfulness to life. Rejection of true authority sacrifices people's purposes and vision, while adherence to authority protects people's purposes and produces personal vision and the confidence to fulfill it. When everyone understands his purpose and role in light of the Creator's purposes, this knowledge creates the smooth functioning of social relationships and the exercise of personal authority.

WITHOUT AUTHORITY…

Without authority, there is no basis for accountability, and people therefore feel insecure because they don't know what they can expect from others. "Freedom" without law or responsibility eventually becomes chaos.

Without true authority….

+ life has no order.
+ there can be no confidence.
+ purpose has no protection.
+ there is no effective functioning.

- destiny is abandoned.
- power is wasted.
- energy is abused.
- potential is miscarried.

The authority that has eroded in our world needs to be reestablished. When true authority is put in place, it renews a sense of security, so that people experience less stress in their lives and reduced tensions in their relationships. This is why restoring true authority will promote national and global security, peace, and growth.

The following are keys for reestablishing legitimate authority in the earth:

KEY #1: ACKNOWLEDGE THE CRISIS OF AUTHORITY

To restore legitimate authority, we first need to acknowledge that there is a widespread lack of genuine authority in all the basic realms of society—including our families, local and national governments, churches, and businesses—and that this is a critical problem that needs to be addressed.

Reestablishing legitimate authority will not happen if we think that some unnamed "group" or "the government" will fix things for everyone. It begins with each of us, individually, as we rediscover true authority ourselves and then communicate its truths and principles to others.

KEY #2: REDEFINE AUTHORITY, EXPLAINING ITS TRUE NATURE

In communicating what authority is, we have to clearly define it. Authority has lost its meaning for most people, and they often mistake it for oppression or control. That is why I devoted several chapters in this book to defining and explaining the true nature of authority. The term must be reconceptualized and renewed in people's minds. Authority is not inherently evil or even a necessary evil but rather a means for good.

AUTHORITY IS NOT INHERENTLY EVIL OR EVEN A NECESSARY EVIL BUT RATHER A MEANS FOR GOOD.

You can utilize the principles throughout this book, but especially in part one, to help others understand the true definition and purpose of authority. You can also build on the positive aspects of authority that people recognize from everyday life. For instance, when people attend weddings, they usually hear the clergyman or justice of the peace say something like, "By the authority (or powers) vested in me by the state of _____, I now pronounce you husband and wife." Or, when a university confers academic degrees on those who have completed their educational requirements, the president or academic dean will say something similar to, "By the power vested in me by the Board of Regents of _____ University, I confer upon you the degree of _____, along with all the rights, privileges, and responsibilities associated with it."

These are positive and joyful aspects of authority that establish new families and reward personal effort and achievement rather than oppress and constrict. In addition, personal and corporate authority involve the granting and exercising of rights and privileges from a higher authority.

KEY #3: RESTORE THE FOUNDATIONS OF GENUINE AUTHORITY

All authority must be based on the Absolute Authority, the Creator, or else it will fall apart. Self-authorization is not authority; this is the historic mistake of what we have come to know as "humanism," which promotes the idea that man is his own measure in life. Since true authority is always delegated, it would seem that the greatest culprit to the erosion of authority in this and previous generations is the elevation of human beings as the ultimate authority. Humans, in themselves, are no authority at all. Instead, people need a solid reference for who God is, especially as our Creator, and for our dependence on Him. "*O* Lord, *you are our Father. We are the clay, you are the potter; we are all the work of your hand*" (Isaiah 64:8).

> ALL AUTHORITY MUST BE BASED ON THE ABSOLUTE AUTHORITY,
> THE CREATOR, OR ELSE IT WILL FALL APART.

In our contemporary societies, many people don't want to accept the idea of absolute authority. Yet, as we saw earlier, the word *absolute* is defined as "fundamental, ultimate." Whatever is outside of God and His ways is lesser or inferior. Again, true authority must be grounded in an author, and therefore, we must first identify our Author. We must begin with a general acknowledgment of our Creator and of His basic laws as recorded in His Word, the Scriptures.

God's first commandment for His people given through Moses confirmed His absolute authority in their lives: *"I am the* LORD *your God, who brought you out of Egypt, out of the land of slavery. You shall have no other gods before me"* (Exodus 20:2–3). Recognizing and serving God as our Creator and Ruler will enable us to rebuild the age-old, sure foundations of society:

> *The* LORD *will guide you always; he will satisfy your needs in a sunscorched land and will strengthen your frame. You will be like a well-watered garden, like a spring whose waters never fail. Your people will rebuild the ancient ruins and will raise up the age-old foundations; you will be called Repairer of Broken Walls, Restorer of Streets with Dwellings.* (Isaiah 58:11–12)

The world needs to come back to its senses; we must return to the reality that there are absolutes, which are fundamental, strong, stable, and supportive to both individuals and society as a whole. As we do, we will be called *"Repairer of Broken Walls, Restorer of Streets with Dwellings."* Communities will be restored and lives rebuilt.

KEY #4: IDENTIFY THE LAWS OF THE CREATOR AS OUR REFERENCE FOR AUTHORITY

The erosion of and disillusionment about authority within our nations can be traced to people's movement away from the pillars of authority established by the Creator for the effective and successful functioning of His creation. The Author of all legitimate authority revealed Himself within the context of the biblical text, which clearly established the fundamental laws and principles by which all living things, including humanity, are to operate.

Building on key number three, then, after relaying the general foundation of the authority of the Creator in our lives, we need to identify His laws and principles, which are our reference for everyday living. This is the only way to effect the true restoration of authority.

Almost all nations are built on law because law produces and maintains a functioning and stable society. For healthy national development to take place, the whole nation must agree on what the law, or authority, will be. Many nations have a constitution, which we can define as "the basic principles and laws of a nation, state, or social group that determine the powers and duties of the government and guarantee certain rights to the people in it."

A constitution establishes what has been called the "rule of law," in which it is ultimately the law that rules the nation, not the president or prime minister, congress or parliament. Although we often repeat the phrase that "no one is above the law," this principle has to return in practice. When people think they ultimately rule the nation based on their own opinions, then authority is weakened and even cancelled because people's opinions can be arbitrary and changeable.

> **GOD'S AUTHORITY, WHICH HE PROVIDES THROUGH HIS WORD, IS STABLE; IT DOESN'T CHANGE ON A WHIM.**

Governing through opinion polls might sound fair, until we see how inconsistent people's attitudes can be from week to week and from month to month, depending on the immediate circumstances of their own lives and the events in the communities and world around them. This is why a solid foundation for governing can be found only in the fixed nature of established laws and principles.

Again, God's authority, which He provides through His Word, is stable; it doesn't change on a whim. Another definition of *absolute* that we looked at earlier is "independent of arbitrary standards of measurement." We also saw that the word *ruler* refers to a Latin word meaning "to keep straight, direct." True authority gives us a reference point, a clear direction in which to go.

The reality of the current crisis in our nations and the world is that we need to decide what our fundamental authority is and what direction to go in. To solve our problems, legitimate authority has to be instated, and this will happen only as nations learn to align their laws in keeping with the Creator's principles.

Where there is no authority, there is no law. When there is a return to a respect for authority, there will be orderly development in a country. For example, if people value the law, crime will decrease because people will respect others' property, and there will be fewer broken homes because husbands and wives will take seriously their vows to one another.

In other words, society needs to be reintroduced to its bedrock principles.

> So this is what the Sovereign LORD says: "See, I lay a stone in Zion, a tested stone, a precious cornerstone for a sure foundation; the one who trusts will never be dismayed. I will make justice the measuring line and righteousness the plumb line."   (Isaiah 28:16–17)

We have to bring back the Creator's justice and righteousness as our measurement for living. That will be the precious cornerstone of our individual relationships, communities, and nations. We need a cornerstone that has been tested and proven to be immovable—a solid Rock.

An anchor can sometimes be a good analogy for stability, but my experience growing up in the Bahamas has shown me that if a storm comes, an anchor is useless without a rock. Rocks don't move, but anchors certainly can, and boats may be pulled away from their moorings and into dangerous waters. The Authorized Dealer, who is *"the chief cornerstone"* (Ephesians 2:20), is the One who leads us back to the Creator God and our stability as human beings. He said,

> Everyone who hears these words of mine and puts them into practice is like a wise man who built his house on the rock. The rain came down, the streams rose, and the winds blew and beat against that house; yet it did not fall, because it had its foundation on the rock. But everyone who hears these words of mine and does not put them into practice is like a foolish man who built his house on sand. The rain came down, the streams rose, and the winds blew and beat against that house, and it fell with a great crash.   (Matthew 7:24–27)

KEY #5: TEACH THAT EVERYONE MUST BE ACCOUNTABLE TO AUTHORITY

The next key is that people must understand that everyone is accountable to authority and that submission is a voluntary surrendering of one's independence for a greater personal or corporate good. We can never succeed in isolation. Life doesn't permit that because we were created and designed for relationships.

In fact, if people don't learn to submit voluntarily, society may make them submit. For example, when a judge sentences someone to prison for violating the law, he is simply taking a lawless person and placing him under authority again. A prisoner is told when to get up, when to go to bed, when to eat, when to bathe, what to wear, what work he can do, when to start working, when to stop working, who can see him and for how long, and so on. His life is subject to a strict authority under which his personal desires are set aside. So, even though the prisoner disregarded authority, he is made to live under it nevertheless.

It is much better to respect authority and receive its benefits than to suffer for ignoring it. Many people suffer from ignoring authority. They may not be in prison, but their lives are disordered, unsettled, and unproductive.

We must communicate to others that true authority and submission are for the purpose of giving and receiving what is good for our lives. Just as we submit to the oxygen that the plants produce, we keep one another thriving by respecting others' authority and receiving what they are authorized to give. If you know what your authority is and what it is not, then you can respect other people's authority as they provide you with what you need but do not have. We are not to control others but to use our authority to serve them, and we are accountable for the service that we use it for. Let us encourage people to trust others' authority, respect it, and allow them to exercise their inherent gifts as we exercise ours.

KEY #6: HOLD AUTHORITY ACCOUNTABLE TO ITS AUTHORITY

In the various realms of life, we have the right to hold someone in authority accountable to whoever is his higher authority, whoever has delegated power to him. This is essential for restoring legitimate authority to the earth. No one can be above authority, or he will misuse and abuse others. Parents, politicians, pastors and priests, and business leaders are in positions to either help or hurt others by their attitudes and behavior in their positions of authority.

> **WHEN PEOPLE UNDERSTAND THE TRUE NATURE OF AUTHORITY AND SUBMISSION, IT WILL BECOME CLEAR THAT THERE ARE MORE ADVANTAGES TO SUBMISSION THAN TO REBELLION.**

For example, what contributed to the economic crisis that began in the first decade of the twenty-first century was that corporations were not held to responsible business practices. A reinstatement of authority in the form of safeguards and regulations is helping to address this problem. This type of reinstatement of sound principles is at the heart of restoring a culture.

KEY #7: TEACH THE BENEFITS OF AUTHORITY

People must especially understand the benefits of true authority if it is to be reestablished in the world. We have been taught the dangers of false authority for so long that we often don't know that it is a distortion of something that is positive and life affirming. When people understand the true nature of authority and submission, it will become clear that there are more advantages to submission than to rebellion.

The benefits of personal authority have been highlighted throughout this book, but particularly in chapter 8: originality, awareness of intrinsic value, personal fulfillment, confidence, no competition, no comparison, no jealousy, no fear, internal motivation and passion, and authenticity. The primary purposes of authority, outlined in chapter 6, are also advantages to authority that address the crisis in our world today. True authority brings order, maximum production, preservation, representation through validity and defense, safety, promotion, freedom, identity, and reality.

In effect, living in one's authority leads to a clear and uncluttered life: When you understand authority, you know who you are, what you are meant to do, and whom you can appeal to when a problem or need arises. Thus, authority is the source of order and peace. It is the substance of simplicity.

KEY #8: DISCOVER YOUR PERSONAL AUTHORITY SO THAT YOU CAN DELEGATE AUTHORITY

Another essential key is to make sure we discover our own personal authority so that we will be qualified and equipped to delegate true authority to others. We can't help to restore others if we haven't been restored ourselves.

Make it a priority to ask the Creator to clarify your personal authority, and answer the questions in the Personal Authority Profile section at the back of this book. In this way, you will not only experience personal fulfillment but will be able to show others how to enter into their true authority, as well.

KEY #9: ALLOW PEOPLE TO PURSUE THEIR AREAS OF AUTHORITY

A ninth key to reestablishing legitimate authority is to allow people to pursue their areas of authority and to encourage others to do the same.

> AUTHORITY GIVES US TOTAL FREEDOM WITHIN THE BOUNDARIES OF OUR PERSONAL DOMAIN.

Authority gives us total freedom within the boundaries of our personal domain and therefore lets us be who we were created to be without limitation. What are the boundaries? We are not to infringe on others or their authority, or we will be trespassing. If we have a clear idea of our authority—as in key eight, above—then we will know when we are overstepping another person's boundary. Again, we must acknowledge that everybody is a leader as he carries out his God-given authority on earth, and that we are an authority only in the area of our personal purpose.

We can also enable others to pursue their gifting by creating environments for them to find and release their personal authority. Parents can make a special contribution in this regard. If a child discovers early in his life what his personal authority is and what his position and role in the family is, and if he is taught what his position and role will be when he is an adult, then he will have clear guidance in how to live his life.

As people discover and start to exercise their personal gifting, the whole structure of interdependent authority will begin to be put back into place.

KEY #10: RECOGNIZE THAT WE ARE ACCOUNTABLE TO THE SOURCE OF ALL AUTHORITY

Key number ten brings us full circle to an acknowledgment of God as our Author. We cannot just recognize the Source of our authority and not be answerable to Him. In the end, He is the one to whom we will give a report of our lives and how we have used the authority He has given us. Paul said, "It is written: 'As surely as I live,' says the Lord, 'every knee will bow before me; every tongue will confess to God.' So then, each of us will give an account of himself to God" (Romans 14:11–12).

Reestablishing legitimate authority in the world will naturally include responsibility and accountability, and these qualities should begin with us. We therefore must be conscious of the fact that we will be judged and made to give an account for our lives before our Creator. And, as we discover, enjoy, and fulfill our personal authority, we can remember that…

God is not unjust; he will not forget your work and the love you have shown him as you have helped his people and continue to help them. We want each of you to show this same diligence to the very end, in order to make your hope sure. (Hebrews 6:10–11)

FIFTEEN

FOUR BASIC REALMS OF AUTHORITY

RESTORING FOUNDATIONS OF AUTHORITY IN THE FAMILY, IN GOVERNMENT, IN THE CHURCH, AND IN BUSINESS

In the last chapter, we saw that to reestablish legitimate authority on earth, we must acknowledge the absolute authority of our Creator and identify specific laws and principles on which we should base our lives. To help you begin to do this, this chapter provides foundational Scriptures that correspond to the nature of authority in four basic realms of human relationships: the family, government, the church, and business. Each of these areas involves important interactions between people that need guidelines for the proper exercise of authority.

As you review the four realms, please keep these points in mind:

+ Authority can be compared to electricity: the same force that is used to empower people has the potential to destroy them if it is not regulated and submitted to the right purpose.

+ Authority produces and maintains order—in families, in societies, in nations, in the world—because it establishes the reference for all relationships in life. When someone is functioning according to authority, he knows where he is supposed to be and what he is meant to do based on the authority he has been given. It is never a matter of someone being "greater" or more important but of what each person's authority is for the well-being, protection, and security of all involved. It is also a matter of creating an environment in which each person can thrive in his personal authority and contribute to the community.

+ Authority and submission are interdependent. In relationships, people both give and receive. When you give, you are exercising a certain degree of authority; when you receive, you are operating under a certain degree of submission. Authority doesn't function without submission, and submission is invalid and meaningless if it is not in the context of true authority. In fact, submission is dangerous without genuine authority because what is sometimes called "submission" is actually a belittling and oppression of others.

+ Authority, power, and position are interrelated. *Authority* is delegated right, or permission. *Power* is ability, might, or enabling strength. *Position* is one's place in relation to order. Your personal authority is your domain, or "home," in the order of things and is the key to your power and effectiveness.

+ When you understand the purpose of authority, you know that you need to respect, cooperate with, and love others; that others are able to give you something you lack; and that you are able to supply something others lack.

+ Since it is authority that releases authority and power, understanding the role of authority in each realm of life gives us the opportunity to exercise the full potential of our personal authority.

The following is not a comprehensive manual on these four realms of authority, since an entire book could be devoted to each area. Rather, it is designed to refer you to noteworthy Scriptures that pertain to each realm so that you can begin to apply them in your life in conjunction with the other principles of authority in this book. However, I have included a somewhat more in-depth discussion of the realm of the family because there has been much confusion and contention in society about the roles of men and women, their inherent makeup, and their similarities and differences, and these issues need to be noted in relation to authority.[1]

THE REALM OF THE FAMILY

What was the first area of authority that God established on earth? It wasn't "religion" or the church or even the state—it was the family. One of the reasons the family is the most important realm of authority is that it contributes to all the other realms of authority—the future participants in the state, the church, and business are first raised and trained in the context of a family. Therefore, the quality of the leaders in all the other realms depends on what the family produces. The kind of children that come out of our families determine the kind of society we will have.

> William J. Bennett...once said that the family is the original Department of Health, Education and Welfare. Society has yet to invent a better means of raising healthy, well-adjusted people than by placing them in loving and intact families that live under godly principles.... The family, church and government occupy separate spheres of life, but depend on each other."[2]

Why is authority really needed within a family? Again, we return to the primary purposes of authority. Authority is needed in a family for order, maximum production, preservation, representation through validity and defense, safety, promotion, freedom, identity, and reality.

What is the nature of authority in the family, and how should those relationships be conducted? The structure within the family that carries out the above purposes of authority is (1) the husband as leader, (2) the wife as coleader, and (3) the submission of the children to both parents. Let us look at the scriptural basis for this order, because a misunderstanding of these roles has led to the tragic misuse and abuse of the woman in marital relationships, in family relationships, and in society, both today and throughout much of human history.

THE SOURCE OF AUTHORITY FOR HUSBAND AND WIFE

When our Author created human beings, He began with a man, Adam, whose body He formed from the ground, and whose spirit and soul were drawn from God Himself. Moses recorded, "*The LORD God formed the man from the dust of the ground and breathed into his nostrils the breath of life, and the man became a living being*" (Genesis 2:7).

The male was created first, but he was not meant to live in isolation or to fulfill his authority on his own. He was intended to do so in collaboration with the female. The woman is therefore a coleader who works alongside the man to accomplish what they were both created to do.

> *The LORD God said, "It is not good for the man to be alone. I will make a helper suitable for him."... So the LORD God caused the man to fall*

into a deep sleep; and while he was sleeping, he took one of the man's ribs and closed up the place with flesh. Then the LORD *God made a woman from the rib he had taken out of the man, and he brought her to the man. The man said, "This is now bone of my bones and flesh of my flesh; she shall be called 'woman,' for she was taken out of man."*

(Genesis 2:18, 21–23)

The word *"rib"* in Genesis 2:22 is the Hebrew word *tsela*. It does not necessarily mean a rib as we understand the word. It could mean "side" or "chamber." The point is that God drew the woman from a part of the man because the "receiver" has to be exactly like the "giver," or the source. Just as man was created as essentially spirit in order to receive love from God and be in relationship with Him, the woman had to be of the same essence as the man in order to receive love from him and be in relationship with him.

We must realize that while males and females are of the same essence, God actually made them using different methods. The Bible says that the man was *"formed"* of the dust of the earth (Genesis 2:7). The Hebrew word translated *"formed"* is *yatsar*, meaning "to mold," as a potter molds clay. However, God *"made"* the woman (Genesis 2:22). The Hebrew word translated *"made"* is *banah*, which means to "build" or "construct."

When Paul wrote, *"Man did not come from woman, but woman from man"* (1 Corinthians 11:8), he was referring to this passage in Genesis. God took the woman out of the man and "built" her. If God had gone back to the soil to fashion another person when He formed the female, she would not have come from the male, and she would therefore not have been made of the same essence as the male. God took exactly what was needed from the male to make the female.

The woman was so much in likeness to the man that, when God presented her to him, the man's first words were, *"This is now bone of my bones and flesh of my flesh"* (Genesis 2:23).

Note that since God made the second human being from Adam and not from another mound of earth, all people who have ever lived essentially came from Adam, who can be considered our earthly, biological source. None of us is independent; none of us can say that we are "self-made," because we all were born in relation to someone else who came before us—most directly from our own parents, but then all the way back to Adam.

ADAM'S TIMING IN CREATION

In chapter 3 of this book, we saw that an author or creator is always the source of the authority of his work. The source of a product has the legitimate right to state the framework of the authority he puts into his product and the way the product functions best. This framework is what we call the principles or laws governing it and through which it operates. Men and women were created by their Source with complementary designs that reflect their individual roles in the larger purposes of authority for which they were created by Him.

> **GOD CREATED MALES AND FEMALES BOTH SIMILARLY AND DIFFERENTLY SO THEY COULD FULFILL HIS PURPOSES FOR THEM.**

So, God created the male first, gave him information about how he was to live on earth, and then placed him in a garden. The female was created after this.

> The LORD God took the man and put him in the Garden of Eden to work it and take care of it. And the LORD God commanded the man, "You are free to eat from any tree in the garden; but you must not eat from the tree of the knowledge of good and evil, for when you eat of it you will surely die." (Genesis 2:15–17)

Adam's timing in creation is significant in relation to authority. He was the first to be made and to be given information. He was the first one on the scene in the world and the first to receive instruction from the Creator, and this made him a legitimate authority. We see an example of this type of authority in a court of law. During a trial, a witness is considered credible and especially valuable if he was on the scene first and can describe what he saw. This is the reason Adam was ultimately responsible when the serpent deceived Eve, and both of them disobeyed the laws of the Creator by doing what He had told them not to do. The man had been given the original instructions, and it was his responsibility to pass them along and to ensure that they were followed.

Therefore, ever since the creation of humanity, the family has had a structure of authority. This structure doesn't make the man better or more intelligent than the woman but instead provides order and parameters for human relationships.

*"God created man in his own image, **in the image of God he created him; male and female he created them"*** (Genesis 1:27). Male and female together are "man." God didn't create the woman from the soil but from the man, and there is thus a need for mutual cooperation, for mutual submission, and for interdependency. Problems begin when this cooperation and dependency are challenged. We don't outgrow the nature God has given us. Women's struggle for rights under God is legitimate. But to say that men and women have exactly the same authority is inaccurate according to the scriptural record. Authority can only be given; it can never be taken, and men and women have different types of authority.

Paul wrote, *"I want you to realize that the head of every man is Christ, and the head of the woman is man, and the head of Christ is God"* (1 Corinthians 11:3). He was saying that there is an order to human relationships in the family, beginning with the man, then the woman, and extending to the children, whom we will discuss shortly. Note that *"the head of Christ is God."* Christ Himself submits to the Father, even though He is one with the Father, and so, again, submission does not reflect worth, only position.

FALSE AUTHORITY AND ABUSE IN MARRIAGES

There is much argument between males and females today about who is "inferior" or "superior." May that attitude be far from us! No such contention was ever planned by God. There is tension, argument, and antagonism between male and female because of their confusion about authority, and ignorance of authority breeds conflict. As we have seen, an absence of authority produces chaos and tyranny. Without authority, life has no order. Without authority, purpose has no protection. Without authority, there is no effective functioning. Without authority, destiny is abandoned. Without authority, power is wasted. Without authority, energy is abused. Without authority, potential is miscarried.

Christ is the head of the husband, and the husband is the head of the wife, so that everyone is under some authority in life and not independent. Since the woman came out of the man, he is, in that sense, her source and sustainer. God designed a woman to receive her authority from her "source." This doesn't give husbands the right to exercise false authority in the form of tyranny or the "boss spirit." On the contrary, the husband is the woman's protection or covering.

> **MEN HAVE TO UNDERSTAND THAT IF THEY'RE NOT UNDER THE AUTHORITY OF GOD, THEY CAN'T EXPECT ANYONE ELSE TO RESPOND TO THEIR AUTHORITY.**

Men have to understand that if they're not under the authority of God, they can't expect anyone else to respond to their authority. This applies not only to the realm of the family but to all realms of authority. As more men come to understand this, it will bring order back to the mess we are experiencing in the world, because everything starts with the family.

The man is accountable to God for this headship of the family, particularly if he uses authority for the wrong reasons. The safety of the woman is in her awareness that the man is accountable to God—that God will deal with him. In cases of abuse, the woman has to protect herself and find shelter. At the same time, she should appeal in prayer to the Creator, who is the authority of the man, the One to whom he is ultimately accountable.

When either the male or the female is out of position in the family, authority breaks down. Remember from the book of Jude that the demons moved out of their proper position. Now, they try to get human beings out of position. We need to stay under authority so that we don't attract demons, or evil spirits. If you are in agreement with demonic thinking, if demons become your "friends" because you are no longer in the proper position, then you cause problems—not only for yourself but also for your family. The demons became tormented when they left their positions. I know that there are women who feel they are living tormented lives because their husbands are not under the authority of God, and their family lives are disordered and stressful.

"*The head of every man is **Christ**"* (1 Corinthians 11:3). A man who is not submitted to Christ's authority is a "headless" man. He also has no power over demons who are tempting him and otherwise attacking him. Likewise, when a woman is out of position, the spirit world knows that she lacks true authority. If she does not stay in her order under the covering of the man, she, too, becomes like a "demon," one who has left her true position. Remember that if Jesus hadn't submitted to the authority of John the Baptist, He wouldn't have been able to withstand the temptations of the devil. The ability to have victory over evil spirits is therefore related to a proper response to authority and position.

> **WHEN EITHER THE MALE OR THE FEMALE IS OUT OF POSITION IN THE FAMILY, AUTHORITY BREAKS DOWN.**

THE HIGHEST EXAMPLE OF HUMAN SUBMISSION

How do husbands and wives live out their authority in marriage? In Paul's letter to the Ephesians, we read,

> *Submit to one another out of reverence for Christ. Wives, submit to your husbands as to the Lord. For the husband is the head of the wife as Christ is the head of the church, his body, of which he is the Savior. Now as the church submits to Christ, so also wives should submit to their husbands in everything. Husbands, love your wives, just as Christ loved the church and gave himself up for her to make her holy, cleansing her by the washing with water through the word, and to present her to himself as a radiant church, without stain or wrinkle or any other blemish, but holy and blameless. In this same way, husbands ought to love their wives as their own bodies. He who loves his wife loves himself.*
>
> (Ephesians 5:21–28)

In its genuine form, marriage may be the highest human example of authority and submission. Paul also wrote,

> *In the Lord, however, woman is not independent of man, nor is man independent of woman. For as woman came from man, so also man is*

born of woman. But everything comes from God.

(1 Corinthians 11:11–12)

"Submit to one another out of reverence for Christ" (Ephesians 5:21). Recall that true submission is a voluntary and natural act as part of the interdependent nature of authority. Marriage is the submission of two people to each other in all things: their bodies, gifts, talents, energy, achievements, possessions, finances, and more. It is not just the submission of one person to another or the partial submission of one person to the partial submission of the other. The modern concept of marriage lacks true authority because it does not reflect this characteristic of submission to one another in all things but instead encourages people to create qualifications, such as "I'll give 50 percent, and you'll give 50 percent" to reach a supposed 100 percent commitment, or prenuptial agreements in which one or both parties holds back something from the other.

Ephesians seems to sum up the beauty of mutual submission and unity in marriage as the Creator designed it: *"Husbands ought to love their wives as their own bodies. He who loves his wife loves himself.... Each one of you also must love his wife as he loves himself, and the wife must respect her husband"* (Ephesians 5:28, 33).

The authority structure of the family that was established by the Manufacturer is under great stress today. It is being threatened in its very nature, and when the family is threatened, all other authority structures are threatened, as well. This is why it is critical that we begin to restore the foundations of authority by focusing on this first realm.

Let us move on now to authority in the family in relation to children.

THE SOURCE OF AUTHORITY FOR CHILDREN

As the basic, foundational unit of society, the family is responsible for teaching authority to children, who are society's future leaders and participants. Therefore, the family needs to be kept intact and not be tampered with. For example, when two homosexual men or two lesbian women adopt and raise a baby, the authority structure of a father, a mother, and children is broken, and the children do not come to understand authority as the Creator established it.

Children learn genuine authority by observing it in the context of a true family structure. Someone who is not taught to respect his own parents will almost always not respect authority in other realms of society. By living in a family, children learn that people's lives need order if there is going to be peace and productivity. The biblical commands for children to obey and honor their fathers and mothers are a large part of their own training for authority, as well as for their protection and welfare. Safeguarding and preserving the priority of authority in the family is therefore vital.

> **BY LIVING IN A FAMILY, CHILDREN LEARN THAT PEOPLE'S LIVES NEED ORDER IF THERE IS GOING TO BE PEACE AND PRODUCTIVITY.**

Family relationships are not to be engaged in haphazardly but purposefully by the parents in order to fulfill the divine design for teaching authority within social relationships. If a child learns the principles of authority in the home first, then he can apply them to his relationships with his supervisors and coworkers on his job, to his relationships with the members of his church and the community or cultural organizations he is connected with, to his interactions with those in government and civic positions, and in all other relationships that may occur in his life. When you have been given good training as a child and have made a point to receive that training, you develop moral standards and ethical positions, so that you respect others' persons and property, the laws of the land, and so forth.

The following are some Scriptures that teach children truths and principles about their parents' authority in their lives and the importance of obeying and following their instructions.

Children, obey your parents in everything, for this pleases the Lord. Fathers [and mothers], *do not embitter your children, or they will become discouraged.*   (Colossians 3:20–21)

Children, obey your parents in the Lord [as those whom God has set over you], *for this is right. "Honor your father and mother"—which is the first commandment with a promise—"that it may go well with you and that you may enjoy long life on the earth." Fathers, do not exasperate your children; instead, bring them up in the training and instruction of the Lord.*   (Ephesians 6:1–4)

My son, keep your father's commands and do not forsake your mother's teaching. Bind them upon your heart forever; fasten them around your neck. When you walk, they will guide you; when you sleep, they will watch over you; when you awake, they will speak to you. For these commands are a lamp, this teaching is a light, and the corrections of discipline are the way to life.   (Proverbs 6:20–23)

The eye that mocks a father, that scorns obedience to a mother, will be pecked out by the ravens of the valley, will be eaten by the vultures [the child's life will be "devoured" and his potential wasted in some form].   (Proverbs 30:17)

A fool spurns his father's discipline, but whoever heeds correction shows prudence.   (Proverbs 15:5)

Rejecting God's established authority in the family obviously leads to serious consequences for children. For example, the Scriptures say that children should obey their parents so that they will enjoy long life on earth. Conversely, if they disobey their parents, they will not enjoy long life. I don't believe this refers only to physical life. The essence of this statement is that if you violate the authority the Creator has placed over you, life is going to "kill" you. You will not experience the richness and enjoyment of it that you were meant to.

Note that the instructions for parents are just as important. The parents generate the environment in the home for their children's understanding of the Creator and His principles and laws, as well as for the development of the children's own personal authority. Embittering or exasperating the children will not teach them the nature of the Creator or promote an understanding of the blessings and protection of true authority.

If a child is obedient and submitted to his father and mother as long as he is living in their house, then his moral life will be preserved. Even when Satan tries to defeat him or situations threaten to destroy him, if he has been in proper relationship with authority, God will go into action to protect him. Therefore, length of life and quality of life can be directly tied to authority.

Finally, even after children are no longer living in their parents' home, they should continue to respect them. We should always respect and honor our parents as our initial authority, under God, in our experience as human beings.

THE REALM OF GOVERNMENT

The next realm of authority is that of government, which would include national, regional (such as state and provincial), and local governments, and the relationships between governmental leaders and citizens.

GOD INSTITUTED GOVERNMENTAL AUTHORITY

First, governmental authority was instituted by God. Another Greek word that is translated *authority* several times in the Scriptures is *dunastes*. For example, in Acts 8:27, we read, "*A man of Ethiopia, a eunuch of great authority [dunastes] under Candace the queen of the Ethiopians, who had charge of all her treasury,…had come to Jerusalem to worship*" (NKJV). This word *dunastes* means "a ruler or officer:—of great authority, mighty, potentate."

Earthly authorities can release authority and power, but God Himself is the *Omni*-potent (omnipotent) one. He is the Potentate above all potentates. All legitimate authority that exists on earth—whether the authority of a king, queen, mother, father, boss, or anyone else—finds its origin in God. Again, if God doesn't give someone authority, then he has none.

Let us look at some general Scripture passages in regard to the earthly authority of governments, and then some principles that follow. I believe that "*judgment*" in the first passage refers to self-destruction.

> *Everyone must submit himself to the governing authorities, for there is no authority except that which God has established. The authorities that exist have been established by God. Consequently, he who rebels against the authority is rebelling against what God has instituted, and those who do so will bring judgment on themselves.* (Romans 13:1–2)

Keeping a close watch on [Jesus], [the religious leaders] sent spies, who pretended to be honest. They hoped to catch Jesus in something he said so that they might hand him over to the power and authority of the governor. So the spies questioned him: "Teacher, we know that you speak and teach what is right, and that you do not show partiality but teach the way of God in accordance with the truth. Is it right for us to pay taxes to Caesar or not?" He saw through their duplicity and said to them, "Show me a denarius. Whose portrait and inscription are on it?" "Caesar's," they replied. He said to them, "Then give to Caesar what is Caesar's, and to God what is God's." They were unable to trap him in what he had said there in public. And astonished by his answer, they became silent. (Luke 20:20–26)

Submit yourselves for the Lord's sake to every authority instituted among men: whether to the king, as the supreme authority, or to governors, who are sent by him to punish those who do wrong and to commend those who do right. (1 Peter 2:13–14)

GOVERNMENTAL OFFICIALS ARE ACCOUNTABLE TO GOD

Since God establishes authority, government officials are responsible before God for their actions, and they are accountable to Him for how they carry out their authority. Likewise, citizens are to consider these officials as "God's servants."

The lips of a king speak as an oracle, and his mouth should not betray justice.... A throne is established through righteousness.
(Proverbs 16:10, 12)

Rulers hold no terror for those who do right, but for those who do wrong. Do you want to be free from fear of the one in authority? Then do what is right and he will commend you. For he is God's servant to do you good. But if you do wrong, be afraid, for he does not bear the sword for nothing. He is God's servant, an agent of wrath to bring punishment on the wrongdoer. Therefore, it is necessary to submit to the authorities, not only because of possible punishment but also because of conscience.
(Romans 13:3–5)

WE ARE TO RESPECT GOVERNMENTAL OFFICIALS

God sometimes gives governmental authority even to those who don't seem to acknowledge Him, and He uses them in His purposes. Remember that Jesus told Pilate, *"You would have no power over me if it were not given to you from above"* (John 19:11). While we might not always understand why this is so, we should respect and obey all governmental authority, as far as we are able to in accordance with God's principles. We should give the Creator honor for the authority He has over all the earth and also respect His earthly authority.

> ### SINCE GOD ESTABLISHES AUTHORITY, GOVERNMENT OFFICIALS ARE RESPONSIBLE BEFORE GOD FOR THEIR ACTIONS.

Remind the people to be subject to rulers and authorities, to be obedient, to be ready to do whatever is good, to slander no one, to be peaceable and considerate, and to show true humility toward all men.

(Titus 3:1–2)

This is also why you pay taxes, for the authorities are God's servants, who give their full time to governing. Give everyone what you owe him: If you owe taxes, pay taxes; if revenue, then revenue; if respect, then respect; if honor, then honor. Let no debt remain outstanding, except the continuing debt to love one another, for he who loves his fellowman has fulfilled the law.

(Romans 13:6–8)

One of the characteristics of freedom in a republic, a democracy, or a constitutional monarchy is that the citizens can question the elected officials in relation to the trust that has been given to them—what they are doing and saying. It's the citizens' right to do this; they are expected to do it in order to keep elected officials accountable in relation to their positions.

Yet holding officials accountable sometimes disintegrates into relentless criticism that offers no support or concrete suggestions and doesn't allow leaders to lead. There is a difference between requiring responsibility from officials and mocking, slandering, and gossiping about them and dispensing unproductive blame. This behavior is contrary to the teachings of the Scriptures. We should respect the positions of governmental officials.

WE ARE TO PRAY FOR GOVERNMENTAL OFFICIALS

Instead of complaining and mocking, citizens who are living under the Creator's principles and laws are called to pray for governmental officials—that they would exercise genuine authority and have wisdom for the decisions they need to make. Paul wrote,

> I urge, then, first of all, that requests, prayers, intercession and thanksgiving be made for everyone—for kings and all those in authority, that we may live peaceful and quiet lives in all godliness and holiness. This is good, and pleases God our Savior, who wants all men to be saved and to come to a knowledge of the truth. (1 Timothy 2:1–4)

How many of us truly respond to Paul's urging? When we understand the principles of authority, we take this responsibility seriously. Since all rulers and leaders are ultimately under God's authority, then He is the authority we can appeal to in relation to their decisions and behavior.

GOD'S AUTHORITY SUPERSEDES EARTHLY AUTHORITY

We must realize that when earthly authority figures try to compel us to do what would conflict with or be contrary to the Creator's higher principles and laws, we cannot obey the earthly authority but must obey God, instead. Jesus's followers in the first century encountered this situation:

> "We gave you strict orders not to teach in this name," [the high priest] said. "Yet you have filled Jerusalem with your teaching and are determined to make us guilty of this man's blood." Peter and the other apostles replied: "We must obey God rather than men! The God of our fathers raised Jesus from the dead—whom you had killed by hanging him on a tree. God exalted him to his own right hand as Prince and Savior that he might give repentance and forgiveness of sins to Israel. We are witnesses of these things, and so is the Holy Spirit, whom God has given to those who obey him." (Acts 5:28–32)

Note that Peter, who wrote, *"Submit yourselves for the Lord's sake to every authority instituted among men"* (1 Peter 2:13), also told those in authority, *"We must obey God rather than men!"*

When we find ourselves in such circumstances, we have this encouragement from the Authorized Dealer, Jesus Christ:

> *When you are brought before synagogues, rulers and authorities, do not worry about how you will defend yourselves or what you will say, for the Holy Spirit will teach you at that time what you should say.*
>
> (Luke 12:11–12)

This is another example of our Ultimate Authority protecting us and being responsible for us.

GOVERNMENT IS INTENDED FOR ORDER, PEACE, AND JOY

True authority is derived from eternal truths and principles, and this authority produces order. That is why "law and order" may be found together.

> *When the righteous are in authority, the people rejoice; but when a wicked man rules, the people groan.* (Proverbs 29:2 NKJV)

> TRUE AUTHORITY IS DERIVED FROM ETERNAL TRUTHS AND PRINCIPLES, AND THIS AUTHORITY PRODUCES ORDER.

Sadly, the eternal truths and principles of authority are not being taught in many schools, which are often sponsored and overseen by governments. Teachers are instructing children that there is no absolute truth, and so the basis for the foundation of authority is eroded. Teachers are told by their principals and educational organizations that they aren't to exercise authority over the children in the form of correcting them, and this approach spirals down to influence the children's behavior. When children have no respect for authority, it leads to a deterioration of relationships with their teachers and principals to the point where the teachers can't do their jobs, and some children are now killing each other and their teachers *in* the schools. Then we wonder why the system is broken. Again, where there is no genuine authority, there will eventually be chaos.

In contrast, wherever people have good, genuine law, based on the principles of the Creator—and obey it—there is order and peace in their communities. George Washington wrote in his farewell address as the first president of the United States,

> Of all the dispositions and habits which lead to political pros-perity, Religion and morality are indispensable supports. In vain would that man claim the tribute of Patriotism, who should labour to subvert these great Pillars of human happiness, these firmest props of the duties of Men & citizens. The mere Politican, equally with the pious man ought to respect & to cherish them. A volume could not trace all their connections with private & public felicity.[3]

JESUS CHRIST IS KING OF KINGS

Ultimately, all government on earth will be that of order, peace, and joy because it will be under the direct authority of our Authorized Dealer:

> *For to us a child is born, to us a son is given, and the government will be on his shoulders. And he will be called Wonderful Counselor, Mighty God, Everlasting Father, Prince of Peace. Of the increase of his govern-ment and peace there will be no end. He will reign on David's throne and over his kingdom, establishing and upholding it with justice and righteousness from that time on and forever.* (Isaiah 9:6–7)

> *On* [Jesus's] *robe and on his thigh he has this name written:* KING OF KINGS AND LORD OF LORDS. (Revelation 19:16)

THE REALM OF THE CHURCH

The realm of the church is sometimes mistaken for the "institution" of the church. And while the life of the church is manifested in individual churches, denominations, and other religious groups, the true realm of the church consists in the fellowship of all those throughout the world who have been restored to God through the Authorized Dealer, Jesus Christ.

JESUS CHRIST IS THE HEAD, OR PRIMARY AUTHORITY

*For [God] has rescued us from the dominion of darkness and brought us into the kingdom of the Son he loves, in whom we have redemption, the forgiveness of sins. [Jesus] is the image of the invisible God, the firstborn over all creation. For by him all things were created: things in heaven and on earth, visible and invisible, whether thrones or powers or rulers or authorities; all things were created by him and for him. He is before all things, and in him all things hold together. And **he is the head of the body, the church;** he is the beginning and the firstborn from among the dead, so that in everything he might have the supremacy. For God was pleased to have all his fullness dwell in him.*

(Colossians 1:13–19)

God established the church, Jesus Christ is its "Head," and He delegates authority to certain people to lead in this realm.

And in the church God has appointed first of all apostles, second prophets, third teachers, then workers of miracles, also those having gifts of healing, those able to help others, those with gifts of administration, and those speaking in different kinds of tongues.   (1 Corinthians 12:28)

It was [Christ] who gave some to be apostles, some to be prophets, some to be evangelists, and some to be pastors and teachers, to prepare God's people for works of service, so that the body of Christ may be built up until we all reach unity in the faith and in the knowledge of the Son of God and become mature, attaining to the whole measure of the fullness of Christ.   (Ephesians 4:11–13)

For through [Christ] we both have access to the Father by one Spirit. Consequently, you are no longer foreigners and aliens, but fellow citizens with God's people and members of God's household, built on the foundation of the apostles and prophets, with Christ Jesus himself as the chief cornerstone.   (Ephesians 2:18–20)

RESPONSIBILITIES OF CHURCH LEADERS

All those appointed with leadership authority and other specific gifts of authority (see 1 Corinthians 12:4–11) in the church are accountable to the Head for how they use their authority, have certain responsibilities in relation to their authority, and must conduct themselves according to God's principles and laws:

> To the elders among you, I [Peter] appeal as a fellow elder, a witness of Christ's sufferings and one who also will share in the glory to be revealed: Be shepherds of God's flock that is under your care, serving as overseers—not because you must, but because you are willing, as God wants you to be; not greedy for money, but eager to serve; not lording it over those entrusted to you, but being examples to the flock.
>
> (1 Peter 5:1–3)

> Here is a trustworthy saying: If anyone sets his heart on being an overseer, he desires a noble task. Now the overseer must be above reproach, the husband of but one wife, temperate, self-controlled, respectable, hospitable, able to teach, not given to drunkenness, not violent but gentle, not quarrelsome, not a lover of money. He must manage his own family well and see that his children obey him with proper respect. (If anyone does not know how to manage his own family, how can he take care of God's church?) He must not be a recent convert, or he may become conceited and fall under the same judgment as the devil. He must also have a good reputation with outsiders, so that he will not fall into disgrace and into the devil's trap. Deacons, likewise, are to be men worthy of respect, sincere, not indulging in much wine, and not pursuing dishonest gain. They must keep hold of the deep truths of the faith with a clear conscience. They must first be tested; and then if there is nothing against them, let them serve as deacons. In the same way, their wives are to be women worthy of respect, not malicious talkers but temperate and trustworthy in everything. A deacon must be the husband of but one wife and must manage his children and his household well. Those who have served well gain an excellent standing and great assurance in their faith in Christ Jesus. (1 Timothy 3:1–13)

Since an overseer is entrusted with God's work, he must be blame-less—not overbearing, not quick-tempered, not given to drunkenness, not violent, not pursuing dishonest gain. Rather he must be hospitable, one who loves what is good, who is self-controlled, upright, holy and disciplined. He must hold firmly to the trustworthy message as it has been taught, so that he can encourage others by sound doctrine and refute those who oppose it. (Titus 1:7–9)

AUTHORITY IS NOT A MATTER OF AGE BUT POSITION

To exercise authority in the church, a person must be mature in his faith and lifestyle, yet age—whether someone is older or younger than you are—does not disqualify that person from being your authority in the church if God has placed him there. Paul wrote to Timothy, *"Don't let anyone look down on you because you are young, but set an example for the believers in speech, in life, in love, in faith and in purity"* (1 Timothy 4:12). We don't submit to people because of their age but because of their position.

Moses's older sister, Miriam, had a problem submitting to position. She was jealous of Moses's authority even though she had been granted authority, as well. (See Micah 6:4.) When she stepped out of order by crit-icizing Moses's leadership (along with Aaron, Moses's brother), God was angry with her, but Moses, her authority, intervened and saved her life. (This is still another instance of how authority will protect, preserve, keep, and save you.) Miriam underwent discipline, however, because she was a visible authority figure among the people and so that she would learn to understand the nature of God's authority. (See Numbers 12:1–15.)

> ## WE DON'T SUBMIT TO PEOPLE BECAUSE OF THEIR AGE BUT BECAUSE OF THEIR POSITION.

Remember that when Jesus submitted to John, He said, in effect, "It is proper for us to do this to fulfill all righteousness." Yet, some people who are under a younger pastor might think, "Me, submit to him? I'm old enough to be his father!" That may be true, but your submission to him is proper to "fulfill all righteousness," because he is the pastor.

I have been the pastor of my siblings who are older than I am. That doesn't mean I am better than they are. It is a matter of position, and it can be a difficult position to be in because they know me better than almost anyone else! Their submission to me as their pastor has been a revelation of their understanding of order. They know they can't pastor themselves.

God placed in the body of Christ apostles, evangelists, prophets, pastors, and teachers to instruct and guide His people. Whoever wants to be spiritually trained has to find those who are functioning in these ministry gifts. If the apostle, evangelist, prophet, pastor, or teacher happens to be someone who is younger or older than you are, then, again, the position is more important than the person. We need to follow the authority in our lives, for the sake of righteousness.

RESPONSIBILITIES OF CHURCH MEMBERS

Paul wrote to Titus, "*Encourage and rebuke with all authority. Do not let anyone despise* ["*disregard*" NASB] *you*" (Titus 2:15).

Unfortunately, there seems to be much disregarding and despising of authority going on in churches today. The culture of democracy that has led to an attitude of individualism in other realms also gravitates against authority in the realm of the church. I don't think that the average Christian understands the nature of authority. The same unproductive criticism of governmental leaders we talked about in the previous section is leveled at leaders in the church, as well. Because of this, people verbally abuse and disrespect their pastors, criticize church leaders behind their backs, close their eyes to the sound instruction and teaching of the Word of God, and fail to pay their leaders a decent wage for their service.

Another reason people disregard authority in the church is that many churches have "overdosed" on the concept of grace at the expense of obedience. Grace has been used as an excuse by people to ignore the instruction of pastors and teachers that calls them to align their lives with God's principles and laws.

God's grace is real, wonderful, and necessary for us. We couldn't receive His forgiveness and new life through the Authorized Dealer without it. "*If we confess our sins, he is faithful and just and will forgive us our sins and purify us from all unrighteousness*" (1 John 1:9). Yet, as Paul said, we are not to treat

God's grace lightly: *"Shall we go on sinning so that grace may increase? By no means! We died to sin; how can we live in it any longer?"* (Romans 6:1–2).

Instead, members of the church are to respect and honor their leaders and to submit to their urgings and warnings about living according to the nature of God:

> *Now we ask you, brothers, to respect those who work hard among you, who are over you in the Lord and who admonish you. Hold them in the highest regard in love because of their work. Live in peace with each other.* (1 Thessalonians 5:12–13)

> *The elders who direct the affairs of the church well are worthy of double honor, especially those whose work is preaching and teaching. For the Scripture says, "Do not muzzle the ox while it is treading out the grain," and "The worker deserves his wages."* (1 Timothy 5:17–18)

> *Obey your leaders and submit to their authority. They keep watch over you as men who must give an account. Obey them so that their work will be a joy, not a burden, for that would be of no advantage to you.* (Hebrews 13:17)

WOMEN IN AUTHORITY IN THE CHURCH

The last point I would like to discuss in the realm of the church relates to a question that is still controversial in many people's minds: Should women be in leadership positions? This issue is too broad to discuss in depth in the context of this book, so I will give you what I believe are important guidelines in relation to authority for women who are serving as pastors and teachers.[4]

> **MEMBERS OF THE CHURCH ARE TO RESPECT THEIR LEADERS AND SUBMIT TO THEIR URGINGS ABOUT LIVING ACCORDING TO THE NATURE OF GOD.**

Based on the order of authority outlined in the above section "The Realm of the Family," in which we saw that the male was created first and the female was created from the male, I believe that an unmarried female pastor or teacher should find a male authority who will serve as her covering and protection, and as the one to whom she is accountable as an authority figure herself. Healing evangelist Kathryn Kuhlman had a powerful ministry, but when she stood up to minister, she always told her audience who her pastor was, placing herself under his authority for her ministry. She voluntarily submitted to him as her covering.

For a woman who is a pastor or teacher and who is also married, it is important that she be submitted to her husband and not be operating outside of their relationship of authority as husband and wife. She should also have a female accountability partner or an accountability group to which she belongs within the ministry setting, but her first priority in keeping a proper authority relationship before God would be her relationships with God and her husband.

THE REALM OF BUSINESS

In chapters 11 and 12 of this book, the discussions of authority, mentorship, and submission give a number of practical principles and guidelines that can be particularly applied to the realm of business, and I suggest that you review those chapters with this realm in mind, as well.

HONEST TRANSACTIONS

Those who own and run businesses, and the consumers who use their services and buy their products, must treat one another fairly and honestly.

The LORD abhors dishonest scales, but accurate weights are his delight. When pride comes, then comes disgrace, but with humility comes wisdom. The integrity of the upright guides them, but the unfaithful are destroyed by their duplicity. Wealth is worthless in the day of wrath, but righteousness delivers from death. (Proverbs 11:1–4)

The wicked man earns deceptive wages, but he who sows righteousness reaps a sure reward. The truly righteous man attains life, but he who pursues evil goes to his death. (Proverbs 11:18–19)

Honest scales and balances are from the Lord; all the weights in the bag are of his making.… The highway of the upright avoids evil; he who guards his way guards his life. Pride goes before destruction, a haughty spirit before a fall. Better to be lowly in spirit and among the oppressed than to share plunder with the proud. (Proverbs 16:11, 17–19)

Whatever you do, whether in word or deed, do it all in the name of the Lord Jesus, giving thanks to God the Father through him.
(Colossians 3:17)

RELATIONSHIPS BETWEEN EMPLOYERS AND EMPLOYEES

Employers and employees, in the same way, must treat one another justly. The following are Scriptures that originally referred to the relationships between slaves and masters, but they also teach us vital truths for the workplace. See if you recognize these principles and guidelines in the below Scriptures: (1) God is our Ultimate Authority, who will reward our work as it is done for Him; (2) we should be diligent and sincere in our work, whether anyone is watching us or not; (3) we need to treat one another with respect and kindness; (4) employers must provide proper working conditions and pay for their employees; (5) employees must not steal from or cheat their employers but put in a good day's work; (6) we are to respect the position of someone in an authority role.

Whatever you do, work at it with all your heart, as working for the Lord, not for men, since you know that you will receive an inheritance from the Lord as a reward. It is the Lord Christ you are serving.… Masters, provide your slaves with what is right and fair, because you know that you also have a Master in heaven.
(Colossians 3:23–24; 4:1)

Slaves, obey your earthly masters with respect and fear, and with sincerity of heart, just as you would obey Christ. Obey them not only to win their favor when their eye is on you, but like slaves of Christ, doing the will of God from your heart. Serve wholeheartedly, as if you were serving the Lord, not men, because you know that the Lord will reward everyone for whatever good he does, whether he is slave or free.

Masters, treat your slaves in the same way. Do not threaten them, since you know that he who is both their Master and yours is in heaven, and there is no favoritism with him. (Ephesians 6:5–9)

Slaves, obey your earthly masters in everything; and do it, not only when their eye is on you and to win their favor, but with sincerity of heart and reverence for the Lord. (Colossians 3:22)

Teach slaves to be subject to their masters in everything, to try to please them, not to talk back to them, and not to steal from them, but to show that they can be fully trusted, so that in every way they will make the teaching about God our Savior attractive. For the grace of God that brings salvation has appeared to all men. It teaches us to say "No" to ungodliness and worldly passions, and to live self-controlled, upright and godly lives in this present age, while we wait for the blessed hope— the glorious appearing of our great God and Savior, Jesus Christ, who gave himself for us to redeem us from all wickedness and to purify for himself a people that are his very own, eager to do what is good. (Titus 2:9–14)

All who are under the yoke of slavery should consider their masters worthy of full respect, so that God's name and our teaching may not be slandered. Those who have believing masters are not to show less respect for them because they are brothers. Instead, they are to serve them even better, because those who benefit from their service are believers, and dear to them. (1 Timothy 6:1–2)

Show proper respect to everyone: Love the brotherhood of believers, fear God, honor the king. Slaves, submit yourselves to your masters with all respect, not only to those who are good and considerate, but also to those who are harsh. For it is commendable if a man bears up under the pain of unjust suffering because he is conscious of God. But how is it to your credit if you receive a beating for doing wrong and endure it? But if you suffer for doing good and you endure it, this is commendable before God. (1 Peter 2:18–20)

If we read, study, and apply the scriptural principles in this chapter to all the major realms of human life, we will make great strides toward understanding authority and how it is meant to function on earth. We will also see more clearly how to restore the structures of order and peace in our families, communities, nations, and world.

EPILOGUE:
AUTHORITY, THE BEAUTIFUL PRINCIPLE

In chapter 2, I wrote that I like to call genuine authority the "beautiful principle" because, contrary to false authority, it's not about "lording it over" others. Instead, it is a means of providing the resources, protection, refreshment, growth, accomplishment, fulfillment, and satisfaction we all need in life.

THE "YOKE" OF AUTHORITY IS EASY AND LIGHT

The Authorized Dealer, Jesus Christ, is the only One who can restore our relationship with the Creator, lead us to our personal authority, enable us to live in collaboration with others, and reestablish true authority in the world. He does this as we recognize His authority in our lives and as we learn about Him and His ways. Jesus said,

> *All things have been committed to me by my Father. No one knows the Son except the Father, and no one knows the Father except the Son and those to whom the Son chooses to reveal him. Come to me, all you who are weary and burdened, and I will give you rest. Take my yoke upon you and learn from me, for I am gentle and humble in heart, and you will find rest for your souls. **For my yoke is easy and my burden is light**.* (Matthew 11:27–30)

Jesus's invitation highlights the nature of God's authority and what we can receive from Him. A yoke is traditionally "a wooden bar or frame by which two draft animals (as oxen) are joined at the heads or necks for working together." Most people consider a yoke to represent something confining and oppressive. They are weary and burdened in life, and they think that running away from authority is the answer.

Yet Christ invites us to experience a different kind of yoke, one that joins us to Him in the shared purpose of fulfilling God's plans for us and for the world. Our being joined to Him allows us to walk through life with a sure step as He guides us. His yoke of authority brings spiritual and personal "rest" because, by it, we become who we were meant to be, and we are able to do what we were born to do in life.

WHAT IT MEANS TO "TAKE HIS YOKE"

To give us this rest, Christ, our Authorized Dealer, first asks us to *"come"* and acknowledge that true authority and purpose cannot be found apart from Him.

Second, He asks us to "take His yoke" upon ourselves so we can learn from Him. Note that *we* are the ones who *voluntarily* take His yoke because we want to work alongside Him to fulfill the Creator's plans. He doesn't put the yoke on us. In this way, once again, we see that submission is always a voluntary act on our part to fulfill a God-given purpose.

Taking Christ's yoke involves walking alongside Him as we discover and accept our inherent realms of authority, learn the truths and principles of authority in God's Word, and live according to them.

> CHRIST'S YOKE IS "EASY" BECAUSE, AS WE WALK BESIDE HIM, HE GUIDES US IN THE WAY WE SHOULD GO

In this process, we are guided by the One who made us and who deeply loves us. He is not an angry authority figure ready to strike us down, as some have imagined. His *"gentle and humble"* attitude toward us draws us to Him and enables us to learn from Him and to become what He created us to be. *"For God did not send his Son into the world to condemn the world, but to save the world through him"* (John 3:17).

Christ's yoke is *"easy"* because, as we walk beside Him, He guides us in the way we should go. What we carry is *"light"* because it consists of truths and principles that set us free. It is also light because it is *natural*, and because, when we live in that naturalness, we are no longer weighed down by false authority and the dead-end roads of fearful and self-centered living.

THE PRINCIPLE, POWER, AND PROTECTION OF AUTHORITY

Through the "yoke" of genuine authority, you can live in the joy of your personal domain in God's great design. You can release the principle, power, and protection of authority into your life and circumstances. It is my prayer that this book will bring healing and restoration of order to all realms of society, throughout the nations of the world. People all over the earth need the peace, confidence, and security of genuine authority. We therefore need to reverse the misunderstanding, misuse, and abuse of authority worldwide, so that we will increasingly have more of the *right* kind of authority and less of the *wrong* kind of authority.

You have been invited by your Creator to "come" and "take" your God-given authority to fulfill His purposes for you and your generation. Will you accept His invitation?

AUTHORITY AND A WORD TO THE THIRD WORLD

ESTABLISHING REAL FREEDOM THROUGH GENUINE AUTHORITY

Many Third World peoples have become suspicious of the concept of authority as a result of the way they have been historically misused and abused by other nations and groups. Postcolonial countries experienced the oppressive abuse of domineering kingdoms that exercised control over their territories. Many of these powers annihilated cultures while raping the resources of their colonies, subjugating those who were native to these conquered areas and trading in human labor and life; in essence, they reduced humanity to commodities and chattel.

These experiences resulted in two diverse attitudes among the oppressed: (1) they promoted a defeatist, surrendered outlook, and (2) they ignited a fierce resolve to throw off any form of perceived authoritative control and to establish the pursuit of freedom as the ultimate ideal. Significantly, both of these attitudes have often been accompanied by a rejection not only of false authority but also of legitimate authority.

> ### PEOPLE'S MISUNDERSTANDING OF GENUINE AUTHORITY AND TRUE FREEDOM IN THE THIRD WORLD HAS ACTUALLY LED TO NEW FORMS OF OPPRESSION.

Consequently, Third World peoples have embraced the worldwide trend toward pure democracy that has clouded the clear boundaries of authority. This trend causes people to continually test the parameters of "freedom." If the present movement in the evolution of democracy continues, without the reestablishment of clear absolutes of authority, then I believe the "American experiment" and other experiments in democracy will fail because authority preserves, protects, and defends that which submits to it.

Two principles of authority that I have emphasized in this book are (1) ignorance of true authority is the father of anarchy, and (2) without true authority, purpose has no protection. Unfortunately, we see these principles unfolding in developing countries. A misunderstanding of genuine authority and true freedom in the Third World has actually led to new forms of oppression.

People will do almost anything if they think it is vital to their survival, and that is why we are seeing some native Third World leaders abusing their own people in an attempt to gain something for themselves. They have been in the land of scarcity for so long that they think they should grab hold of whatever they can, while they can. Yet we can never lift ourselves up by tearing others down. We are called to protect not only our individual purposes but our collective purposes, as well. Our policies and our actions should promote the good of all.

To do this, we must come to the place where we realize—and exemplify the fact—that freedom and authority are not incompatible. Rather, freedom comes through authority, and the two support and complement one another. Remember that God took a group of slaves—the Hebrews—brought them out of Egypt, and made a large and powerful nation out of them. However, what was the first thing He gave them in establishing their freedom? He didn't tell them that now they could do anything they wanted to do (which was their continual tendency). Instead, He gave them a solid authority on which they could build their lives. He gave them His law, through Moses, as their source of authority. And He gave them His presence to support and guide them.

GENUINE AUTHORITY IS THE ONLY PATH TO ESTABLISHING REAL FREEDOM.

The key concept we must embrace is that recognizing Absolute Authority—God's authority, with the principles and laws of His Word—is essential for entering into the true freedom of personal and corporate authority in developing nations. *"Jesus said, 'If you hold to my teaching, you are really my disciples. Then you will know the truth, and the truth will set you free'"* (John 8:31–32). Drawing on our Absolute Authority is also essential for delegating our inherent authority to those around us who need our support and assistance to enter into the power of their own personal domains.

Genuine authority is the *only* path to establishing real freedom. We cannot deny either ourselves or others in the developing world the opportunity to build on what has been accomplished so far. And we will reverse and perhaps even destroy what has been accomplished if we reject the principles of authority.

Instead, let us enter into all the liberties, all the possibilities, and all the advancement of a life authorized and designed by our Creator and given to us for our enrichment and His pleasure.

NOTES

CHAPTER FOUR

1. See Merrill F. Unger and William White Jr., eds., *Vine's Complete Expository Dictionary of Old and New Testament Words* (New York: Thomas Nelson Publishers, 1985), 45, s.v. *Author*, number 2, *archegos*.

CHAPTER FIVE

2. Larry Donnithorne, *The West Point Way of Leadership* (New York: Currency Books [Doubleday], 1993), 19.

CHAPTER TEN

1. See, for example, NBA.com Staff, "Legends Profile: Michael Jordan," NBA History, https://www.nba.com/news/history-nba-legend-michael-jordan.

2. See, for example, Andrew R. Chow, "'Craziness on a Daily Basis': Michael Jordan's White Sox Teammates Remember His 1994 Season," *Time*, May 10, 2020, https://time.com/5833121/michael-jordan-baseball-the-last-dance/.

3. Chow, "Craziness on a Daily Basis."

CHAPTER FIFTEEN

1. For a detailed discussion of the inherent makeup and roles of men and women, please refer to the author's books *Understanding the Purpose and Power of Women* (Whitaker House, 2018) and *Understanding the Purpose and Power of Men* (Whitaker House, 2017).

2. Tom Minnery, "The Relationship Between Church, Family and Government," *Focus on the Family* magazine, July 1998, 12, 10.

3. George Washington, presidential farewell address, page 20, http://gwpapers.virginia.edu/documents/farewell/transcript.html.

4. For a biblical discussion of women and leadership, please refer to the author's book *Understanding the Purpose and Power of Women*, chapter 11, "Should Women Be in Leadership?" (Whitaker House, 2018).

MAXIMIZING YOUR PERSONAL AUTHORITY

PRINCIPLES AND EXAMPLES OF AUTHORITY

To maximize your personal authority, review the following principles and scriptural examples of authority, which are essential for discovering and executing your purpose in your generation, pleasing your Author, and bringing personal satisfaction and significance to yourself.

GENERAL PRINCIPLES OF AUTHORITY

+ God is a God of authority.

+ God is the Source of all authority.

+ God created everyone and everything with inherent authority.

+ Authority is a natural law and a principle of creation.

+ Authority is natural to a person.

+ Personal authority is determined by gifts, talents, natural abilities, and inner passion.

+ Personal authority is the Author's permission for you to become yourself.

+ Purpose is what you were authorized to do; your assignment is your purpose.

+ Authority is the source of true power and the means to the full release of that power.

+ Authority makes life easier and also makes life *look* easy to others.

+ Authority establishes its own freedoms and limitations.

+ Authority can only be given, never taken.

+ Authority protects delegated authority and its power.

+ Authority is always accountable.

+ Authority needs no self-defense; its decisions are validated by its source.

+ Submission to authority releases authority and protects purpose.

+ Authority is the key to life and proper function, as well as the foundation of effectiveness; it guarantees maximum performance.

+ Authority gives life significance.

+ Authority is the guarantee of fulfillment.

+ Authority is the measure of success.

+ Authority is based on faith and produces confidence.

+ Authority leads to order and peace.

+ Ignorance or absence of authority produces confusion and chaos.

+ Disobedience to authority sacrifices purpose and cancels vision.

+ The unauthorized can only abuse.

+ One can be gifted, talented, skilled, and experienced and still be unauthorized by not fulfilling one's God-given potential and personal authority.

+ One must not only discover his authority but also release it and *remain* in it.

+ If one has strayed from authority, he should immediately submit to it again so that his gifting can be renewed within him.

SELECT EXAMPLES OF AUTHORITY AND ITS POWER IN THE SCRIPTURES

+ Genesis 1:1: God is the Author of all creation.

+ Genesis 1:11–12: The seed of everything is in itself; authority is inherent.

+ Genesis 1:16–17: God created two lights to *"govern"* the day and the night.

+ Genesis 1:24–25: God created the animals according to their kinds.

+ Genesis 1:26–28: Man (male and female) was made in God's image and given personal authority as well as dominion over the earth.

+ Genesis 6:13–22: Noah was authorized to build the ark.

+ Genesis 12:1–3: Abraham was authorized to be the father of a new people and nation.

+ Exodus 3:7–10: Moses was authorized to go to Pharaoh and to bring the Israelites out of Egypt.

+ Matthew 3:13–17: John was authorized to baptize people and to prepare the way for the Authorized Dealer (Jesus), or the Messiah.

+ Luke 4:31–36: Jesus operated under the authority and power of God so that the people were *amazed at his teaching, because his message had authority,*" and "*with authority and power he* [gave] *orders to evil spirits and they* [came] *out.*"

+ John 21:19–22: Peter was authorized to follow Jesus only in his own personal authority and was not to trespass on the authority of anyone else.

+ Matthew 16:18; John 21:15–17: Peter was authorized to care for and build up the church.

+ Acts 26:12–18: Paul was given authority to go to the Gentiles "*as a servant and as a witness*" of Jesus.

+ John 1:12: Those who are restored to the Creator are authorized to become "*children of God.*"

+ Matthew 28:18–20: Those who are reconnected to the Creator are given general authority to communicate to the world that all people can be restored and reconnected to Him and receive the benefits of coming under His eternal warranty and discovering their own personal authority.

PERSONAL AUTHORITY PROFILE

(MAKE A COPY OF THIS SAMPLE PROFILE AND ANSWER THE
QUESTIONS TO HELP YOU EVALUATE AND SUMMARIZE YOUR
AUTHORITY, GIFTING, AND PERSONAL DOMAIN.)

KEY #1: WHAT IS MY DEEPEST DESIRE?
(Not what I have a general or passing "interest" in, but rather a deep yearning or aspiration to do.)

KEY #2: WHAT AM I TRULY PASSIONATE ABOUT?
(What do I really care about? What gifts and abilities do I especially enjoy using?)

KEY #3: WHAT MAKES ME ANGRY?

(Not destructive anger, which is selfishly motivated, but constructive anger that is based on compassion for others and a desire for people to be treated right, anger that is grieved by injustice and that leads to positive action to remedy problems.)

KEY #4: WHAT IDEAS ARE PERSISTENT IN MY HEART AND THOUGHTS?

(What recurring dreams do I have for my life? What idea never leaves me?)

KEY #5: WHAT DO I CONSTANTLY IMAGINE MYSELF DOING?

(What do I dream about becoming? What gifts or skills would I use and develop in order to become this?)

KEY #6: WHAT DO I WANT TO DO FOR HUMANITY?

(What kind of impact would I like to have on my community? What do I want to pass along to the next generation? What would I like to be remembered for?)

KEY #7: WHAT WOULD BRING ME THE GREATEST FULFILLMENT?

(What three endeavors or achievements have given me the greatest satisfaction and fulfillment in life so far, and why? What motivates and gratifies me the most, and how can I incorporate it into my life as my vocation or life focus?)

KEY #8: WHAT WOULD I DO FOR NO MONEY OR OTHER COMPENSATION?

(What activities am I currently receiving satisfaction from that I'm not being paid for? What am I so dedicated to that I would continue to do it even if I stopped receiving money for it? What would I do for no compensation?)

KEY #9: WHAT WOULD I RATHER BE DOING?

(What do I wish I were doing when I am doing other things? What makes me feel most at home when I am doing it?)

KEY #10: WHAT WOULD I DO IF I KNEW I COULD NOT FAIL?

(What endeavor, enterprise, creative work, project, or plan would I engage in if it were risk-free? If money were no object? If I didn't worry that I had the wrong background, the wrong looks, the wrong job experiences, or the wrong anything else?)

KEY #11: WHAT IS THE MOST IMPORTANT THING I COULD DO WITH MY LIFE?

(Above all other things, what is the most significant thing I could do with my life? What do I want to occur in my life? How do I want to live my life based on my values and beliefs?)

KEY #12: WHAT ENDEAVOR OR ACTIVITY WOULD BEST CONNECT ME TO MY CREATOR?

(What draws me closest to God?)

SUMMARY STATEMENT:
WHAT I BELIEVE I WAS PUT ON THIS EARTH TO DO:

• *Documenting Your Personal Authority*: In what specific ways have I exercised this authority in the past? How can I build on this in the future?

• *Exercising and Refining Your Personal Authority*: In what ways will I develop and apply my personal authority now that I know what it is?

• *Releasing Your Personal Authority*: Who has the knowledge, skills, and commitment to help me to release my authority? (For more information on this, see chapter 11.)

ABOUT THE AUTHOR

Dr. Myles Munroe (1954–2014) was an international motivational speaker, best-selling author, educator, leadership mentor, and consultant for government and business. Traveling extensively throughout the world, Dr. Munroe addressed critical issues affecting the full range of human, social, and spiritual development. The central theme of his message is the maximization of individual potential, including the transformation of followers into leaders and leaders into agents of change.

Dr. Munroe was founder and president of Bahamas Faith Ministries International (BFMI), a multidimensional organization headquartered in Nassau, Bahamas. He was chief executive officer and chairman of the board of the International Third World Leaders Association and president of the International Leadership Training Institute.

Dr. Munroe was also the founder and executive producer of a number of radio and television programs aired worldwide. In addition, he was a frequent guest on other television and radio programs and international networks and was a contributing writer for various Bible editions, journals, magazines, and newsletters, such as *The Believer's Topical Bible*, *The African Cultural Heritage Topical Bible*, *Charisma Life Christian Magazine*, and *Ministries Today*.

He was a popular author of more than forty books, including *The Power of Character in Leadership*, *Understanding the Purpose and Power of Authority*, *Understanding the Purpose and Power of Change*, *Becoming a Leader*, *The Purpose and Power of the Holy Spirit*, *The Spirit of Leadership*, *The Principles and Power of Vision*, *Understanding the Purpose and Power of Prayer*, *Understanding the Purpose and Power of Women*, and *Understanding the Purpose and Power of Men*.

Dr. Munroe has changed the lives of multitudes around the world with a powerful message that inspires, motivates, challenges, and empowers people to discover personal purpose, develop true potential, and manifest their unique leadership abilities. For over thirty years, he trained tens of thousands of leaders in business, industry, education, government, and religion. He personally addressed over five hundred thousand people each year on personal and professional development. His appeal and message transcend age, race, culture, creed, and economic background.

Dr. Munroe earned BA and MA degrees from Oral Roberts University and the University of Tulsa, and was awarded a number of honorary doctoral degrees. He also served as an adjunct professor of the Graduate School of Theology at Oral Roberts University.

The parents of two adult children, Charisa and Chairo (Myles Jr.), Dr. Munroe and his wife, Ruth, traveled as a team and were involved in teaching seminars together. Both were leaders who ministered with sensitive hearts and international vision. In November 2014, they were tragically killed in an airplane crash en route to an annual leadership conference sponsored by Bahamas Faith Ministries International.

A statement from Dr. Munroe in his book *The Power of Character in Leadership* summarizes his own legacy: "Remember that character ensures the longevity of leadership, and men and women of principle will leave important legacies and be remembered by future generations."